PR 573 CLA

WITHDRAWN
FROM STOCK
QMUL LIBRARY

Class and the Canon

Also by Kirstie Blair

FORM AND FAITH IN VICTORIAN POETRY AND RELIGION

VICTORIAN POETRY AND THE CULTURE OF THE HEART

Also by Mina Gorji

JOHN CLARE AND THE PLACE OF POETRY

Class and the Canon

Constructing Labouring-Class Poetry and Poetics, 1750–1900

Edited by

Kirstie Blair
University of Glasgow, UK

and

Mina Gorji
University of Cambridge, UK

Introduction, selection and editorial matter © Kirstie Blair and Mina Gorji 2013
Individual chapters © contributors 2013

All rights reserved. No reproduction, copy or transmission of this publication may be made without written permission.

No portion of this publication may be reproduced, copied or transmitted save with written permission or in accordance with the provisions of the Copyright, Designs and Patents Act 1988, or under the terms of any licence permitting limited copying issued by the Copyright Licensing Agency, Saffron House, 6–10 Kirby Street, London EC1N 8TS.

Any person who does any unauthorized act in relation to this publication may be liable to criminal prosecution and civil claims for damages.

The authors have asserted their rights to be identified as the authors of this work in accordance with the Copyright, Designs and Patents Act 1988.

First published 2013 by
PALGRAVE MACMILLAN

Palgrave Macmillan in the UK is an imprint of Macmillan Publishers Limited, registered in England, company number 785998, of Houndmills, Basingstoke, Hampshire RG21 6XS.

Palgrave Macmillan in the US is a division of St Martin's Press LLC,
175 Fifth Avenue, New York, NY 10010.

Palgrave Macmillan is the global academic imprint of the above companies and has companies and representatives throughout the world.

Palgrave® and Macmillan® are registered trademarks in the United States, the United Kingdom, Europe and other countries.

ISBN 978–1–137–03032–0

This book is printed on paper suitable for recycling and made from fully managed and sustained forest sources. Logging, pulping and manufacturing processes are expected to conform to the environmental regulations of the country of origin.

A catalogue record for this book is available from the British Library.

A catalog record for this book is available from the Library of Congress.

10 9 8 7 6 5 4 3 2 1
22 21 20 19 18 17 16 15 14 13

Printed and bound in Great Britain by
CPI Antony Rowe, Chippenham and Eastbourne

Contents

Acknowledgements vii
Notes on Contributors viii

1. Introduction 1
   Kirstie Blair
2. Was Burns a Labouring-Class Poet? 16
   Nigel Leask
3. Constructing the Ulster Labouring-Class Poet: The Case of Samuel Thomson 34
   Jennifer Orr
4. Sociable or Solitary? John Clare, Robert Bloomfield, Community and Isolation 55
   John Goodridge
5. John Clare and the Triumph of Little Things 77
   Mina Gorji
6. 'No more than as an atom 'mid the vast profound': Conceptions of Time in the Poetry of William Cowper, William Wordsworth, and Ann Yearsley 95
   Kerri Andrews
7. The Pen and the Hammer: Thomas Carlyle, Ebenezer Elliott, and the 'active poet' 116
   Marcus Waithe
8. Samuel Ferguson's Maudlin Jumble 136
   Matthew Campbell
9. Courtly Lays or Democratic Songs? The Politics of Poetic Citation in Chartist Literary Criticism 156
   Michael Sanders
10. Edwin Waugh: The Social and Literary Standing of a Working-Class Icon 174
    Brian Hollingworth

| 11 | William Barnes's Place and Dialects of Connection
Sue Edney | 191 |

Index 211

Acknowledgements

This collection received its initial impetus from a conference we organized in 2008 on the theme of 'Class and the Canon', and the lively discussions we had with participants on that day. We are grateful to all the speakers and attendees for their inspiring work on labouring-class poetics, and to the British Association for Victorian Studies and the University of Glasgow for funding this event. We would also like to thank all the contributors to this volume for their patience and willingness in revising their work, and the reader for Palgrave Macmillan for their helpful suggestions for revision.

Kirstie completed the editing work and wrote the Introduction for this collection while holding a visiting professorship, as Margaret Root Brown Professor of Robert Browning and Victorian Studies at the Armstrong Browning Library, Baylor University. She is very grateful to the ABL and Baylor for the research leave funding that supported these tasks. She would also like to thank Matthew Creasy and Corinna Creasy for providing childcare at a crucial moment.

Mina would like to thank John Beer, Heather Glen and Subha Mukherjee for their incisive and helpful comments on her essay. She is grateful to Sara Lodge for permission to quote from her forthcoming article. She would also like to thank Zach Beer for helping her clarify and shape her thoughts – and cheering and sustaining all the while.

Notes on Contributors

Kerri Andrews is a lecturer at the University of Strathclyde, and has previously taught at the Open University, Nottingham Trent University and the University of Leeds. Her general research interests are in eighteenth-century literature, particularly labouring-class poetry, women's writing, and print culture of the Romantic period. She is the editor of *The Collected Works of Ann Yearsley* (4 vols), forthcoming in 2013, and of the forthcoming monograph *Ann Yearsley and Hannah More, Patronage and Poetry: The Story of a Literary Relationship* (2013). She is secretary of the British Association for Romantic Studies, and a member of the British Society for Eighteenth-Century Studies and the Robert Bloomfield Society.

Kirstie Blair is Senior Lecturer at the University of Glasgow, and has published widely in the field of nineteenth-century poetry and poetics. She is the author of *Victorian Poetry and the Culture of the Heart* (2006) and *Form and Faith in Victorian Poetry and Religion* (2012), and has edited and co-edited collections on John Keble and on Tractarian poetry and poetics. Her published work on labouring-class poetry and poetics includes an essay in *Victorian Literature and Culture*, 37 (2009), and a chapter on 'Tennyson and the Victorian Working-Class Poet' in *Tennyson Among the Poets*, ed. Seamus Perry and Robert Douglas-Fairhurst (2009).

Matthew Campbell is Professor of English at the University of York. His research falls into three main areas: Victorian poetry, nineteenth-century Irish poetry in English, and contemporary Irish poetry. In 1999 he published *Rhythm and Will in Victorian Poetry*, and from 1999–2004 he was editor of the *Tennyson Research Bulletin*. He also co-edited *Memory and Memorials, 1789–1914* (2000, with Jacqueline M. Labbe and Sally Shuttleworth), and contributed a chapter on the nineteenth-century funeral ode. He has published a series of articles on nineteenth-century Irish poets, including Thomas Moore, William Allingham, Samuel Ferguson, James Clarence Mangan, and W. B. Yeats. A recent chapbook, *Jeremiah Joseph Callanan and 'The Last Home of the Bards'* (2004) published a manuscript of Callanan's 'Gougane Barra' (1826) which he discovered in the British Library. He wrote the chapter on Victorian Irish Poetry in English for the *Cambridge History of Irish Literature* (2006). He is currently finishing a major monograph, *Irish*

Poetry in the Union, 1801–1899. In the field of contemporary poetry, Professor Campbell edited and introduced *The Cambridge Companion to Contemporary Irish Poetry* (2003).

Sue Edney lectures in English at Bath Spa University where she completed her PhD. Her research covers aspects of poetic language, especially in constructions of place through dialect poetry of the eighteenth and nineteenth centuries. Her published essays include '"Times be badish vor the poor": William Barnes and his dialect of disturbance in the Dorset "Eclogues"', *English*, 58 (2009): 206–29; 'Printed Voices: Dialect and Diversity in Mid-Nineteenth-Century Lancashire', *Place, Writing, and Voice in Oral History*, ed. Shelley Trower (2011) and 'Recent Studies in Victorian English Literary Dialect and its Linguistic Connections', *Literature Compass* 8/9 (2011): 660–74.

John Goodridge is Professor of English at Nottingham Trent University and an eighteenth and nineteenth-century specialist with particular interests in 'recovery' research and labouring-class poetry. He has published widely on pastoral and georgic, Romantic and labouring-class poets including Bloomfield, Clare, Mary Collier and John Dyer. He has written two Cambridge monographs, *Rural Life in Eighteenth-Century English Poetry* (1994) and *John Clare and Community* (2012) and is the General Editor of two series of *English Labouring-Class Poets* (2003 and 2006). He is a Vice-President of the John Clare society and a Fellow of the English Association.

Mina Gorji is a lecturer at Cambridge University and a Fellow of Pembroke College where she works on eighteenth and nineteenth-century poetry. Her published writing includes a monograph *John Clare and the Place of Poetry* (2009) and essays on Robert Bloomfield in *Lyric, Class and the Romantic Canon*, eds Simon White, John Goodridge and Bridget Keegan (2006), and on William Hone's popularization of writers such as Keats, Spenser and Clare in the early nineteenth century (in *Romanticism and Popular Culture*, ed. Phillip Connell and Nigel Leask (2008)). She has also edited a collection of essays *Rude Britannia* (2007) which examines the forms and forces of rudeness in British culture.

Brian Hollingworth is a retired Head of Literature Studies at Derby University and formerly a lecturer in Education at Leeds University. His interests include vernacular language, its significance in education and general culture, and its use in literature. His writing has covered the development of English studies in nineteenth-century secondary and primary education, and the use of the vernacular in Caribbean literature and in British literature. He has published *Songs of the People: Lancashire Dialect Poetry of the Industrial Revolution* (1977), *Maria Edgeworth's Irish Writing: Language, History, Politics* (1997), and most recently privately published *The Diary of Edwin Waugh: Life in Victorian Manchester and Rochdale 1847–1851* (2008).

Nigel Leask holds the Regius Chair of English Language and Literature at the University of Glasgow. He was previously Reader in Romantic Literature in the English Faculty at Cambridge University, and a Fellow of Queens' College, Cambridge. His first book *The Politics of Imagination in Coleridge's Critical Thought* was published in 1988. Subsequently, he has published widely in the area of romantic literature and culture, with a special emphasis on empire, orientalism and travel writing. His *British Romantic Writers and the East: Anxieties of Empire* (1992) was a pioneering study of the anxieties and instabilities of Romantic representations of the 'Orient' in the writings of Byron, Shelley, De Quincey, Southey, Moore and others. In 1997 he edited Coleridge's *Biographia Literaria* for Everyman with a new introduction, text and notes. His monograph *Curiosity and the Aesthetics of Travel Writing, 1770–1840* (2002) is the first study of its kind to explore the Romantic obsession with the 'antique lands' of Ethiopia, Egypt, India and Mexico from a post-colonial perspective. He edited an anthology of Romantic Period Travel Narratives of Spanish America and the Caribbean, volume 7 of *Travels, Explorations and Empires: Writings from the Era of Imperial Expansion 1770–1835* (2001). He has in addition co-edited two essay collections: (with David Simpson and Peter De Bolla) *Land, Nation and Culture, 1740–1840: Thinking the Republic of Taste* (2004) and (with Phil Connell) *British Romanticism and Popular Culture* (2008). His most recently completed research project is a study of Robert Burns and British Romanticism, and (more generally) Anglo-Scottish literary relations in the late eighteenth-century, *Robert Burns and Pastoral: Poetry and Improvement in Late Eighteenth-Century Scotland* (2010).

Jennifer Orr is a graduate of the Universities of Oxford and Glasgow where she produced her doctoral thesis examining the life and works of the Irish romantic poet Samuel Thomson (1766–1816). She works for the University of Oxford and has recently produced the first scholarly edition of correspondence from the poetic circle of Samuel Thomson, *The Correspondence of Samuel Thomson (1766–1816)* (2012).

Michael Sanders is Senior Lecturer in Nineteenth-Century Writing at the University of Manchester. He has recently completed a monograph on Chartist poetry, entitled *The Poetry of Chartism: Aesthetics, Politics, History* (2009). This study argues that 'Chartist poetry' currently exists as a complex of aesthetic, historical and sociological problems rather than a properly defined category of literary history. Further publications include: a scholarly edition of Benjamin Disraeli's first novel *Vivian Grey* for the Pickering and Chatto series, *The Early Novels of Benjamin Disraeli* (2004), a four-volume collection of primary materials, *Women and Radicalism in the Nineteenth Century* (2001), as well as articles in *Victorian Poetry*, *Victorian Periodicals Review*, *Victorian Literature and Culture*, and *Women: A Cultural Review*.

Marcus Waithe is a University Lecturer and Fellow of Magdalene College, Cambridge. He is the author of *William Morris's Utopia of Strangers: Victorian Medievalism and the Ideal of Hospitality* (2006). That book explored Victorian interest in the treatment of strangers, in the light of literary, architectural and political efforts to define the limits of the good society. The essay included in the current volume is part of a book-length project on representations of literary labour. Dr Waithe has also published articles on John Ruskin, William Empson and Geoffrey Hill. An essay on William Barnes's representation of field labour is forthcoming in *The Oxford Handbook of Victorian Poetry*. In 2010, he launched a web-based 'reconstruction' of Ruskin's St George's Museum (www.ruskinatwalkley.org). Ruskin founded the Museum in the Sheffield suburb of Walkley in 1875, to promote 'the liberal education of the artisan', and to preserve 'memorial studies of Venice'. The project assembles an impression of the original setting and interior from surviving Victorian photographs, and links objects in their original setting to modern museum-quality images.

Introduction

Kirstie Blair

> What! write my Life? my – Life! – and can this be
> From such a Bard – a modest Bard – like me?
> To write, regardless of the wreaths of fame,
> MY OWN MEMOIRS, and print them with my *Name!*
> And no Apology? – no Preface here?
> No page inscribed to Commoner, or Peer?
> 'Tis even so!
> (James Bird, from *Poetical Memoirs*, ll.1–7,
> in McEathron, 2006, p. 237)

James Bird's opening to his *Poetical Memoirs* (1823), a long *ottava rima* poem in the style of Byron's *Don Juan*, is a signal example of the self-consciousness with which labouring-class writers engaged with poetic tradition. Many if not most volumes of eighteenth and nineteenth-century verse by labouring-class authors opened with subscription lists and other statements of patronage; many contained prefaces authored by better-known poets or critics; many introduced their authors not simply by name, but by profession or political affiliation – 'Lactilla, Milkwoman of Clifton' (Ann Yearsley), 'The Factory Girl' (Ellen Johnston), 'The Corn-Law Rhymer' (Ebenezer Elliott), 'Surfaceman' (Alexander Anderson). Whether in the words of the poet him or herself, or their patron, an apology for the poet's lack of learning or skill, a reference to his or her difficulties in achieving the education and the leisure time necessary to produce poetry, was also standard. These were the expectations which governed the publishing of 'labouring-class poetry' from the 1700s well into the Victorian period, and framed it for readers and critics.

In Bird's ironic tone we hear a chorus of imagined higher-class reviewers and readers, shocked at his temerity in abandoning the required apologetics. When he qualifies 'Bard' (in itself, a loaded term) with 'modest', it is deliberately ambiguous whether he is referring to himself as 'modest', 'having a moderate or humble estimate of one's own abilities or achievements' (*OED* 3(a)) and thus ambitious in attempting to write his memoirs, or whether 'modest' is a term that his imagined audience would apply to him, in the sense 'of a person's origins or social circumstances: undistinguished on the social or economic scale' (*OED* 4). This latter kind of modesty should, the implication is, bar him from straying into genres and subjects associated with more 'distinguished' poets. Bird's point is, of course, that the two are indistinguishable: poets 'undistinguished on the social and economic scale' are – if they want to be published – required to perform humility. In stating his intention to break with these conventions, Bird also subscribes to them, because he makes it clear that his poetry can be read within the tradition he satirizes. By noting that he is not following the standard practice of 'modest' poets, he suggests that he might, in fact, be one of them.

Bird provides a good example with which to open this collection, because it is not so much that he *is*, self-evidently and indisputably, a 'labouring-class poet', as that he is aware that he will be constructed as such, and participates in this construction himself. His social or class position was ambiguous: he was the son of a farmer, educated to a manual trade as a miller and in precarious economic circumstances, yet he later moved into a more 'literary' profession as a bookseller in Yoxford, Suffolk. Like many labouring-class poets, he had a strong local presence and was assisted into print by the editor of the *Suffolk Chronicle*, but he was also very well read and wrote a number of poems on London institutions and traditions (McEathron, 2006, pp. 235–6). Scott McEathron comments that 'our understanding of his place within the tradition must take into account the fact that he was – in relative terms – a learned, successful and worldly figure' (p. 236). In Bird's learning, his ambition, and his display of these through the reworking of poetic forms and styles popularized by a more established poet, he is very similar to many of the poets discussed here. In addition, he presents an instance of how important the work of twentieth and twenty-first century literary critics and editors can be in constructing a labouring-class tradition. Far from a well-known figure, it is through his inclusion in Pickering & Chatto's 6-volume *Eighteenth and Nineteenth-Century English Labouring-Class Poets* (Goodridge, 2003, 2006), a landmark collection in the field, that Bird is most likely to come to the attention of scholars and students working in this area.

The late twentieth and early twenty-first centuries have seen an explosion of scholarship on labouring-class poetry and poetics in the eighteenth and nineteenth centuries. Thanks to online resources such as the Labouring-Class Writers Project at Nottingham Trent or the 'Minor Victorian Poets and Authors' database, dedicated to Gerald Massey and his contemporaries, and to new anthologies, such as *Eighteenth and Nineteenth-Century Labouring-Class Poets*, Kevin Binfield's *The Writings of the Luddites* (2004) or Florence S. Boos' *Working-Class Women Poets in Victorian Britain* (2008), scholars have a far wider range of available resources and information in this field than ever before.[1] Yet with the recovery of so many poets, it has also become clear how much remains to be said about these writers and their importance in the literary cultures of their time, not to mention in their political, social and religious contexts. Since Robert Southey's foundational essay of 1831, 'The Lives and Works of the Uneducated Poets', labouring-class poets have often been judged *sui generis*, placed in a particular category and most frequently assessed in terms of their relationships with others within that category. The many outstanding monographs on labouring-class poetry and poetics, by critics such as Martha Vicinus, Donna Landry, William J. Christmas and Bridget Keegan, frequently compare these poets to each other, highlighting the existence of connections and a sense of community within this specific tradition. As Keegan observes:

> Despite the efforts of many patrons and early critics to capitalize upon the supposed uniqueness and rarity of the figure of the labouring-class genius, these poets were well aware of one another's work, often writing poems addressing or commenting upon fellow authors. (2008, p. 2)

John Goodridge's essay in this collection is an excellent example of one such relationship between John Clare and Robert Bloomfield, two of the best-known labouring-class writers of their period. Tracing such connections is vital in showing how conscious these poets were about their own place within a rapidly changing landscape of labouring-class literature. Yet, as these critics invariably acknowledge, the construction of a labouring-class tradition is a tricky process, because it inevitably involves situating a poet with regard to his or her personal circumstances, and judging these circumstances as either qualifications or disqualifications for labouring-class status. Christmas, for instance, whose focus is on 'occupation-specific poems', decides to define this strand of poetics as 'plebeian' and includes 'only those poets who have some form of labouring experience in their background' (2001, pp. 23, 29). In discussing her decision to include some eighteenth-century women poets in her study and not others, Landry refers to their 'borderline status', observing that 'signs of genteel social connection work against equating "laboring class" with what it might mean to be of "humble" or "obscure" birth' (1990, pp. 9, 8). These critics are aware of the difficulties in locating a poet within a particular class, but they still have to make the choice about whether to do so or not. As others build on this foundational work, however, these constructed categories begin to seem more and more porous. Nigel Leask's work on Robert Burns, here and in his recent *Robert Burns and Pastoral* (2010), is a particularly strong example. Burns did have labouring experience, but he was working in the fields alongside men who were his employees. Was a tenant farmer in mid-eighteenth century Ayrshire labouring class, or not? Such research, by uncovering the complexities of social standing in a particular time and place, quietly works against over two centuries of constructing Burns as the typical labouring-class poet, and shows the question to be, if not moot, unanswerable. Many of the essays in this collection similarly focus on poets whose status as 'labourers' is, at most, liminal. Samuel Thomson and William Barnes, for instance, were schoolmasters, and Barnes eventually acquired a university education. Ann Yearsley may have started out working in a dairy, but as Kerri Andrews implicitly shows, by the time she produced her later poetry she was (at points) relatively well-off, and unquestionably well read. If poets managed to write their way out of a more precarious existence dependent on hard manual labour, were they still labouring class? Or if they came from more 'middle-class' backgrounds, like Barnes, but wrote in a linguistic mode strongly associated with labouring-class poetics, is their poetry then 'labouring class' even if they themselves were not? What the essays on individual poets in this collection show is that eighteenth and nineteenth-century poets, journalists and critics were also engaged with these questions, and involved in efforts to locate their own work and that of others in relation to a perceived notion of a labouring-class poetic tradition.

If the notion of 'labouring' is not at all straightforward, 'class' is, of course, equally tricky. E. P. Thompson, whose shadow still looms large in literary criticism on this topic, influentially argued that 'we must exert caution against any tendency to read back subsequent notations of class' in relation to the eighteenth century, a period when 'class was not available within people's own cognitive system' (1978, p. 148). The arguments of Gareth Stedman Jones, which prompted a 'linguistic turn' in class-based historical studies, made the important point that what matters is the language that particular groupings (in his case, the

Chartists) used, and used of themselves. It was not so much the concept of class, as the word itself, that was 'not available' to eighteenth-century poets, as Christmas notes in his helpful discussion of this issue.[2] In the title of this volume, we have retained 'class' as a useful shorthand for indicating how the poets and critics discussed here located themselves within their societies, whether 'high' or 'low', 'polite' or 'rude', rich or poor. Of course, the division between 'labouring class' (most often used to refer to poets from the long eighteenth century) and 'working class' (most often used to refer to poets from the Victorian period) is also problematic, not least because it helps to create artificial divisions between so-called literary periods. The span of this volume, more than a century, follows recent work, such as Keegan's, that notes the continuity of a poetic tradition across eighteenth-century, 'Romantic' and 'Victorian' categories: discussing the Victorian poet and postman Edward Capern, Keegan comments that he 'wryly shows his awareness of how the limited expectations for what a labouring-class poet can and should produce have not changed greatly from the 1730s to the 1870s' (2008, p. 178). Victorian labouring-class poets, whose knowledge of contemporary poetry was often relatively limited due to its high cost, often had a stronger relationship as readers with eighteenth-century predecessors than with the poets of their own time, and still wrote very much in the shadow of Burns. Of the individual poets discussed here, only Ebenezer Elliott potentially fits into the notion of a 'working-class' poet in the sense of a worker in the newly industrialized Victorian city – and, as Marcus Waithe demonstrates, this was in large part wishful thinking and deliberate misrepresentation on the part of contemporary critics like Carlyle rather than an actual reflection of Elliott's circumstances.

Eighteenth and nineteenth-century poets were operating in a period when, it has been argued, notions of a 'canon' of English poetry, consisting of its 'classics', were being solidified. Jonathan Brody Kramnick pronounces, in the opening lines of his study, 'The English literary canon achieved its definitive shape during the middle decades of the eighteenth century' (1998, p. 1). Thomas F. Bonnell, while differing from Kramnick's emphasis on the importance of Shakespeare, Spenser and Milton in this canon, agrees that the 'multi-volume poetry collections that sprang from the British press after 1765' offered 'for the first time in material form a presumptive canon of English poetry' (2008, p. 1). By the Victorian period, it is safe to assume that certain English poets were more or less definitively canonized, or, in Paul Thomas Murphy's helpful term '"established" – that is, having a strong and reasonably steady reputation among other classes, particularly among the middle class' (1994, p. 3). Of course, labouring-class writers did not always have access to the works of these 'established' writers, nor did they necessarily share the high estimate in which they were held. Murphy's seminal *Toward a Working-Class Canon* demonstrates that working-class journalists in the nineteenth century made a deliberate effort to promote 'a canon for their class' that, Murphy argues, 'had very little in common with that of the middle class': 'The journalists looked at every work they quoted or reviewed from a completely new, class-based point of view' (p. 53). Further studies, such as Mike Sanders' in-depth examination of the poetry columns of the Chartist press, have investigated in detail the significance of poetry in political cultures and the shifting ways in which Chartist literary critics and poets engaged with questions of canonicity. Sanders' essay here, and also the essays by Matthew Campbell and Waithe, focus specifically on the construction of a labouring-class 'canon' by nineteenth-century critics in their periodical and newspaper criticism. As Waithe and Campbell show, however, this project also engaged critics writing for more established middle-class periodicals, such as *Blackwood's Edinburgh Magazine* or its new, ambitious imitator, the *Dublin University Magazine*. Much was at stake for writers like Carlyle and Samuel Ferguson – both personally and politically – in championing particular forms of labouring-class verse.

The effort to push the labouring-class poet into a particular mould is not unique to eighteenth and nineteenth-century critics and patrons, from Southey onwards. As noted above, twentieth and twenty-first century critics have productively engaged in attempts to define a canon of labouring-class poetry and poetics, as well as trying to introduce this poetry into the classroom and make it part of the institutionalized 'canon' of texts taught to undergraduate students. The most recent criticism, however, is often notable for its attempts to complicate perceptions of labouring-class poets as valuable for the 'authenticity' of their representation of 'class-specific labour experience', a view dating back to the eighteenth century at least but still remarkably persistent, which has led to certain more 'authentic' poems being valued above others (Christmas, 2009, p. 26). In Aruna Krishnamurthy's edited collection *The Working-Class Intellectual in Eighteenth and Nineteenth-Century Britain*, which helpfully demonstrates the extent to which a range of working-class writers were knowingly operating within literary tradition, Christmas argues that the canonization of Stephen Duck's *The Thresher's Labour*, long seen as his defining poem, rests on a valuation of 'originality and independence' over 'imitation and assimilation' that misrepresents Duck's own ambitions and interests and ignores a substantial and interesting part of his later poetic career (2009, p. 45). Landry, in a 2003 essay on Mary Collier and Mary Leapor, emphasizes that their use of 'poetic forms previously associated with polite rather than plebeian culture . . . should not be viewed as a regrettable aesthetic choice' and that the 'artistry of both poets is at least as significant as their testimony of labouring-class experience' (p. 224). Christmas and Landry's joint introduction to a special edition of *Criticism* on labouring-class poetics further stresses that 'formal and aesthetic questions' are coming to the fore in new work in the field (2005, p. 414). And Goodridge, another extremely influential critic in this area, suggests in several of his works that in studying and teaching labouring-class poetry, we might profitably consider how labouring-class poets 'use canonical and classical forms and models' (2010, p. 20), as Landry does in considering Collier's remaking of the georgic, Christmas does in discussing Duck's Horatian verse and imitation of Alexander Pope, or Mina Gorji does in assessing Clare's reworking of the Spenserian stanza (2008, pp. 57–76).[3]

There is clearly a shift in such work (and that of many other critics) away from the 'biographical and ideological approach' to labouring-class poets that dominated earlier criticism (see Scrivener, 2011, p. 235). This is in part due to seminal research by critics such as William St Clair and Jonathan Rose, that has served to complicate and deepen our understanding of reading practices in the eighteenth and nineteenth centuries, and in particular, to emphasize that working class readers and writers were astute and experienced.[4] The relationships between labouring class poets and more established writers, their appropriations of form and language, their allusiveness, are important in this critical shift, and are crucial in many of the essays in this collection. Examining such relationships can also have the effect of restoring to our view poems by labouring-class writers that might previously have been dismissed as 'Parnassian', derivative, or as less relevant to our concerns because of their apparent lack of political force and biographical reference.[5] To take only one of myriad possible examples, John Critchley Prince's sonnet 'On Receiving from a Friend the Poems of Keats', from *Hours with the Muses* (1841) displays many of the complexities of these relationships:

> Thanks for the Song of Keats – as rich a boon
>   As ever poet unto poet sent;
>   Oh! thou hast pleased me to my heart's content,
> And set my jarring feelings all in tune.
> 'Twere sweet to lie upon the lap of June,

> Half hidden in a galaxy of flowers,
> Beneath the shadow of impending bowers,
> And pore upon his page from morn to noon.
> 'Twere sweet to slumber by some calm lagoon,
> And dream of young Endymion, the boy
> Who nightly snatched a more than mortal joy,
> From the bright cheek of the enamoured moon.
> Thanks for the Song of Keats, whose luscious lay
> Hath half dissolved my earthly thoughts away.
>
> (Prince, 1841, p. 71)

Like many of the poems in Prince's first collection, this nods towards the existence of a local community of labouring-class poets who shared and discussed their favoured poems. Indeed, after he moved to Manchester, later in 1841, Prince became an important figure in one such poetic community, centred on the Sun Inn. Prince's vision of Keats focuses on the soothing affect of Keats's poetry and its ability to make the reader forget everyday cares: his view of Keats's poetics as dreamlike and otherworldly is typical of early Victorian representations. In Keatsian language, like 'sweet', 'enamoured' and 'luscious', Prince hints at the sensuousness if not sensuality of Keats's poetry, and his vision of a fantasy reading scenario of bowers and lagoons alludes to the landscapes of poems such as 'Endymion'. In the context of *Hours with the Muses*, however, this is perhaps not such an untroubled celebration of another poet's work as it might seem. If half the poet's mind is on poetry, the other half is on less ethereal concerns. The explicitly political 'Song of Freedom', immediately preceding this poem, speaks of 'oppression, strife and despair', and opens its second stanza with:

> Rejoice! Oh, ye Sons of Industry! Rejoice!
> List, list to the sound of a glorious voice
> 'Tis the sweet hymn of Freedom that gladdens the gale
>
> (p. 69)

What casts a shadow over this poem is not 'impending bowers' but impending Chartist revolution, and the 'jarring feelings' evident in it are not entirely cancelled out by the succeeding sonnet.[6] The two poems together indicate the shift, identified by Anne Janowitz, from politicized, communal labouring-class verse, to more individualistic lyrical poems that focused on poetry as an affective force through its aesthetic beauties.[7]

Prince's high valuation of poetry's emotional power, here and throughout his volume, is held in tension with a more political and, most importantly, economic valuation of verse. *Hours with the Muses* included a 'Sketch of the Author's Life' that elaborated on Prince's difficult early life and impoverished background, and on his work as a reed-maker, machinist and yarn warehouseman. Prince's preface to the first edition, in its studied humility and emphasis on patronage and subscription, equally deliberately situated him as a self-made working poet who needed financial assistance. When this sonnet states that it would be sweet to 'lie upon the lap of June' or 'slumber . . . and dream', it envisages the joys of leisurely reading, of daydreaming and escapism; luxuries rarely if ever available to Prince, who worked six days a week. He composed poetry at his desk in the factory or once, a significant anecdote from the biographical sketch reports, in a tavern 'amid the riot and noise of a number of coal-heavers and others', on paper bought with his last cash from the sale of his waistcoat, in a desperate bid to write something he could sell to stave off imminent starvation (Prince, 1841, p. xx). That the poems of Keats might provide an antidote to the harsh circumstances of real life is seen as a positive good in 'On Receiving from a Friend the Poems of Keats', a poem which, in its established poetic form and smooth rhymes, also sets out to mimic the comforting effects it describes. But readers of the whole volume would know this escape to be temporary, fantasy rather than reality.

This sonnet would still be highly unlikely to make it into an anthology of labouring-class poetry, or a university seminar on the topic, or to receive critical attention when compared to Prince's more politicized verse, such as 'The Death of the Factory Child'. Yet its relation to questions of class and canonicity in its own time is fascinating and complex. To investigate it further, we would have to know what 'cultural capital' (to borrow John Guillory's important term) Keats held in 1841, and whether his reputation was the same for middle-class readers as for working-class readers, and to trace in particular, perhaps, whether Keats's own radicalism and arguably labouring-class background could have been known to Prince at the time when this sonnet was composed. More specifically, we would want to know what the labouring-class poets of Manchester and the surrounding areas thought of Keats, and whether others discussed him in their writings. We would have to establish what a volume of Keats's poems cost at this time and how widely available it would be, to assess whether this poem is more likely to refer to a loan (labouring-class poets frequently shared one volume between many readers) or a gift, and if the latter, what its value said about the friendship between Prince and the giver. We would have to assess what it meant for a labouring-class poet to write in a 'canonical' genre, the sonnet. All these questions have broader implications in terms of how labouring-class poets operated in a particular time and place. If there is not space here to consider them, contributors in this collection do ask similar questions of other poets, in differing times and locations. What Thomson may have been doing when he reworked poems by Burns, in late eighteenth-century Ulster; what another Irish Protestant, Samuel Ferguson, attempted to achieve in his translations of 'peasant' poetry in Gaelic, in mid-nineteenth century Dublin; the tradition into which John Clare entered when he chose the sonnet form for poems of natural observation; what was at stake in Edwin Waugh or Barnes's choices to write in dialect, and why the stakes were different in Lancashire and Dorset: it is the specificity of these questions, and their attention to formal poetic choices located within detailed historical contexts, that situates this collection within new approaches to labouring-class poetry and poetics.

This volume opens, appropriately, with Leask's essay on Burns, a figure who dominated the field of labouring-class poetry from the late eighteenth century onwards. As noted above, Leask highlights many of the concerns that run through the collection as a whole, by interrogating not just what it might mean to be 'labouring class', but what the precise issues concerning 'labour' and 'poetry' might be in mid-eighteenth century Scotland, and even more particularly, in Ayrshire. The Burns that emerges from Leask's work is not unfamiliar, but more nuanced than popular cultural representations of Scotland's national bard might have us imagine. Jennifer Orr's work on Thomson follows Leask's chronologically, but also traces the impact of Burns – a vital role-model for Thomson – on the culture of Ulster-Scots poetry in this period. Orr's meticulous work in recovering the publication contexts of Thomson's poetry, and situating these in relation to his sometimes shifting political views, shows the importance of local knowledge, for these poets and for those researching them, and highlights the poetic lines of influence between Ulster and Scotland. Thomson is still relatively little-known, though Orr's recent edition of his letters will hopefully draw more critical attention to his work (Orr, 2012). The succeeding two essays, however, focus on the best-known labouring-class poet other than Burns, and perhaps the only other labouring-class poet who has indisputably entered the 'canon' of writers taught on introductory undergraduate courses, John Clare. Goodridge considers questions of class and community in focusing on Clare's connections, personal and poetic, to Bloomfield, who was hugely influential in his day and is also returning to prominence in critical discussions. Like Leask and Orr, Goodridge conveys a strong sense of the sociability of labouring-class poets, their embeddedness within literary communities and networks of connection. But he also comments on their investment in images of loneliness and isolation, and on how Clare in particular was later constructed as a solitary, isolated poet. Mina Gorji's study of 'littleness' in Clare's poetics investigates not simply Clare's brilliant linguistic and formal engagement with tiny details, minute observation and small spaces, but also how Clare's investment in the 'little' is a self-conscious reference to constructions of the labouring-class poet and his or her poetry as little in the sense of inferior or ephemeral, by Burns and Bloomfield as well as by contemporary critics. As Gorji has shown elsewhere, Clare was very alert to literary tradition and aware of his place within it (Gorji, 2008). If he knew the negative connotations of littleness, he also knew that attention to detail could signify refinement and delicacy, and, adapting the sonnet form to record small incidents and minute observations, he works with both these conventions.

Kerri Andrews' essay situates Yearsley within a literary tradition and a 'community' of poets. Through close reading of extracts from Yearsley's later poems, she shows that these repay close attention, in their allusions to other poems and poets, their engagement with science, and their prefiguring of later, better-known poetic considerations of the role of time and memory. In particular, by suggesting that through Yearsley, we might better understand some of the most-discussed passages from Wordsworth's poems, Andrews' essay strongly relates to recent studies that integrate labouring-class writers and the 'major' Romantic poets, such as Simon J. White's 2007 monograph on Bloomfield, which opens by comparing *The Farmer's Boy* to *The Prelude*. White's comment that 'Because we are so conditioned by Wordsworthian poetics we fail to see subtly different kinds of "Romanticism" in less well-known poetry' (p. 7) nicely relates to Andrews' emphasis on Yearsley's poetic themes and strategies as precursors of these themes in later poets.

If the first five essays in this collection focus on individual poets and (on the whole) on how they defined themselves as poets in relation to canons of labouring-class and established poetry, the next three have a stronger concentration on the role of critics in constructing the figure of the labouring-class poet and defining traditions of labouring-class poetics. Waithe, as noted above, assesses Carlyle's important essay on Ebenezer Elliott, the 'Corn-Law Rhymer'. By considering Carlyle's personal and ideological investment in the concept of the poet as artisan, Waithe shows that this influenced his determination to position Elliott as the archetypal 'labouring' poet. Carlyle's version of Elliott was highly influential, yet it ignored or neglected significant aspects of Elliott's poetic output and assigned him a class position that was, in many ways, at odds with his actual social circumstances. Campbell's essay, similarly, shows us a critic struggling to make labouring-class poetry mean what he wished it to mean for his personal, political – and, in this case, also religious and national – aims. While the Gaelic poems that Samuel Ferguson discussed and translated in his important series of periodical articles are outside the eighteenth and nineteenth-century labouring-class tradition, Ferguson was trying to draw this 'peasant' poetry into his version of a canon of Irish literature. His interpretation of these poems and their authors draws on some of the stock clichés applied to labouring-class writing, but is given a twist by Ferguson's nationalistic aims. Like Leask and Orr, Campbell draws to our attention the fact that labouring-class canons have national and regional biases, and like Waithe and Sanders, he emphasizes that these canons were often invented by critics. Sanders' essay differs, however, in that while Carlyle and Ferguson were both established critics writing from a middle-class perspective, the anonymous critics that Sanders discusses were writing for working-class Chartist periodicals aimed at an audience of working-class readers. Sanders' study of what the *Chartist Circular* had to say about the canon and the function of poetry more generally is a significant addition to his other work on poetry in Chartist culture.

The final two essays work together as explorations of a vital area in labouring-class poetics: dialect. Edwin Waugh was one of Victorian Britain's best-known and widely-read dialect poets. Brian Hollingworth's exploration of Waugh's persona as a labouring-class poet (which included deliberately positioning himself as a successor of Burns) takes in Waugh's own accounts from his diary, while also considering how critics and biographers interpreted Waugh and placed him within a dialect tradition, smoothing over many of the problematic aspects of his biography as they did so. Sue Edney's discussion of William Barnes, a poet who, as she notes, is highly rated by critics but still marginal in terms of a 'canon' of Victorian poetry, is a wide-ranging consideration of what writing in dialect meant in mid-late Victorian Britain, as well as what it meant to Barnes. She shows how important dialect was for Barnes in terms of his investment in local landscapes and cultures, and examines its operation within some of his key poems.

What these essays have in common is that they demonstrate how conscious eighteenth and nineteenth-century poets and critics were of the ongoing task of shaping both a recognizable image of the 'labouring-class poet', and a labouring-class canon, while defining the relationship of both to established poets and established literary genres and forms. They also show how influential these constructions have been on our own critical practices. By paying close attention to the aesthetic choices of poets and critics, the language and forms they used, as well as their historical contexts, the critics here, as Michael Scrivener urges in a recent survey of the field, 'read the aesthetic ideologically and the ideological aesthetically' (2011, p. 235). Above all, perhaps, this collection shows how important poetry as a genre was for labouring-class writers and critics in these centuries. Whatever role they thought poetry could play within society, whether as a direct intervention in the circumstances affecting their time and place or as an escape from them, they never doubted that its role was significant, and that poetry was a medium within which they could explore their relationship to broader social, literary and political contexts.

Notes

1. Labouring-Class Writers Project: human.ntu.ac.uk/research/labouring classwriters/index.htm. 'Minor Victorian Poets and Authors': gerald-massey. org.uk/.
2. See Jones, 1983. Christmas concludes that in the eighteenth century, 'languages of class' emerged that 'predate the existence of a specifically working-class consciousness' and are 'not dependent on the actual use of the term itself' (2001, p. 44, see also pp. 42–5).
3. See also Goodridge and Burke, 2010 and the essays in this special issue, which includes several of the authors featured in this collection.
4. Rose, 2001; St Clair, 2004. Several critics have focused in depth on responses to particular 'canonical' figures. For recent work on Shakespeare and working-class readers, for example, see Murphy, 2008 and Prince, 2008, especially pp. 16–36.
5. For a helpful account of 'Parnassian' working-class poetry and a selection of such poems, from one of few critics to take this genre seriously, see Maidment, 1987.
6. Prince's nineteenth-century biographer works hard to disassociate him from Chartism and emphasizes his dissatisfaction with some of its aspects, but also indicates that Prince had considerable sympathy with the movement (Lithgow, 1880).
7. See Janowitz, 1998 and also Sanders, 2009 and below.

Bibliography

Bonnell, Thomas F. (2008) *The Most Disreputable Trade: Publishing the Classics of English Poetry, 1765–1810* (Oxford: Oxford University Press, 2008).

Christmas, William J. (2001) *The Lab'ring Muses: Work, Writing and the Social Order in English Plebeian Poetry* (London: Associated University Presses).

———. (2009) '"From threshing Corn, he turns to thresh his Brains": Stephen Duck as Laboring-Class Intellectual', in *The Working-Class Intellectual in Eighteenth and Nineteenth-Century Britain*, ed. Aruna Krishmamurthy (Aldershot: Ashgate), pp. 25–48.

———. and Donna Landry (2005) 'Introduction', in 'Learning to Read in the Long Nineteenth Century: New Work on Laboring-Class Poets, Aesthetics and Politics', ed. William J. Christmas and Donna Landry, *Criticism*, 47 (2005), 413–20.

Goodridge, John, gen. ed. (2003) *Eighteenth-Century Labouring-Class Poets, 1700–1800*, 3 vols (London: Pickering & Chatto).

———. gen. ed. (2006) *Nineteenth-Century Labouring-Class Poets, 1800–1900*, 3 vols (London: Pickering & Chatto).

———. (2010) 'Labouring-Class Poetry', in *Teaching Romanticism*, ed. Sharon Ruston and David Higgins (Basingstoke: Palgrave Macmillan), pp. 11–23.

———. and Tim Burke (2010) 'Retrieval and Beyond: Labouring-Class Writing', *Keywords* 8, 1–14.

Gorji, Mina (2009) *John Clare and the Place of Poetry* (Liverpool: Liverpool University Press).

Guillory, John (1993) *Cultural Capital: The Problem of Literary Canon Formation* (Chicago: University of Chicago Press).

Janowitz, Anne (1998) *Lyric and Labor in the Romantic Tradition* (Cambridge: Cambridge University Press).

Jones, Gareth Stedman (1983) *Languages of Class: Studies in English Working-Class History, 1832–1982* (Cambridge: Cambridge University Press).

Keegan, Bridget (2008) *British Labouring-Class Nature Poetry, 1730–1837* (Basingstoke: Palgrave Macmillan).

Kramnick, Jonathan Brody (1998) *Making the English Canon: Print-Capitalism and the Cultural Past, 1700–1770* (Cambridge: Cambridge University Press, 1998).

Krishnamurthy, Aruna, ed. (2009) *The Working-Class Intellectual in Eighteenth and Nineteenth-Century Britain* (Aldershot: Ashgate).

Landry, Donna (1990) *The Muses of Resistance: Laboring-Class Women's Poetry in Britain, 1739–1796* (Cambridge: Cambridge University Press).

———. (2003) 'The Labouring-Class Women Poets: "Hard Labour we most cheerfully pursue"', in *Women and Poetry 1660–1750*, ed. Sarah Prescott and David Shuttleton (Basingstoke: Palgrave Macmillan).

Leask, Nigel (2010) *Robert Burns and Pastoral: Poetry and Improvement in Late Eighteenth-Century Scotland* (Oxford: Oxford University Press).

Lithgow, R. A. Douglas (1880) *The Life of John Critchley Prince* (Manchester: Abel Heywood).

Maidment, Brian (1987) *The Poorhouse Fugitives: Self-Taught Poets and Poetry in Victorian Britain* (Manchester: Carcanet).

McEathron, Scott, ed. (2006) *Nineteenth-Century Labouring-Class Poets*, I, 1800–1830, gen. ed. John Goodridge (London: Pickering & Chatto).

Murphy, Andrew (2008) *Shakespeare for the People: Working-Class Readers, 1800–1900* (Cambridge: Cambridge University Press).

Murphy, Paul Thomas (1994) *Toward a Working-Class Canon: Literary Criticism in British Working-Class Periodicals, 1816–1858* (Columbus: Ohio State University Press).

Orr, Jennifer (2012) *The Correspondence of Samuel Thomson (1766–1816)* (Dublin: Four Courts Press).
Prince, John Critchley (1841) *Hours with the Muses* (London: Simpkin, Marshall & Co.).
Prince, Kathryn (2008) *Shakespeare in the Victorian Periodicals* (New York: Routledge).
Rose, Jonathan (2001) *The Intellectual Life of the British Working Classes* (New Haven: Yale University Press).
Ruston, Sharon and David Higgins, ed. (2010) *Teaching Romanticism* (Basingstoke: Palgrave Macmillan).
Sanders, Mike (2009) *The Poetry of Chartism* (Cambridge: Cambridge University Press).
Scrivener, Michael (2011) 'Laboring-Class Poetry in the Romantic Era', in *The Blackwell Companion to Romantic Poetry*, ed. Charles Mahoney (Oxford: Blackwell), pp. 234–50.
St Clair, William (2004) *The Reading Nation in the Romantic Period* (Cambridge: Cambridge University Press).
Thompson, E. P. (1978) 'Eighteenth-Century English Society: Class Struggle Without Class?', *Social History*, 3, 133–65.
Vicinus, Martha (1974) *The Industrial Muse: A Study of Nineteenth-Century British Working-Class Literature* (London: Croom Helm).
White, Simon J. (2007) *Robert Bloomfield, Romanticism and the Poetry of Community* (Aldershot: Ashgate).

2
Was Burns a Labouring-Class Poet?

Nigel Leask

Writing in the *Edinburgh Review* in 1809, Francis Jeffrey reflected on the widespread contemporary view of Robert Burns as a 'peasant poet'; 'certainly by far the greatest of our poetical prodigies – from Stephen Duck down to Thomas Dermody. *They* are forgotten already; or only remembered for derision. But the name of Burns, if we are not mistaken, has not yet "gathered all its fame".' Jeffrey canvassed the case for locating Burns in the company of Wiltshire-born Stephen Duck (1705?–1756), tragic paradigm of all eighteenth-century labouring-class poets, and the more contemporary Irish poet-prodigy Thomas Dermody (1772–1802), but dismissed the comparison as deeply misleading: 'He will never be rightly estimated as a poet, till that vulgar wonder be entirely repressed which was raised on his having been a ploughman' (Jeffrey, 1809, p. 249).

Jeffrey's disavowal, in what is otherwise a strangely equivocal essay on Robert Burns, has a lot to do with his snobbish distaste for plebeian writing, as well as his special pleading for Scottish literary production, concluding as it does with a swingeing attack on Wordsworth as a poor imitator of Burns's genius. Yet the view of Burns as a labouring-class prodigy derided here was central to the meteoric rise of the poet's fame, which was still (as Jeffrey notes) very much 'on the up' in 1809.[1] Henry Mackenzie's famous description of Burns as a 'Heaven-taught ploughman' in *The Lounger* for 9 December 1786 had been largely responsible for propagating the image of Burns as a peasant-genius, an image Jeffrey dismisses as a 'vulgar wonder' (Low, 1974, p. 70). But it was nevertheless an image that, despite Jeffrey's assault, exerted a massive influence upon subsequent Romantic poets like Wordsworth, when he wrote 'Of him who walk'd in glory and in joy / Behind the plough, upon the mountain-side' ('Resolution and Independence', ll.45–6), as well as poets of the British and Irish working-class tradition who were largely inspired by Burns's success. As doyen of the late-Enlightenment Scottish literati, Mackenzie would have been aware of the poetic licence underlying his description, which artfully echoed James Beattie's influential poem *The Minstrel* (1769–74), where Beattie had enjoined his eponymous peasant-genius; 'let thy heaven-taught soul to heaven aspire, /To fancy, freedom, harmony, resign'd; /Ambition's groveling crew for ever left behind' (Beattie, 1784, p. 4 (I.vii)).

To be fair to Mackenzie, he was only elaborating the 'self-taught' image already constructed by Burns himself in the Kilmarnock volume of 1786, the preface of which proclaimed that 'he sings the sentiments and manners, he felt and saw in himself and his rustic compeers around him, in his and their native language' (Burns, 1786, p. iii). Burns's skill in situating his poetry in relation to the late eighteenth-century cult of 'primitive' genius (as promoted by William Duff, Beattie and Hugh Blair) is evinced in the epigraph to the Kilmarnock volume: 'The Simple Bard, unbroke by rules of Art, / He pours the wild effusions of the heart: / And if inspir'd, 'tis Nature's pow'rs inspire; / Her's all the melting thrill, and her's the kindling fire' (Burns, 1786, title page). Although Burns here abandons Scots for the high-strained discourse of sensibility, there is a close link between the 'heaven-taught ploughman' image and what Kilmarnock's title describes as poetry written 'chiefly in the Scottish dialect'. It is important not to flatten out the complex interrelationship of class, language, region and nationality that underpins Burns's poetic self-fashioning in considering his links with subsequent 'labouring-class' poets. As I have recently argued in *Robert Burns and Pastoral* (2010), the eighteenth-century pastoral tradition, especially as modified by Scots vernacular poets Allan Ramsay and Robert Fergusson, permitted licences of language and social observation impossible in other genres, including georgic, the alternative classical mode for writing about rural life.

In an illuminating essay on Burns in the third volume of the Pickering & Chatto anthology *Eighteenth-Century Labouring Class Poets*, Tim Burke proposes that it might even be 'undesirable' to attempt an answer to the question 'was Burns a labouring-class poet', given the 'uses to which the "truth" of (Burns's) class status has been put in the last two hundred years, by commentators of all political hues, employing a variety of methodological perspectives' (Burke, 2003, p. 106). Yet his decision to include Burns in the anthology already presupposes an affirmative answer, as does his description of the Ayrshire poet in the opening sentences of his introduction to the volume, as the 'first international celebrity' of the labouring-class poetic tradition, echoing Carol

McGuirk's more disputable claim that he was 'the only great poet ever to emerge from the British peasant class'.[2]

One might assume that given his own role in constructing the myth of the 'heaven-taught ploughman', as well as his stated ambition (albeit in a letter to a powerful patron, Dr John Moore) 'to please my Compeers, the rustic Inmates of the Hamlet', that inspiring labouring-class imitators would have delighted the democratically-minded Bard (Burns, 1985, I, p. 88). On the contrary, in an April 1789 letter to his patron Mrs Frances Dunlop he argued that 'my success has encouraged such a shoal of ill-spawned monsters to crawl into public notice under the title of Scots poets, that the very term, Scots Poetry, borders on the burlesque' (Burns, 1985, I, p. 382). Lest we think this was aimed merely at poetry in Scots, in another letter of April 1789 he grumbled about an 'inundation of nonsense over the Land' (Burns, 1985, I, p. 400), and elsewhere damned the productions of the Ayrshire poet Janet Little with the faintest of praise (although denominated the 'Scotch Milkmaid', much of her poetry was written in neo-Augustan English) (Burns, 1985, I, p. 438). Subsequent labouring-class poets of the stature of Samuel Thomson, Edward Williams ('Iolo Morgangw'), James Hogg, Robert Bloomfield and John Clare were certainly upfront in admitting Burns as a major inspiration. Of course the Bard's marked lack of enthusiasm for his poetic progeny might have been tempered if he had lived to read the distinguished verse of any of the aforementioned. But as well as inspiring subsequent poets of humble birth, Burns's demise and premature death (especially as moralized by his biographer Dr James Currie) was often served them as a warning by their patrons and 'friends'. In an 1802 letter to the Earl of Buchan, whose patronage Burns had himself struggled to brush off a decade earlier, Robert Bloomfield complained *'Remember Burns* has been the watch word of my friends. *I do remember Burns*, but I am not Burns, neither have I his fire to quench, nor his passion to controll.'[3] Bloomfield's impatience here provides a revealing insight into the double valency of Burns's reputation in the Romantic period.

Axiomatic to the study of 'labouring-class poetry' (or any of its cognates past and present, 'uneducated', 'peasant', 'plebeian', 'working-class' poetry) is the slipperiness of the concept of class as an analytical category. This was something of a hot chestnut for Marxist historiography in the 1970s and '80s, and we would still do well to heed E. P. Thompson's caveat that 'if class was not available within people's own cognitive system, if they saw themselves and fought out their own historical battles in terms of "estates" or "ranks" or "orders", etc., then if we describe those struggles in class terms we must exert caution against any tendency to read back subsequent notions of class' (1978, p. 148). Burns's occupation as a tenant farmer, together with the pastoral title of 'heaven-taught ploughman', have led to mighty confusions about his social class, and (not quite the same thing) class-*consciousness*. He certainly did not regard himself as an 'uneducated poet', despite the disavowal of learning we have seen in the 'Preface' to the Kilmarnock volume, and, famously, in the 'Epistle to John Lapraik': 'Gie me a spark o' Nature's fire, / That's a' the learning I desire' (ll.73–4) (the latter barely disguising its allusions to Pope and Sterne).

This is strongly evident in a lesser-known epistle of 1786 'To James Tennant of Glenconner':

> I've sent you here by Johnie Simson,
> Twa sage Philosophers to glimpse on!
> Smith, wi' his sympathetic feeling,
> An' Reid, to common sense appealing.
>
> (ll.7–10)

Burns here alludes to Adam Smith's *Theory of Moral Sentiments* and Thomas Reid's *Inquiry into the Human Mind on the Principles of Common Sense*, both recent publications at the cutting edge of eighteenth-century Scottish Enlightenment philosophy, which he was lending to Tennant. It is significant that this epistle was never published during the poet's lifetime, as if he sensed the damage it might do to his reputation as a 'heaven taught ploughman'. Burns requested that his friend return the books speedily, lest he be forced to re-peruse works of Calvinist devotion by Brown and Boston; 'Till by an' by, if I haud on, / I'll grunt a real Gospel groan' (ll.23–4). Presbyterian parish schooling had disseminated habits of literacy through the whole social fabric of rural society in eighteenth-century Lowland Scotland: James Tennant's brother David was librarian at the Ayr Library Society, whose up-to-date stock was supplied by William Creech, leading publisher of the Scottish Enlightenment, and to which Burns had access (Leask, 2010, p. 11). Significantly, the poet here confesses to an enlightened interest in Smith and Reid as a salvation from traditional devotional reading of the sort favoured by the Presbyterian 'auld lichts', or orthodox party who dominated Mauchline Parish. It was precisely this concern for enlightenment 'common sense' that inspired his brilliant Kirk Satires, establishing his reputation as a local poet in Tarbolton and Mauchline well before his poetry was first published in 1786.[4]

Contemporary opinion differed widely about the extent of Burns's literacy, and, by extension, his education. Echoing Jeffrey's rejection of the 'heaven-taught' epithet, Sir Walter Scott wrote of Burns that he 'had an education not much worse that the sons of many gentlemen in Scotland' (Low, 1974, p. 258). Contemporary research on the poet's education, as well as the range of reading available to him, suggests that this was no exaggeration (McIlvanney, 2002, pp. 38–63). Close study of Burns's poetry reveals a density of literary allusion to canonical British poets (Shakespeare, Milton, Dryden, Pope, Goldsmith, Shenstone, Beattie, Blair, Barbauld, etc.) equal to Blake or Wordsworth, despite the fact that Burns preferred to limit his indebtedness to Allan Ramsay and Robert Fergusson, his precursors in the Scottish vernacular revival. After Burns's death, Robert Anderson recalled a conversation with him in Edinburgh in 1787 when the poet reviewed his literary and linguistic tool-kit with technical fluency:

> It was, I know, part of the machinery, as he called it, of his poetical character to pass for an illiterate ploughman who wrote from pure inspiration. When I pointed out some evident traces of poetical inspiration in his verses, privately, he readily acknowledged his obligations and even admitted the advantages he enjoyed in poetical composition from the *copia verborum*, the command of phraseology, which the knowledge and use of the English and Scottish dialects afforded him; but in company he did not suffer his pretensions to pure inspiration to be challenged, and it was seldom done where he might be supposed to affect the success of the subscription for his Poems. (Burns, 1968, III, pp. 1537–8)

Here the 'heaven-taught' mask is allowed to slip for a moment, although Burns does express some concerns about the damage such candour might do to his subscription list. He underlines the fact that, rather than struggling with an 'impoverished' or 'restricted' idiom, the Scots poet who commands both 'the English and Scottish dialects' in fact enjoys a peculiar advantage over others limited to standard English poetic diction alone (such a consideration might have determined Burns's final decision to publish 'chiefly' rather than 'exclusively' in 'Scots dialect'). Jeremy Smith argues that Burns's *copia verborum*, ('abundance of words') signifies a language that 'contains sufficient vocabulary for all registers (i.e. elevated, plain, demotic)': and his particular skill was 'to shift from one register of language to another in accordance with the social situation of his language' (Smith, 2007, pp. 76, 84). And as Murray

Pittock reminds us, 'because Burns is a sophisticated writer, writing in Scots is always a poetic option for him, not an educational necessity' (Pittock, 2008, p. 145). Of course this is not necessarily tantamount to denying that Burns was a 'labouring-class' poet (there is nothing to stop a humbly born writer being 'sophisticated' if he or she has been able to overcome their social disadvantages to acquire an education), but it does seriously qualify the claim, or at the very least demand that its criteria are reconsidered, to take account of the specific instance of Robert Burns.

If 'uneducated' will not do for Burns, will 'plebeian' or 'peasant' poet serve him any better? As employed by Thompson in his memorable essay 'Patricians and Plebs', 'plebeian' describes the agency of the unenfranchised eighteenth-century 'mob' or 'crowd' to exert political pressure on the ruling class (Thompson, 1974). However, despite Burns's invocation of mob agency in poems like 'The Author's Earnest Cry and Prayer' (positively) and 'The Ordination' (negatively), the term 'plebeian' seldom appears in Burns's poetry, and when it appears in his correspondence he generally uses it with distaste, to the extent that it implies dependence on the Patrician 'other', to the detriment of Burns's cherished virtue of 'independence'. 'Plebeian' of course takes its origin from the bi-polar social order of classical Rome, lacking an upwardly-mobile 'middling sort' of the kind that was rapidly emerging in eighteenth-century Britain.

The class consciousness that does emerge in Burns's Kilmarnock poems is defined in both negative and affirmative terms. In negative terms it is marked by a disdain for aristocracy and the vertical relations of patronage ('not the mercenary bow over a counter, but the heart-throbbing gratitude of the Bard' (Burns, 1786, p. v)); in affirmative terms, by a sense of horizontal solidarity with men like Davie Sillar, John Lapraik and James Ranken, the addressees of the volume's verse epistles. Struggling tenant farmers, linen-drapers, grocers, school-teachers, these men were the nascent petit bourgeoisie of rural Ayrshire, well-educated in the aspirational ideology of improvement and popular enlightenment, their social trajectory blocked by the elitism of the old society, and severely undercapitalized or indebted as a result of the recent Douglas Heron Bank crash of 1772, and similar crises of credit. The epistles seek to vindicate the exchange of Scots poetry or 'crambo-jingle' (in what the poet called 'plain braid Lallans' ('To Willie Simson, Ochiltree', l.119)), affirming the values of social solidarity and 'good-heartedness' in consolation for worldly failure. Burns's disdain for the 'paughty feudal *Thane*' and the 'purse proud' *'city-gent'* ('Second Epistle to Lapraik', ll.67, 61) targets both the rank-renting old gentry and the new merchant class which was rapidly replacing them in the new capitalist society. The subscription publishing of the Kilmarnock volume in 1786 was largely based on this horizontal network, although as I will argue below, Burns was obliged to solicit more genteel patronage in pursuing his poetic ambitions after the success of the 1786 volume. Although the democratic language and sentiment of the verse epistles absorb a traditional spirit of plebeian resistance to social hierarchy, they do seem to articulate the resentment of the 'middling sort', rather than the traditional values of the peasantry idealized in 'The Cotter's Saturday Night' (the Lowland cotters were in fact in the process of being rapidly cleared from the land, as Tom Devine has recently demonstrated, although Burns nowhere mentions the fact) (Devine, 1994, pp. 144, 136–64; Leask, 2010, pp. 215–31).

The social location of this horizontal class consciousness is particularly evident in Burns's invocation of his muse in the 'Second Epistle to Lapraik', as Liam McIlvanney has pointed out (McIlvanney, 2002, p. 72). In the tradition of Ramsay's personification of his muse as a 'vogy jade', Burns personifies poetic creativity as a reluctant plebeian female;

> The tapetless, ramfeezl'd hizzie,
> She's saft at best an' something lazy,
> Quo' she, 'Ye ken we've been sae busy
>   This month an' mair,
> That trouth, my head is grown right dizzie,
>   An' something sair'.
>
>   (ll.13–18)

The well-worn connubial excuse of a bad headache suggests this Muse resembles a tenant's hired labourer, maybe a mistress from the servant class rather than a wifely Jean Armour figure (i.e. rather like Agnes Brown's servant Elizabeth Paton who bore Burns's illegitimate child in 1786). Like the tenant farmer he is, the poet commands his Muse's labour, like the cottage spinner with her 'rock and wee pickle tow' (distaff and reel) hard pressed to spin rhymes ('So dinna ye affront your trade, / But rhyme it right', he orders her (ll.23–4)). Female labour was a crucial element of the eighteenth-century Scottish agricultural economy, and could make all the difference to the farmer's income; as such it was particularly harsh and unremitting.

Burns's poetry and prose written in the revolutionary decade of the 1790s often shows a more defiant championship of plebeian resistance to the vertical order of the old society, but it is noteworthy that in his rousing democratic anthem 'Is there for Honest Poverty' (1794/5) he preferred the non-class specific word 'honest' (with its strongly Paineite connotations) to 'plebeian'; 'the honest man tho' e'er sae poor / Is king o' men for a that' (ll.15–16). Although Burns never mentions Tom Paine by name, the radicalization of his views of social class in the 1790s pervades his verse and correspondence in the revolutionary years. Writing to Frances Dunlop from Dumfries in January 1796 during the war-induced famine, he cited Burke's derogatory term for the populace: 'we have actual famine, & that too in the midst of plenty. How long the *Swinish Multitude* will be quiet, I cannot tell: they threaten daily' (Burns, 1985, II, p. 355). Of course by this time Burns's membership of the Dumfries Volunteers would have determined that he was one of the men charged with defending William Pitt's rule of law against the food rioters, although the historical record remains silent as to whether or not this came to pass.

Finally, then, was Burns a 'peasant'? Published as an appendix to the third volume of the *Statistical Survey of Scotland* was an anonymous letter addressed to its editor Sir John Sinclair of Ulbster, describing the formation of the Monklands Friendly Society Library, Dumfries. The letter was in fact written by Burns himself, who had been instrumental in assisting his friend and patron Robert Riddell of Glenriddell to establish the library, and it is redolent of the spirit of improvement and popular enlightenment promoted by the *Statistical Account*. Burns's letter addressed 'every country gentleman, who thinks the improvement of that part of his own species, whom chance has thrown into the humble walks of the peasant and the artisan, a matter worthy of his attention' (Burns, 1985, II, p. 107). After a rather patronizing snipe at some of the 'trash' purchased by the plebeian subscribers to the Monklands library (mainly Calvinist theology and popular novels), Burns lists some of the better quality works purchased, including books by the luminaries of the Scottish Enlightenment like Blair, Robertson and Hume, as well as the *Spectator, Mirror, Lounger, Observer,* etc. He concludes with the thought that 'a peasant who can read, and enjoy such books, is certainly a much superior being to his neighbour, who, perhaps, stalks beside his team, very little removed, except in shape, from the brutes he drives'. Wishing success to Sinclair's 'patriotic exertions', Burns signed off, with characteristic panache, as 'A PEASANT' (Burns, 1985, II, p. 108). This was at least in part ironic, to the extent that the oxymoronic idea of an 'enlightened peasant' exposed the social prejudice underlying the word's common usage.

Early reviews of Burns tended to shy away from describing him as 'a peasant', however, preferring either the vague designation 'of a low station in life', or else, Mackenzie's by-now familiar 'ploughman'. (His Ayrshire provenance remained immensely important both to the poet and his reviewers, encouraging many of his labouring-class imitators to underline their locality in 'branding' their poetry.) 'Ploughman' connoted skilled and purposeful agricultural labour whereas 'peasant' suggested mindless drudgery; and of course the notion that Burns might have been an educated peasant was fatal to the fashionable romantic theory of *poeta nascitur non fit*. It is notable that Wordsworth everywhere shied away from the word 'peasant', preferring to dignify his agricultural characters like Michael with the Lakeland title of 'Statesman'. By contrast, Bloomfield and Clare were both openly promoted as 'peasant' poets, although both regarded Burns as their precursor in this respect. In the case of Clare at least, this may have been due to the enormous influence of Burns's first posthumous editor and biographer Dr James Currie, who in 1800 wrote that 'Robert Burns was, in reality, what he has been represented to be, a Scottish peasant' (I, p. ix). Currie obviously feared that this claim was potentially misleading unless contextualized by an entire prefatory essay entitled 'Observations on the Character and Condition of the Scottish Peasantry'. The gist of his argument is contained in the statement that 'a slight acquaintance with the peasantry of Scotland will serve to convince an unprejudiced observer, that they possess a degree of intelligence not generally found among the same class of men in the other countries of Europe', including, of course, England (Currie, 1800, I, p. x).

Currie, an expatriate Scottish physician residing in Liverpool, hoped that 'this informed and hardy race of men, educated in poverty, and prepared for hardship and danger, patient of labour, and prodigal of life', would spill over the border to 'invigorate' England and Britain's colonies, just as Burns's poetry promised to stimulate an effete and debilitated canon of English literature. Currie's Burns is not really a romantic bard at all, but rather a vehicle for the promotion of Scottish popular enlightenment, industry and domestic virtue across the English border. This 'Whiggish' view of Burns (which Currie shared with his mentor Dugald Stewart and Francis Jeffrey) was later savaged by Thomas Carlyle, son of an Ecclefechan stonemason, who replaced the laurels of natural genius on his brow, writing: 'A Scottish peasant's life was the meanest and rudest of all lives, till Burns became a poet in it, and a poet of it . . . Is not every new genius an impossibility till he appears?' (Low, 1974, p. 360).

According to the current *OED* definition, a 'peasant' is 'a person who lives in the country and works on the land, especially as a smallholder or a labourer: (chiefly sociological) a member of an agricultural class dependant on subsistence farming'. The first part of this applies to Burns, but not the second, and in what remains of my essay I want to clarify the poet's place in the social hierarchy of the rural Lowlands, exemplified by his account of rural labour in 'The Vision'. Burns 'came of age' in the years 1766–77 working on his father's 70-acre, unimproved farm of Mount Oliphant near Alloway. During the period of his major poetic creativity, he assisted his father as tenant of the 130-acre farm of Lochlie (1777–84) in the parish of Tarbolton in upland Ayrshire. Subsequently, together with his brother Gilbert, he was himself tenant of the nearby 118 acre Mossgiel (1784–6), a farm on the Loudoun estates in the parish of Mauchline, sublet by the Mauchline lawyer Gavin Hamilton, to whom he dedicated the Kilmarnock volume. In the years 1788–91, in the wake of his literary triumph in Edinburgh and before his disgruntled abandonment of farming for a career in the Excise, he cultivated the large 170-acre farm of Ellisland, outside Dumfries, leased from the banker and entrepreneur Patrick Miller of Dalswinton.

As a tenant farmer in the 1780s Burns occupied the middle rung on the social hierarchy of the rural Lowlands, although he remained, even in the Ellisland years, the kind of farmer who believed in labouring alongside his men. In 'The Inventory' he provided 'a faithfu' list, / O gudes an' gear, an' a' my graith' (equipment) (l. 2–3) at Mossgiel, prompted by Pitt's 1786 taxes on horses, carriages and servants. He depicted his three servants (a 'gaudsman' or ploughboy, a thresher and a cowherd) with sardonic affection, describing how he 'rul(ed) them . . . discreetly' and 'labour(ed) them compleately':

> For men, I've three mischievous boys,
> *Run de'ils* for rantin' an' for noise;
> A gaudsman ane, a thrasher t'other,
> Wee Davoc hauds the nowt in fother[5]
>
> (ll.34–7)

Socially, then, Burns ranked above cotters and farm servants, the 'rustic compeers' whose 'sentiments and manners' he described in 'his and their native language', and whose manual labour he hired. On the other hand, he ranked below freehold farmers (in Scotland dubbed 'bonnet lairds', although they were thin on the ground in a country which had the highest density landownership in Europe), and certainly below the lairds of the gentry and aristocracy to whom he paid rent. The fact that improving landowners frequently charged rent on the potential post-improvement, rather than actual, value of their land, meant that tenants (upon whom the practical burden of enclosing, draining and liming land actually fell), accrued mounting debts, a situation exacerbated by appalling harvests in the mini ice-age of the 1770s and early 80s. This helps explain why the landowning class often appear in Burns's poems as objects of bitter satirical resentment, as well as (less frequently, and to the extent to which Burns himself subscribed to the ideology of improvement) of patriotic panegyric.

As an improving tenant farmer Burns was at the cutting edge of an unprecedented agricultural revolution that transformed lowland Scotland during the decades of his lifetime. As both agent and victim of improvement, his poetry absorbed the social energy of that revolution, and represents a dialectical engagement with the forces of modernity. In addition to agricultural revolution, the decades of the 1760s, 70s and 80s saw the rise of manufactures, religious and cultural enlightenment, country banking and the booms and busts of the new credit economy, global expansion, war and empire. Agrarian capitalism, not urban manufacturing, was the cutting edge of the new economic order: and Burns's social station as an undercapitalized tenant farmer, struggling to meet the demands of improving landlords, interpellated him into the vertical social structure and patronage networks of the eighteenth-century rural Lowlands. The result of a 'nostalgic' view of a ruralist Burns has been to sunder his life and work both from the agricultural revolution of eighteenth-century Scotland, and its major intellectual context in the Scottish Enlightenment.

The Vision

I will conclude with a brief examination of Burns's poem 'The Vision', the most ambitious poem published in the Kilmarnock volume to the extent that it explores the relationship between his two vocations as farmer and poet, and stakes a claim (against the horizontal solidarity of the epistles) for genteel patronage. The first eight habbie stanzas of

'The Vision', written in full Scots (giving way to English poetic diction in the remainder of the poem) evoke the harsh winter world of the Ayrshire farmer, exhausted by labour, and meditating gloomily on his alternative vocation as a poet:

> The sun had clos'd the *winter-day*,
> The Curlers quat their roaring play,
> And hunger'd Maukin taen her way,
>   To kail-yards green,
> While faithless snaws ilk step betray
>   Whare she has been.
>
> The Thresher's weary *flingin-tree*,
> The lee-lang day had tir'd me;
> And when the Day had clos'd his e'e
>   Far i' the West,
> Ben I' the *Spence*, right pensivelie,
>   I gaed to rest.
>
>   (ll.1–12)

While other country folk have been enjoying the 'roaring play' of the curling stones, while scavenging 'maukins' (hares) have filled their bellies by raiding 'the kailyard green', the farmer-poet has been condemned to hard physical labour. He has worked all day at 'The Thresher's weary *flingin-tree*', separating the grain from the *caff* or straw, the most tedious task of the farming year (l.7). (The 'flinging tree' is the hand-held 'swingle of the flail'). On the evidence of these stanzas alone, there is no doubt that Burns was indeed a labouring poet, if not a labouring-*class* poet.

Quite possibly the choice of threshing (rather than Burns's more iconic labour of ploughing) connects 'The Vision' with Stephen Duck's counter-pastoral 'The Thresher's Labour' (1730). (Duck had also published a poem called 'The Vision', in which the weeping figure of Britannia informs him of the death of his patroness, Queen Caroline). Although we saw Jeffrey comparing Burns and Duck in his 1808 review, the Ayrshire poet never mentions Duck in his poetry or correspondence, although, as it happens, neither did Bloomfield nor Clare.[6] Here are some well-known lines from Duck's 'The Thresher's Labour':

> No intermission in our Works we know;
> The noisy Threshall must for ever go.

Their Master absent, others safely play;
The sleeping Threshall does it self betray . . .
Can we, like Shepherds, tell a merry Tale?
The Voice is lost, drown'd by the noisy Flail . . .
'Tis all a dull and melancholy Scene,
Fit only to provoke the Muses Spleen.

(ll.46–9; 52–3; 62–3)

Duck complains that the thresher cannot take a break without the silence of the flail betraying him to his master: there is simply no opportunity for exhausted labour to take repose. The difference in Burns's version is that the master is co-labourer, albeit by economic necessity, given the high labour wages in 1780s Ayrshire, matched by equally high rents, which squeezed the tenant middleman. Burns elsewhere remarked that he had become a dextrous ploughboy in his early teens at Mount Oliphant (Burns, 1985, I, p. 137) when his father William had been unable to afford hired labour, and the effects of hard manual labour on his boyhood frame caused some permanent deformity in the mature poet.

But like Duck in the famous frontispiece to the 1730 edition of *Poems on Several Subjects*, Burns represents himself as being distracted from farming by his alternative vocation as poet. In the image Duck holds a copy of Milton in his right hand and fixes it with an attentive eye, while in his left he ineffectually brandishes a flail. John Blane, one of three labourers employed by the Burns brothers at Mossgiel, later recalled how:

> in the laborious employment of husbandry, the Peculiarities of Burns's mind were easily discernible – While engaged in Thrashing, it was evident that his mind was particularly occupied, from the varied alternations from slow to quick which rendered it dangerous & even impossible for another to Keep time with him but in an hour or two he was quite exhausted & gave in altogether. (qtd Mackay, 1992, p. 142)

The 'southing' of poetry in Burns's mind cut across the rhythm of threshing, even to the point of putting his labourers in some danger, and exhausting the bard himself.

Despite the hardship of agricultural labour, however, 'The Vision' portrays a relatively privileged world, both in terms of Burns's access to privacy ('lanely, by the ingle-cheek') and the physical space available for retreat ('And when the Day had clos'd his e'e, / Far i' the

West, / Ben i' the *Spence*, right pensivelie, / I gaed to rest' (ll. 9–12). As Gavin Sprott comments, 'although the best room in Mossgiel was still called *the Spence*, it was not the *ben* room of the older Ayrshire houses, but part of a modern house built only a few years before by Gavin Hamilton who had sublet the farm' to the Burns brothers (1990, p. 23). (Hamilton was a Mauchline 'writer' or lawyer who served as a factor to the Earl of Loudoun.) The 'spence' was a theatre for reflection, a site for cultivating poetic inwardness which, in the language of the 1786 Preface, offered 'some kind of counterpoise to the struggles of a world, always an alien scene, a task uncouth to the poetical mind' (Burns, 1786, p. iv). It is this very inwardness, symptomized by Burns's poetic ambitions, upon which he blames his failure as a tenant farmer:

> All in this mottie, misty clime,
> I backward muse'd on wasted time,
> How I had spent my *youthfu' prime*,
>   An' done nae-thing,
> But stringing blethers up in rhyme
>   For fools to sing.
>
> Had I to guid advice but harket,
> I might, by this, hae led a market,
> Or strutted in a Bank and clarket
>   My *Cash-Account*;
> While here, half-mad, half-fed, half-sarket,
>   Is a' the amount.
>
>   (ll.19–30)

In his discussion of the Scottish banking system in *Wealth of Nations*, Adam Smith explained that Bankers 'granted what they called cash accounts, that is by giving credit to the extent of a certain sum . . . to any individual who could procure two persons of undoubted credit and good landed estate to become surety for him' (Smith, 1999, I, p. 395). The purpose of this easy credit, and the flood of paper money issued by the bank, was the patriotic motive of advancing 'the whole capital which was to be employed in those improvements of which the returns are the most slow and distant, such as the improvement of land' (Smith, 1999, I, p. 412).

Writing in the mid-1780s, when the repercussions of the Ayr bank crash were still being felt in southwest Scotland (Burns's epistolary correspondent John Lapraik was imprisoned as a bankrupt in 1785 as a result), it is unlikely that Burns would have been able to 'strut into a Bank and clark his Cash Account', even if he possessed better credit than would have been available to the son of William Burness, the ruined tenant of Lochlie. Tenants simply shouldered the debts incurred by the landowning class; David McClure, landlord of Lochlie, was himself bankrupted as an indirect result of the Ayr Bank crash, and even the 5th Earl of Loudoun, from whom Gavin Hamilton rented Mossgiel Farm (sublet to Robert and Gilbert Burns) was driven by his debts to commit suicide in 1786.

Burns committed himself to poetry around 1783 (a commitment signalled by his decision to keep a commonplace book in April of that year) at the very nadir of his family's fortunes at Lochlie, when McClure was initiating litigation against his father. Is there a causal link here? Burns certainly did not simply aim to make money, given the reiterated attack on 'catch the plack' and on 'ye selfish, warly race' in the epistles written to his fellow 'bardies' in these same years. In the event Burns may have made £54 profit from the Kilmarnock volume, and as much as £700 from the Edinburgh volume, the copyright of which he sold to William Creech for one hundred guineas; at any rated, he donated £180 from the profits of the latter to his brother Gilbert, a capital sum equivalent to nearly two years rent, which enabled the latter to struggle on as tenant farmer until 1797 (Mackay, 1992, p. 236).

But Smith's definition of 'Cash Account' suggests that Burns was after something more valuable than cash in hand, namely 'credit', which in the eighteenth-century carried a complicated range of meanings, going well beyond a favourable balance. In the opening stanzas of 'The Vision', Burns blamed his poverty on poetry, not on the contingencies of bad harvests, bank collapses or social oppression. In proleptically romantic mood, the poetic vocation becomes a figure for failed credit. But just as the poet swears a solemn oath to be *'rhyme proof /* Till my last breath' (ll.35–6), to dedicate himself to farming, his self-centred gloom is shattered by the advent of Coila, that 'tight, outlandish *Hizzie'* whom he instantly recognizes as 'some SCOTTISH MUSE', the personification of his native district of Kyle. The georgic vision of Ayrshire's improving gentry depicted upon Coila's mantle represents Burns's claims as a labouring poet to both inhabit and transcend his 'humble sphere' via his regional self-identification as a poet of Ayrshire first, and Scotland second. Regional as well as national solidarity here overcomes class difference (see Leask, 2010, pp. 103–14).

As a humble tenant farmer, even a 'peasant' to the extent to which he worked rather than owned the land, Burns is mired within the partiality of a 'mechanical' view. As crowned by Coila's holly crown at the conclusion of 'The Vision's' second Duan, however, a symbol of the local patronage that the poem artfully solicits, he imagines himself gaining new credit as Ayrshire's local, and Scotland's national, poet. His bardic coronation relieves him from the self-doubts he has suffered in his rural shades. Coila represents him as the 'rustic bard', in contrast to Thomson, Shenstone or Gray, a 'lowly Daisy' to the 'unrivall'd Rose', or a 'juicy Hawthorn' to the oak tree's 'army shade' (ll.253–8). Yet something is stirring in the undergrowth, although I do not agree with Liam McIlvanney that the hawthorn here prefigures the liberty tree (McIlvanney, 2002, p.73). Quite the reverse here in fact, because we are told at line 245–6 that the fame of Burns's 'manner-painting strains' has ensured that 'some, the pride of *Coila's* plains, / Become thy friends'. As we all know, Burns did later discover the means to criticize a corrupt ruling class and political system in the idiom of the liberty tree. But not in 'The Vision', where Coila, with her georgic mantle, is a figure for the poet's prospective credit with the Ayrshire gentry, holding out a more productive relationship of patronage than the hopeless dependence of the tenant farmer.

Coila as a figure for patronage therefore has the power to transform the poet's credit from the horizontal 'subscription' network of the Kilmarnock volume to a vertical relationship with 'the pride of Coila's plains', on condition that the poet 'never murmur nor repine; / Strive in thy *humble sphere* to shine' (ll.259–60). What is remarkable about these lines is that in 1786 this was still *virtual* patronage, although it was a relationship that the poet's subsequent fame managed to embody as a set of *real* social relations, the credit of which was worth more than money could buy. Many of course would argue that it was the *success* of Burns's quest for patronage, avidly pursued during the Edinburgh sojourn and finally realized in the Excise commission that saw the end of his labouring on the land, which destroyed the poet in the man. For the labouring-class poets who sought to emulate his fame (however much they were also expected to take a warning from his alleged decline into dissipation and premature death), Burns's skill in soliciting patronage was subsumed in his self-created myth of independence and self-help, as he disavowed servility in addressing his noble dedicatees in the Edinburgh preface: 'Nor do I present this Address with the venal soul of a servile Author . . . I was bred to the Plough, and am independent.'[7]

Notes

1. I have followed Christmas in preferring the latter to 'working class' to the extent that it represents 'a kind of preindustrial compromise to the specifically industrial, Marxist connotations of 'working class' and 'proletariat' (2010, p. 41).
2. Burke, 2003, p. xvii; McGuirk, 1985, p. 1. As Burke points out (p. 112), this claim looks unsustainable in the light of recent reassessments of the poetry of John Clare, as well as other 'peasant poets'.
3. Fulford and Pratt (2009), letter 75, To Earl of Buchan, 19th Jan, 1802. romantics.arhu.umd.edu/editions/Bloomfield Letters/HTML.
4. See Leask, 2010, chapter 6, 'Hellfire and Commonsense'.
5. 'feeds the cattle'.
6. Christmas notes that 'by 1800 Duck seems to have dropped out of the collective consciousness of the most prominent rural plebeian poets, in part because of the influence and popularity of Burns, in part because times had changed' (2001, p. 268).
7. Preface to the 1787 Edinburgh edition, in Burns, 1896, I, p. 5. Griffin (1996) has shown that Burns's tone here was a normal convention for poetic dedications in the later eighteenth century.

Bibliography

Beattie, James (1784) *The Minstrel, in Two Books* (London: n.pub.)
Burke, Tim (2003) 'Robert Burns', in *Eighteenth-Century English Labouring-Class Poets*, gen. ed. John Goodridge, 3 vols (London: Pickering & Chatto), III (1780–1800), ed. Tim Burke, pp. 103–15.
Burns, Robert (1786) *Poems Chiefly in the Scottish Dialect* (Kilmarnock: John Wilson).
——. (1896) *The Poetry of Robert Burns*, 4 vols, ed. W. E. Henley and T. F. Henderson (London: Blackwood).
——. (1968) *The Poems and Songs of Robert Burns*, 3 vols, ed. James Kinsley (Oxford: Clarendon Press).
——. (1985) *The Letters of Robert Burns*, 2 vols, ed. G. Ross Roy and J. De Lancey Ferguson (Oxford: Clarendon Press).
Christmas, William (2001) *The Lab'ring Muses: Work, Writing and the Social Order in English Plebeian Poetry, 1730–1830* (London: Associated University Presses).
Currie, James (1800) *The Works of Robert Burns, with an Account of his Life, and a Criticism of his Writings. To which are prefixed, Some Observations on the Character and Condition of the Scottish Peasantry*, 4 vols (Liverpool, London and Edinburgh: n.pub).
Devine, Tom (1994) *The Transformation of Rural Scotland: Social Change and the Agrarian Economy, 1660–1815* (Edinburgh: Edinburgh University Press).
Fulford, Tim and Lynda Pratt, eds. (2009). *The Letters of Robert Bloomfield and His Circle.* Romantic Circles Electronic Edition (University of Maryland). www.rc.umd.edu/editions/bloomfield_letters/.
Griffin, Dustin (1996) *Literary Patronage in England, 1650–1800* (Cambridge: Cambridge University Press).
Jeffrey, Frances (1809) 'Reliques of Burns', *Edinburgh Review*, XIII, 249–76.

Leask, Nigel (2010) *Robert Burns and Pastoral: Poetry and Improvement in Late Eighteenth-Century Scotland* (Oxford: Oxford University Press).
Low, Donald A., ed. (1974) *Robert Burns: The Critical Heritage* (London: Routledge).
Mackay, James (1992) *R. B.: A Biography of Robert Burns* (Edinburgh: Mainstream).
McGuirk, Carol (1985) *Robert Burns and the Sentimental Era* (Athens: University of Georgia Press).
McIlvanney, Liam (2002) *Burns the Radical: Poetry and Politics in Late Eighteenth-Century Scotland* (East Lothian: Tuckwell).
Pittock, Murray (2008) *Scottish and Irish Romanticism* (Oxford: Oxford University Press).
Smith, Adam (1999) *The Wealth of Nations*, 2 vols, ed. Andrew Skinner (London: Penguin).
Smith, Jeremy (2007) '*Copia Verborum*: Linguistic Choices in Robert Burns', *Review of English Studies*, 58 (2007), 73–88.
Sprott, Gavin (1990) *Robert Burns, Farmer* (Edinburgh: National Museums of Scotland).
Thompson, E. P. (1974) 'Patrician Society, Plebeian Culture', *Journal of Social History*, 7, 382–405.
——. (1978) 'Eighteenth-Century English Society: Class Struggle Without Class?', *Social History*, 3, 133–65.

3
Constructing the Ulster Labouring-Class Poet: The Case of Samuel Thomson

Jennifer Orr

Samuel Thomson (1766–1816), a native of the Presbyterian, Scots-speaking townland of Carngranny in South Antrim, was in his own lifetime a respected poet and instigator of an early Romantic coterie of fellow poets in the north of Ireland. He was the first of his circle to produce a published volume of verse, *Poems on Different Subjects, Partly in the Scottish Dialect* (1793), and assaulted the literary marketplace on several fronts, marketing himself in the Belfast radical press as a brother poet of Robert Burns; as a master of both Scots vernacular and Augustan pastoral poetry; and as a tutelary figure in a specifically Northern school of Irish poetry. His early popular success spurred him on to publish two further and more complex editions of poetry, *New Poems on a Variety of Different Subjects* (1799) and *Simple Poems on a Few Subjects* (1806).

Thomson's importance as a poet lies not only in his own individual work but in his position as mentor who fostered protégés, and nurtured the love of literature in others. His County Antrim cottage became known colloquially as 'Crambo Cave', named after the Scots verse parlour game, and the cottage became a byword for fraternal and poetic activity. Although he appears to have remained in the same region of Ireland, his methods of communication were dictated by the increasingly fragmented nature of social contact occasioned by economic migration, war and the growing Belfast metropolis. By initiating correspondence with fellow poets, often through the public verse epistle, he was able to incorporate himself appropriately within what William Dowling describes as the eighteenth-century epistemological 'moment' (1991, p. 21). Thomson has been recognized by some as an important regional poet but it has only been in the last twenty years that significant emphasis has been placed on his political and intellectual centrality within a circle of mostly labouring-class men, many of whom were connected to Irish patriot movements such as the Volunteers and the United Irish Society.

This essay argues that notions of class and canonicity are central to Thomson's poetic project given that his rise to fame was facilitated by an unprecedented proliferation of lower-class poetry in the north of Ireland. This period of literary activity took place mostly in the Belfast radical press from 1791 onwards, during the height of radical political optimism occasioned by the French Revolution. The apparent success in France of Enlightenment values such as liberty, equality and fraternity created an expectation among politically-minded Irish men and women that their nation could throw off the shackles of the ruling Ascendancy class, comprised mostly of Anglican descendants of Plantation settlers. As a member of a Scots-speaking Presbyterian minority in the north of Ireland, Thomson was subject to the same Penal Laws that afflicted his Roman Catholic neighbours. Although he was a well-educated member of the rural classes, he was a descendant of Scottish immigrants to Ulster and spoke an Ulster variety of the vernacular Lowland Scots tongue. He was, therefore, conscious of a unique, hybrid Scottish-Irish identity which was modified by his wide reading of standard English canonical texts. Finally, as a member of the Seceder sect of Presbyterianism, his confessional identity was defined largely against the Anglican Ascendancy whose religion was sponsored by the British Hanoverian monarchy. Thomson's minority class identity was therefore complex in affiliation and defined largely in opposition to the dominant Ascendancy culture in Ireland.

Thomson's position within the canon is further complicated by his own sense of class and his colloquial status as the 'Bard of Carngranny', the popular title which conferred on him a political obligation to inspire national pride among his own community. As a relatively well-educated schoolmaster, Thomson does not fit nicely into the category of labouring class, and his rural 'hedge-school' employment within a fairly prosperous, dissenting weaving community during one of the greatest constitutional upheavals in Irish history afforded him a degree of superiority. He was positioned slightly above his labouring peers as one of the most intellectual men in the neighbourhood who had the added responsibility of educating the sons of labourers who showed promise, affording them some degree of upward mobility. As with contemporary Ulster poets from John Hewitt to Seamus Heaney, Thomson recognized that his national identity was a nuanced mixture of cultural and religious influences. In Thomson's case his unique poetic vision emanated from his Irish birth, rural life experience, close proximity to nature, and patriotic struggle on one hand, and his Scottish ancestry and Presbyterian religious tradition on the other. In a poem of 1806 he summarized this identity as 'IRISH all without . . . /ev'ry item SCOTCH within' (Thomson, 1806, p. 85), reflecting both his birth and life in the north of Ireland and the powerful, Romantic influence of his Scottish vernacular language and ancestral heritage. During the last fifteen years of his life Thomson's political radicalism cooled in line with his growing religious devotion but, though this occurred in tandem with the growing influence of Presbyterian evangelicalism during the nineteenth century, Thomson remained among the minority of Presbyterian evangelicals who never fully accepted the parliamentary Union of 1801 that united Britain and Ireland. He remained an Irishman with a spiritual attachment to his ancestral land of Scotland.

Thomson's mixed cultural affiliations and indistinct class status have effectively limited his inclusion in the Irish literary canon which, in the wake of partition, has been defined by a rigid national paradigm. The reasons for this critical neglect are largely attributable, again, to the issues of class and canonicity. In the twentieth century, the classification of Irish poets was largely reinforced by a narrative which portrayed the postcolonial nation as the logical and inevitable outcome of political struggle. The foremost of this school was Daniel Corkery whose essentialist criteria for Irish literature comprised the following three elements: 1) 'The religious consciousness of the people'; 2) Irish Nationalism; and 3) The Land. This, in Corkery's view, defined the Irish author as one who is a conflated figure of political nationalism, non-Ascendancy status and Roman Catholicism, the obvious definition of Corkery's 'religious consciousness' (1991–2002, pp. 1008–13). This paradigm accounts largely for a century of critical neglect of Thomson's work. The return of Thomson to public attention as a central figure in the 'Rhyming Weaver' movement was laudable, though inevitably coloured by a Marxist, regionalist agenda that has pervaded criticism ever since. In *Rhyming Weavers and Other Country Poets of Antrim and Down* (1974) the Belfast broadcaster and poet John Hewitt called attention to a vibrant 'long' eighteenth-century Ulster tradition of 'braid' Scots writing and local community subject matter. Thomson's class presented Hewitt the anthologist with several problems: he was from an overwhelmingly labouring-class community and yet he was, according to Hewitt, uncommonly well-educated, well-connected in the metropolis, and a passionate lover of nature who displayed exactitude of description in his nature poetry. The most significant omission in Hewitt's study is that he noted no political significance in Thomson's work, an oversight which did not begin to be rectified until the 1990s with Philip Robinson and Ernest Scott's re-discovery of Thomson's contributions to the radical Belfast press during the 1790s (1992, p. iii). It would still be many years before critics questioned the idea of the 'rhyming weavers' as an 'untaught' cohesive working-class entity.

In the early 1990s, more compelling evidence of Thomson's connection to the United Irish movement emerged in the work of Ulster critics such as Robinson, and specialists such as Tim Burke and Bridget Keegan drew on this to include Thomson among their studies of labouring-class poetry. These critics began to explore Thomson's ability to assume a neoclassical poetic voice, previously the purview of the upper classes, describing it as a form of 'eco queer camp' and re-focusing attention on the politically radical aspect of Thomson's pastoral (see Keegan, 2004). Finally, several leading Ulster-based critics, again following on from Robinson's foundational work, have begun to reconstruct Thomson's learned position within the community in the context of local reading societies and the Enlightenment reading habits they encouraged, as well as significant evidence of Romantic poetic fraternities throughout Ulster in the 'long' eighteenth century.

I. The 'real language of men' and the emerging vernacular canon

From the outset of his poetic career, Thomson maintained a tension between his bardic representation of lower-class regional life and a desire to associate with men of more intellectual predilections. The emphasis on Thomson's status as a regional poet is drawn largely from his frequent adoption of the vernacular Scots language of his neighbourhood in his early verse. Although one quarter of his verse is written in the vernacular, it should be emphasized that the medium in question was a heavily stylized, literary version of the Scots tongue, not a *verbatim* reflection of that which was spoken throughout the rural north of Ireland. Poems written in this dialect were intended, however, to be recognizable to readers and to call to mind the customs of the rural Scots-descended, Irish residents of his own region which the compilers of the *Ordnance Survey Memoirs* summarized by their 'strong and disagreeably Scottish' tongue, musical knowledge of country airs 'chiefly Scottish', and their physical characteristics which were 'not unaccompanied by a little rudeness, more characteristic of their "Scottish origin"' (Day, McWilliams and Dobson, 1994, p. 120). The cultural affiliation between Ulster and Scotland, presently enshrined in the European recognition of a particular Ulster Scots culture, is often dogged by controversy and cultural embarrassment, but the literary and linguistic relationship between Scotland and Ireland in the eighteenth century evinces an indisputably vibrant cultural exchange, based on a shared Scots language and culture. By the 1790s in Ulster, a particularly literary version of the vernacular Scots language spoken both in Lowland Scotland and throughout the North of Ireland had been raised to prominence by the Scottish poet Allan Ramsay and, during Thomson's lifetime, by his celebrated contemporary Robert Burns. Though it was fashionable to pen vernacular verses in the Belfast press during the 1790s, particularly with the intention of promoting more radical subject matter, the Scots vernacular had by no means been accepted by the Belfast literati as a standard and, until recently, the Ulster poets who used this tongue were often dismissed as Burns imitators. John Hewitt emphasized that although the Ulster poets used Scottish stanza forms, they turned them to distinctly Irish subject matter, concluding that 'the Ulster Vernacular bards were in much the same relationship to Burns as he had been to his predecessors, and were working free-handedly within the same tradition' (Hewitt, 1974, p. 9).

Hewitt's 'same tradition' references Thomson's awareness of canonicity and his desire to strike a delicate balance between innate poetic talent and the deliberate intellectual pursuit of learning. The same tension is present in the work of Thomson's foremost contemporary, Robert Burns, who came from a similar background and who wrote verses on reformist and radical themes in a familiar tongue. Having entered into a friendly correspondence with Burns in 1791 through a verse epistle, Thomson was encouraged to offer the Irish reading public a taste of his own verses and experience. Thomson's enthusiasm for Burns's writings can be contextualized within the scope of the dawning Romantic movement, particularly the fascination with vernacular language and the lives of lower class people. Poverty itself could form a fitting subject for poetry, and Burns's image as a man of independent mind was highly appealing to Thomson, an ardent Presbyterian who longed for political reform that would disseminate benefits beyond the Anglican ascendency. Thomson's epistle to Robert Burns, 'But frae a' the verses e'er I saw,/Your Cotter fairly taks the shine' (Thomson, 1793, p. 86), praised Burns's combination of his own intimate knowledge of the landscape with the vernacular tongue and culture of the populace, most ideally represented in the 'The Cotter's Saturday Night' (1785), an exposition of rural Presbyterian virtue and simplicity that Thomson would build upon to celebrate the ties of fraternal honesty in 'The Fairy

Knowe; or Damon's Birthplace' (1799, p. 108). It must be emphasized that Burns was only one of the many authors appropriated by Thomson in prefatory and embedded quotations; he also demonstrated enthusiasm for the fashionable sentimental idealism of Oliver Goldsmith, William Shenstone and James Beattie, mediated by the realism of writers like George Crabbe. Each of the authors in this creative cauldron was also crucial to the work of the first generation Romantic poets, particularly Wordsworth.

Burns's 'Caledonian shepherd' offered a particularly Celtic labouring-class trope which gave confidence to fellow 'regional' poets to translate neoclassical Augustan pastoral within their own sense of place. Thomson's opening preface to his debut edition of poetry, *Poems on Different Subjects* (1793), clearly engages with a recognizable pastoral trope, taking his persona of 'a lad – he seek's no better name' [sic] from the opening line of Spenser's *Shepherdes Calendar*, 'A Shepeheards boye (no better doe him call)'. The preface also echoes the opening lines of 'Summer. The Second Pastoral' from Pope's *Pastorals* (1709), 'A Shepherd's boy (he seeks no better Name),/Let forth his Flocks along the silver *Thame.*' Pope, in turn, acknowledged his source to be Theocritus's first Idyll: 'A Shepherd's Boy (no better do him call)', suggesting that Thomson's motivation may have been to create a literary paper trail in the use of this one line (Pope, 1965, p. 129; Spenser, 1912, p. 421). The poet paints a picture of a perfect agricultural republic, in which fraternal honesty flourishes. He undoubtedly valued the fact that his profession as a schoolmaster afforded him a degree of independence from labour, and leisure to enjoy his native landscape, over which he gained a sense of ownership:

> Hail happy place! Whose master kind,
> Blest with a strong untainted mind;
> Consistent, liberal, warm, humane,
> Can look on sceptres with disdain,
> And laugh at all the titled clan –
> An independent, truly honest man.
>
> (Thomson, 1799, p. 103)

This poem, 'Lyle's Hill, a Rhapsody inscribed to Damon' (1799), subverts the traditional concept of the prospect poem, as it is the humble rural bard rather than the landowner who looks down on the landscape below, claiming a sense of ownership. Thomson appears to be referring to himself as the master of Carngranny, crowned with the Irish shamrock and looking down the slopes of Lyle's Hill toward Castle Upton, the residence of Lord Viscount Templetown who was the legal owner of the seat. Beneath the surface of Thomson's pastoral, once dismissed as apolitical, there is a constant assertion of the poet's intimate knowledge of nature and the natural, reclaiming the gaze of the aristocrat in Augustan prospect poetry.

Thomson's political poetry was doubtless informed by the members of his early literary network, few of whom were untouched by reformist or radical opinions. In spite of their varying class statuses they were brought together by a love of literature, not least in a political capacity. Thomson was a prominent member of the Roughfort Bookclub which later merged to become the Four Towns Bookclub in 1796, enabling him to lend and borrow books with other young men of literary predilections. Often the members of the club were connected by family ties but many more still were bonded by deeper Romantic, fraternal ties and placed high value on honesty and candour. In addition, many were politically aware, having been exposed to cutting edge Enlightenment ideals of fraternity, rationality, personal judgement and reason. Many of the circle were both freemasons and Volunteers who would go on to become United Irishmen, such as the weavers James Campbell, James Orr and Luke Mullan. No firm evidence has come to light to prove that Samuel Thomson was a member of any masonic order; however there is strong circumstantial evidence to suggest that he had some connections within what Robinson has called 'hedge' masonry (1986, p. 3). Thomson's close friend, the Ballycarry mason and poet James Orr, signs off a letter of 1807, 'Yours fraternally', a common masonic closing, and the majority of Thomson's correspondents in the 1790s use the word 'fraternal' in their letters and verse epistles. Masonic activity among the labouring classes in the north of Ireland, as Ian McBride has observed, tended to become popular alongside the establishment of the Volunteers, a movement that counted among its members at least three of Thomson's close friends, and Thomson personally solicited a 'system of exercise', presumably a manual instructing local Volunteer leaders in preparing the corps for armed action (McBride, 1997, p. 64; Orr, 2012, p. 187). His circle of correspondents included the Scottish poet and tutor Alexander Kemp, with whom he shared coded, anti-monarchical messages, suggesting that radical subjects were indeed discussed between them: 'I send you a most bitter philippic, two of our deceased *Eccentrics*, against our present *Lacihcranom ynitsed*' ('Monarchical destiny'), 'I need scarcely tell you, suggest the expediency of keeping it *private*' (Kemp to Thomson, in Orr, 2012, p. 112). Kemp later refers to the fact that his own writings were the subject of investigation by the Dublin government who were keeping a close eye on literary activity that stemmed from the Belfast radical press (see Orr, 2012, p. 126). Likewise, Thomson corresponded with the cosmopolitan figure Aeneas Lamont, the typesetter for the radical *Northern Star* newspaper and a Belfast Volunteer who had worked in the newspaper business in Revolutionary America. Notably, while in America, Lamont corresponded with fellow masons of high rank, such as Dr Benjamin Franklin, who perhaps epitomizes the political impact of freemasonry in Revolutionary America (see Orr, 2012, p. 95). A further clue emerged following Lamont's death in 1803, when Mrs Lamont wrote to Thomson, referring to a conversation she had with 'your brother' who confirmed that Thomson '[kept] a school' (Orr, 2012, p. 96). With no existing correspondence between Thomson and a sibling, nor any poetic or biographical mention, it might be surmised that Mrs Lamont referred to a masonic connection. These facts amount to the suggestion that Thomson was at the centre of a sophisticated community of masonic brothers throughout County Antrim and Belfast, which perhaps fostered his lower-class fraternal identity. His published verse epistles demonstrate his desire to showcase the ability of labouring-class men to form strong, intellectual and honest friendships that insulated them from the influence of more powerful men.

II. Thomson the Bard: writing for the radicalized rural landscape and the radical Belfast metropolis

Thomson's attitude to his labouring-class community was by no means uncritical, as in poems such as 'The Simmer Fair' (1792), when an exchange of insults between a cobbler and weaver leads to a general scrum, 'monie a ane, for ither's cause,/Gets bouk and banes weel paiked.'[1] He clearly discriminates between *bona fide* expressions of political discontent and rogue violence. Though it may imply a degree of class snobbery on the part of the poet, it is worth noting that many of Thomson's closest friends were weavers, particularly Luke Mullan and James Orr, both fellow poets and members of the reading society. This group of artisans was inevitably politicized by economic hardship, but their membership of the Reading Society demonstrated a deliberately different choice of company from those men who joined agrarian paramilitary factions such as the Whiteboys and Hearts of Oak, societies which offered a measure of pride and protection for labourers struggling against import tariffs and the adverse economic climate brought about by Britain's wars. The less savoury aspect of these fraternal organizations was their sectarianism, strands of which encouraged the establishment of the Orange Order and Defender movements in County Armagh. In the early 1790s, the majority of Thomson's reading circle shunned such groups in favour of the patriotic Belfast Volunteer movement, an extra-parliamentary group of armed citizens set up during the American Revolutionary War to protect the Irish nation and to act in the interests of the Irish parliament in Dublin. When the Society of United Irishmen was set up in Belfast in 1791, an organization at Templepatrick followed quickly and a fellow member of Thomson's Seceding Presbyterian congregation, James Hope, became a central figure in the movement. Thomson's enthusiastic contributions to the Belfast radical newspaper, the *Northern Star*, throw light upon his early ardent desire for reform and, at times, anger against the oppression of Irish trade. However, there is considerable evidence to suggest that Thomson was deeply uncomfortable with the United Irishmen's shift towards armed struggle, and his initial enthusiasm for the French Revolution gradually wavered following the Terror and, particularly, the rise of Napoleon. He therefore envisioned a need to protect the political integrity of his compatriots within his bardic role.

Given such potent radical connections, it is unsurprising that Thomson's work first excited considerable national attention through the pages of the newly-established Belfast *Northern Star* newspaper (1792–97). One correspondent, calling himself 'A FRIEND TO GENIUS', wrote to the newspaper 'to call forth a suitable degree of public attention to a young man in this neighbourhood, Mr. Samuel Thomson' (*Northern Star*, 1793). Thomson had, at this point, contributed no less than seven items to the newspaper. Alongside its radical political trajectory and support of Irish independence from Britain, the United Irish publication reflected public enthusiasm for poetry penned by men of all classes, particularly underpinned by a strong rural readership. After all, many members of Thomson's circle worked in the Irish linen industry and found their livelihoods directly affected by protectionist British economic policies imposed during the 1780s and 1790s. Thomson's ascent to fame was bound up with the fervour generated by the French Revolution and its political reception in Ireland, generating a ready-made audience of United Irish sympathisers and activists. The extent of Thomson's personal United Irish activity is vague, since it has never been proven that he 'turned out' alongside more openly radical friends during the 1798 Rebellion, but his verses and correspondence demonstrate commitment to politically radical 'moral' force, albeit restrained by a fear of inevitable bloodshed. From the outset, he resisted the polemical kind of verse that pervaded United Irish songbooks like *Paddy's Resource* (1795–6), being determined to strike a balance between the personae of a more refined Augustan poet of idealized rural life and a subversive exposer of true labouring-class life. Most of these initial contributions were not explicitly political, but the dominance of pastorals, such as 'The Contented Shepherd' (1793) demonstrate implicit political radicalism that played on the promotion of labouring-class virtue and identity, as well as the optimism of Paine's 'political summer' (Burke, 2003, p. 41). The shepherd 'Collin' takes a swipe at 'all ye lordlings of *birth*', taunting them with a sneer, 'how vainly expectant ye roam!' and warning them that 'if *happiness* dwells upon earth,/it is with *contentment at home*' (Thomson, 1793, p. 16). The country aphorism creates softer rhetoric than that which might be found in more radical contemporary pieces that might invite the reader to infer that the Anglo-Irish 'lordlings' resident in Ireland do not belong in this landscape and ought to return to Britain. Thomson's approach is much more nuanced as he appeals directly to the absentee landlord who travels the world at the beck and call of Imperial Britain, hence his earlier reference to 'the Indies . . ./and rich mines of Peru' (Thomson, 1793, p. 16). Admittedly he must have been prepared for the poem and its political connotations to fall under the scrutiny of a mixed audience, given that it was published in the pages of the radical *Northern Star* (see Thomson, 1792) and subsequently republished in his first volume of poems, *Poems on Different Subjects* (1793), a volume which took his work to a wider audience that included his own landlord, Viscount Templeton of Castle-Upton.

Templeton was a potential patron, but also an absentee landlord until 1795. On his return to Castle Upton, his Templepatrick seat, Thomson seized the opportunity of offering a welcome note entitled 'Stanzas Addressed to Lord Templeton on his Arrival at Castle Upton, after an absence of several years – with a copy of the Author's Poems' (1795). In speaking on behalf of the residents of Templepatrick, he not only demonstrates his sense of bardic vocation in representing his townland, but also the bold and confident subtext of his 'advice' poem which suggests that the success of his lordship's transition from London back to Ireland will depend entirely on his decision to govern well, 'May nae deceitfu' wanton mouth/Presumptive, dare to bend ye' (Thomson, 1793, p. 173). Having expressed concern that Templeton should not be led astray, the poet emphasizes the reliance of tenants on their landlord, claiming that 'your gay presence back again/Has to mysel' restored me'. He goes on to note Templeton's love of London and thus draws attention once again to his absenteeism – the factor which drives the bard's plea, 'O! wad ye henceforth stay at hame/Content wi' your ain' ha" (p. 174). Thomson increases his familiarity with Templeton, wishing that a speedy marriage might encourage him to settle and, finally, comes to the crux of his plea: ' . . . may ye drive corruption hence,/Wi' fraud an' dissipation' (p. 175). His final lines carry what a post-1798 readership might regard at best as an unfortunate pun on the phrase 'turn out' – the term used of the insurgents who would go into battle on 7 June 1798 – and at worst a foreboding warning of the possibility of a rising: 'I'll yet turn out in fashion,/An be as trig a toun perchance,/As onie in the nation/Some future day' (p. 176).

A more outspoken poem, 'The Bard's Farewell!' (published under the pseudonym 'Carngranny', 1793), was written around the time of Thomson's best friend and fellow poet Luke Mullan's emigration to Britain and expresses outrage against the forced migration of Irish labouring-class people. The bard attributes his emigration to British import tariffs on Irish linen, accusing 'vile *"Ascendancy"'* (l.46) of trying to keep the Irish poor and ignorant, 'Inflaming ignorance, in many a place,/To *trample* knowledge, and *insult* the *wise*' (ll.31–2). Rather than inciting his readership to arms, the bard proposes the revolutionary idea of mass emigration, an act which would leave to the British government an empty Ireland with no labour to exploit. Although Thomson did not emigrate to America, he certainly discussed his options in a letter of 5 June 1795 to James Dalrymple, a friend already living out in New England, who advised the poet that Ireland's condition would not improve without great bloodshed (Orr, 2012, p. 46). Faced with the prospect of potentially irrevocable exodus, Thomson decided to remain in Ireland and his subsequent public print verses took on a splenetic and venomous tone against the ruling classes. Some pieces are so violent in their imagery that they call into question Thomson's apparent intent. 'Epigram to a Rank Aristocrat' (1797) was Thomson's penultimate contribution to the *Northern Star* before the press was destroyed by the loyalist Monaghan Militia and imagines an aristocrat being cooked 'hissing with eggs in a pan' to be 'eat up by some red-hot republican clown/And go to form parts of the MAN' (Thomson, 1797). The self-revelatory violence of the speaker's tone invites questioning of the poet's intention. Was Thomson joining in with the Jacobin propaganda often found in the Irish radical press or was he, like Robert Burns in his religious satire 'Holy Willie's Prayer' (1785), allowing the speaker to reveal his true hypocrisy through the dramatic monologue? The speaker of 'Epigram to a Rank Aristocrat' reveals how far the political ideology of the French Revolution had mutated from the Enlightenment ideals of liberty, equality and fraternity into the very despotism that it originally critiqued. The poet appears to have played a cunning double role, maintaining ambiguity in order to maintain his *Northern Star* readership, but exploiting the half-truth of Augustan satire to expose what he apparently viewed as the hypocrisy of Jacobin republicanism. Once again, Thomson's work encapsulates the nuanced shades of political radicalism, demonstrating uneasiness with the prospect of violent physical force. Through the use of shifting poetic voices, he aims to distinguish between positive political activism and a mob mentality which represents, he implies prophetically, an alternative form of tyranny waiting in the wings.

Like most of his moderate United Irish contemporaries, Thomson expressed civic nationalist sentiments, even outrage against the oppression of the free speech and Irish industry but, as noted above, though there is no evidence that he advocated or took part in armed rebellion, some of his poems were viewed by contemporaries as incitement to patriotic action. Thomson's most effective political work developed in conjunction with his labouring-class persona, where he produced a number of apparently innocent poems which exude the posture of avoiding politics and paying attention to nature. His epistolary contact with the Reverend James Glass is yet another excellent example of political pastoral in which the traditional prospect poem is subverted to enable the poets to look down on their aristocrats, promoting a form of liberty that is won not by armed action but by the exercise of superiority of mind. Thomson's speaker and the poet are transported to an imaginary pastoral scene based on the radicalized Lyle Hill landscape where both poets sit side by side 'in rural state, and smile on a' the *little great*' (Thomson, 1799, p. 151). This rhetoric is typical of Thomson's subversion of the Augustan pastoral order found in poems like Pope's 'Epistle to Burlington' (1731) which describes the Earl of Burlington's estate and praises the God-given inspiration that has resulted in the estate's physical orderliness and, on a more symbolic level, the orderliness of the British nation that is governed by men such as Burlington. By contrast, Thomson's rural bard sets his compatriots up as masters of their own landscape in several poems such as the 'Epistle to James Glass' (1795) and 'Lyle's Hill, a Rhapsody' (1799). Since Thomson was engaged in soliciting the literary patronage of his landlord Lord Templeton from 1803, it is highly significant that he should express the key radical belief of popular ownership of land in 'The Gloaming, a Rhapsody':

> Far distant from the broad highway,
> And out of dissipation's view,
> 'Tis here, ye glittering great and gay,
> The cottager looks down on you.
>
> (Thomson, 1806, pp. 52–6)

That 'The Gloaming' should be positioned midway through *Simple Poems on a Few Subjects* (1806) is not accidental. In addressing this poem to 'the golden great on whirling wing' as if they were birds of prey, Thomson's audacity is even more stark given that *Simple Poems* was explicitly addressed to his landlord, Lord Templeton. This fact alone forms a stern challenge to those critics of Thomson who feared that he had compromised his bardic independence by seeking aristocratic patronage.

Throughout the 1790s Thomson's approach to politics appears to follow a loose trajectory of waning radical enthusiasm. His early radicalism was motivated by a combination of religious and class resentment against Ascendancy abuse of power and compliance with what he viewed as British economic policy designed to weaken Irish trade. His career began with a number of celebrations of rural lower class life such as 'The Simmer Fair' (1791), a 'moral force' appeal to his local landlord for good governance in 'Address' (1793) and a radical call for emigration in 'The Bard's Farewell!' (1793). As tensions in Ulster heightened we see a divergence between Thomson's private misgivings against 'physical force' republicanism and his tendency to echo the republican and Jacobin rhetoric of United Irish public print pieces in 'To the Cuckoo' and 'Epigram to a Rank Aristocrat' (1797). The latter poem's violent rhetoric and satirical undertone suggests that the epigram served to deliberately provoke the reader's criticism not only of the aristocrat described but of the speaker's bloodthirsty vehemence. For Thomson, fulfilling the role of bard of the lower classes did not necessarily entail wholesale support for Jacobin politics. His political poetry is extremely shrewd in teasing out the complexities of class tension on all sides of the 1790s Ulster political divide without endangering the poet's position in relation to the authorities.

Yet however carefully he tried to position himself politically, Thomson had less control over how others interpreted his role as a spokesperson for the oppressed labouring classes. Certainly, James Glass's 'Answer [to Mr Samuel Thomson]' (1797) demonstrated that Thomson's work seemingly inspired patriotic enthusiasm in others:

> Thro' verdant bow'rs and blooming meads to stray
> . . .
> And bid me sing of *Freedom's* glorious fire,
> Which leads the *Patriot* to the hostile field,
> To conquer or to die, but ne'er to yield!
>
> (Glass, 1797)

Glass's high rhetorical flourish and admission that his friend 'speak[s] the real feelings of [his] heart' (l.42) demonstrates further that Thomson was writing in a recognizable vein of radicalism that challenged the right of the aristocracy to land ownership. It seems clear that, given his own success in using pastoral as a cloaking device for radical themes, Thomson's message to Glass to 'quat politics' (l.57) emphasized that the role of a poet was much greater than polemical influence over weaker minds: he must also serve the higher purposes of Art and education, and thus raise the profile of Irish cultural life. James Glass identified Thomson and Burns as kindred spirits in their sympathetic and patriotic engagement with nature through a combination of literary craftsmanship and labouring-class 'modesty', both poets fulfilling the bardic function of inciting the patriot to arms. Thomson set out to prove that, as a labouring-class poet, he was equal in his patriotism to his middle-class Belfast counterparts, while at the same time maintaining the advantage of a direct association with the rural landscape which gave him the additional credibility of representing the *vox populi*.

III. Traitor to *vox populi* or a poet for all people?

In the context of 1790s Ireland and the heightening anticipation of revolution among the radical insurgents, even poems of rural celebration such as Robert Fergusson's 'The Farmer's Ingle' and Robert Burns's 'The Cotter's Saturday Night' carried a heightened radical political currency. Thomson's particular admiration for contemporary Scottish poetic models appears to be based on his interpretation of their special concern with the role of rural, labouring-class life in society. As a result, Thomson's private correspondence from the mid-1790s betrays his growing consciousness of the dangers of touching on political discussion through poetry, including championing labouring-class themes. In advance of publishing, Thomson shared many compositions with his correspondent Alexander Kemp, a Scottish schoolteacher and poet residing in Coleraine, County Antrim. Kemp was a fellow acquaintance of Burns and, like Thomson, he introduced Burns's work into the Belfast newspapers in the late 1780s and early 1790s. Kemp cautioned Thomson against writing on political themes, after reading an excerpt from Thomson's pastoral 'Allan, Damon, Sylvander and Edwin: a Pastoral inscribed to my Rhyme-composing Brother Mr Alexander Kemp' (Thomson, 1799, pp. 32–54), written in the style of Burns's poem 'The Twa Dogs' (1785). Although Kemp stated that he was 'particularly pleased' with Thomson's reworking of Burns's original, he warned that 'however obliquely discussed, or tenderly touched, [political verses] may be productive of serious consequences' (Kemp to Thomson, Orr, 2012, p. 47). Kemp cited his own recent experience of Government investigation into his activities and he clearly identified Thomson's political intent within 'Allan, Damon, Sylvander and Edwin'. Not only does Kemp's reaction confirm that Thomson engaged with political themes steadfastly throughout the period of the Irish Rebellion, but it also suggests that Thomson's methods of re-working Scottish sources, particularly animal fables like 'The Twa Dogs', were not subtle enough to avoid being labelled as political sedition. Thirdly, Kemp appears to sense that, in some respects, Thomson's poem went beyond Burns's radicalism, departing entirely from the Scottish poet's intention in 'The Twa Dogs'.

Burns's 'The Twa Dogs' takes inspiration, in part, from the dialogues of Robert Fergusson, in which humble poverty is pitted against sophistication and manners. Caesar, an aristocrat's pet, and Luath, a poor man's collie, socialize together in spite of their class differences, demonstrating how the animals are more virtuous than their owners. Caesar and Luath have no sense of their social inequality: the great man's dog is devoid of pride, while the ploughman's Collie in part represents Burns himself. Burns's dogs wearily discuss inequality between rich man and poor but come to the ironic conclusion that the rich are, despite their luxuries, more dissatisfied than the poor. The twist of Burns's poem comes as Luath rejects Caesar's sympathy for the poor man because, he argues, he enjoys the most important things such as rest after toil and the company of family. Since the political content and skilful animal fable structure of Burns's poem made the work a mutual favourite of Thomson and Kemp, it is unsurprising that Thomson used it as a model for one of his most ambitious pastoral poems. 'Allan, Damon, Sylvander and Edwin' is an ambitious conversational poem written in the imagined voices of four great eighteenth-century Scottish poets: Allan Ramsay, Robert Fergusson,

Robert Burns and James Beattie. The eclogue envisions a traditional neoclassical singing competition between the four poets, each characterized by their own particular style of poetry. Each competitor is introduced by 'Edwin' – Thomson's imagined version of James Beattie, the author of *The Minstrel* (1771). Beattie is an appropriate invigilator for the poetic competition, having been described by Thomson as 'Sweet Edwin . . . o' bards the best' (1799, p. 110). Thomson's imaginary Burns, referred to in the eclogue by the pastoral pseudonym 'Sylvander', sings a continuation of 'The Twa Dogs', allowing Thomson to turn the political sentiments of Burns's original poem to reflect on contemporary Irish radical politics.

Thomson allows the reader to venture in midway through the dogs' dialogue, as if the piece continues directly from where Burns's poem finishes. The reader is informed that the dogs are discussing 'simple man, again, the lord o' the creation' (1799, p. 42), but Thomson begins by allowing the aristocrat's dog, Caesar, to directly question the justice of man's dominion over animals on the basis of 'this boasted reason, human pride' (p. 43), concluding that there is no difference between man and beast, save two legs. The poor man's collie, Luath, takes Caesar down a peg or two, reminding him that his life of leisure allows for such philosophical enquiries, which perhaps contains a hint of Thomson's parody of those who might have criticized his comparative leisure for learning as a schoolmaster, in contrast to his labouring counterparts. Rather than expressing the characteristic loyalty of Burns's labouring collie, Thomson's Luath reveals that he is dissatisfied with the '*cotter snools*' (p. 44), the cottage fools who feed him, suggesting that Thomson's collie himself may have become dangerously embourgeoised, far from the Burnsian admirer of the noble savage:

> My breakfast grub, a scanty drap,
> Just frae the floor, or *paritch caup   *porridge bowl*
> Then a' day herd unruly brutes,
> Girn, gabble, bark, and bite their *clutes;   *paws*
> While frae their heels, right monie a *skelp *sharp beating*
> My *haffits dree, that gars me yelp;   *cheeks dread*
>
>   (Thomson, 1799, p. 44; gloss added)

In contrast to Burns's collie, Thomson's version of Luath appears to eschew pride in rural virtue, detailing bitterly the many insults and sufferings which he endures. He even goes so far as confessing to Caesar that he would give anything to swap lives: 'I'd gie my tail, but onie strife,/To niffer hames wi' you for life' (p. 44). Thomson performs a particularly interesting intertextual experiment by allowing his version of Caesar to point out the discrepancy between the Luath with whom he now converses, and the Luath of his previous discussion (as imagined in Burns's poem), 'I thought ye had been . . . as independent as a lark' (p. 45), highlighting the contrast between Burns's virtuous representation of poverty and Thomson's bitter reality. Caesar does not pretend to complain of his lot, refusing to even countenance swapping places with his 'lick-plate . . . petty rogue' (p. 44) companion, professing that he 'maist as soon be Hornie's cat' (p. 44). It is Caesar, not Luath, who espouses a much more radical theory: that virtue is no more common in one class of life than in another:

> And Happiness and fair Content,
> Are no to onie station pent –
> Content an' Happiness the same,
> Just in the bosom hae their hame.
> Suppose we somewhat different are,
> But a' the difference hide and hair,
> We're form'd o' ae congenial mind,
> The disinterested, social kind;
>
> (Thomson, 1799, p. 46)

Luath goes on to criticize his own class for their vulgarity and riotous behaviour, complaining of the 'peace-destroying yelps' of the 'vulgar, glutton, mungrell whelps' (p. 46) in the church, mill and marketplace. These lines, a post-1798 addition to the original manuscript, show Thomson implicitly accusing the emergent mercantile classes of encouraging the labouring classes to rise up during the Irish Rebellion. Thomson's Caesar and Luath appear to have arrived at a concept of virtue which is more Christian than civic republican, and both are implicitly critical of the misleading application of Rousseau's philosophy of the noble savage by the revolutionary masses, suggesting that this utopian state of habitation is every bit as unobtainable as Rousseau had himself admitted.

The discussion between Thomson's Caesar and Luath takes a distinctly theological turn, betraying the poet's own excited moral indignation that a virtuous heart does not necessarily merit reward on earth:

> This human life is but a farce,
> Where honest actors are but scarce.

> To see each wealthy blockhead thrive,
> And o'er the tap o' merit drive;
>
> (Thomson, 1799, p. 49)

Thomson's Luath is less of a philosophical collie; not content to say that God wills that some are poor and others are rich, he expresses deep anger at the sinful behaviour of those who hoard wealth. It is left to Thomson's aristocratic Caesar to moderate Luath's position by arguing that 'there's sure a ruling Power on high,/that marks the lot o' dog and man,/Wha out of this confusion can,/And will, bring out a perfect plan' (p. 50). Kemp, who was the recipient of some extracts of the original poem, evidently interpreted it as seditious, warning Thomson to 'shun politics' in his future works (Orr, 2012, pp. 125–6). Yet it is notable that, in the finished 1799 version, it is Caesar who appears to moderate the radical Luath, suggesting that Thomson intended a rather different subtext to be understood; namely, that the sage advice of the aristocracy is still of some value. The fact that Thomson puts pseudo-theological arguments into the mouths of his dogs perhaps takes the poem to a level beyond what Burns' achieves in 'The Twa Dogs' and, in any case, demonstrates that he was prepared to revise Burns's social commentary significantly for his own political context.

This poem is key in that it divulges the heart of Thomson's political philosophy in the wake of the Anglo-Irish Union; and his consciousness that the true class strife lay between men like himself, who were to form the radical masses of 1798, and an emergent bourgeoisie, which in its refusal to pass on the benefits of class mobility, is a common enemy to both the poor man's collie and the aristocrat's pet. Here Thomson imbues his Caesar with an apparently Cobbettian world view in which he modifies his snobbish, anti-aristocratic sentiments towards apportioning blame to corrupt mercantile classes. Caesar identifies that the middle class's success in winning freedoms for themselves comes at the expense of their rural labouring class compatriots, whose opportunity to better themselves has been further narrowed:

> The *Poor*, who make the multitude,
> Untaught and vulgar, squalid, rude:
> The poor, who still the piper pay,
> Are left, alas! To grope their way,
> Instinctive, thro' the cheerless fog
> Of Ignorance, in Slavery's bog!

> Immers'd in darkness, Learning's sun
> Doth never blink their minds upon.
>
> (Thomson, 1799, p. 51)

The accusations against 'Vile *Ascendancy*' levelled against the Irish aristocracy in 'The Bard's Farewell' (1793) are now in 1799 applied to the emergent middle classes, creating some common ground between Caesar and Luath. It is left to the aristocrat's dog Caesar to declare that in spite of this, 'sweet virtue' is still found most often with the poor, but that it is sapped by 'their Clergy, too, a greedy crew' (p. 51), drawing the dogs' dialogue to an end on the note of ecclesiastical avarice and poor education. At this point the poet's voice intrudes as he notes 'the miserable way in which our plebeian youth are educated'. Based partly on his experience as a schoolmaster, Thomson shared the key radical view that literacy and education of the masses would bring about moral reform and, in turn, social reform. Although the poem's speaker ambiguously levels aristocrat with poor man, suggesting that Irish education does few favours for either, the inescapable sentiment is that the uneducated mob share responsibility for allowing themselves to become the front line soldiers for a middle class who will not extend the concessions they have won from the aristocracy.

The poem exposes the agenda of intellectual improvement that lies at the core of Thomson's political radicalism. Thomson appears to advocate strictly meritocratic principles rather than simply calling for a levelling of society; as Luath implies in his sub-Popean last word on 'Dullness' (1799, p. 52), it is not for the rabble to seize power by force of arms, as this results in 'these conflicts' (p. 52) which, notably, extend further beyond Ireland alone to the whole of Britain:

> Hence Science blushes, in a rage,
> And Dullness stupefies the age.
> Hence all these feuds and hellish broils,
> These conflicts that afflict our isles;
> There are exceptions – what the matter,
> The cause is – *people know no better.*
>
> (Thomson, 1799, p. 52)

The poet ends with the dogs' comic sudden recollection that it is supper time, elegantly reminding the reader of the absurdity that such a conversation should occur between two animals, while at the same time, marking the sophistication and relevance of their arguments. Although

Thomson's reworking of the 'Twa Dogs' forms only one section of the entire poem, it is exceptional in its attention to the moral discourse of the Enlightenment, and its application in turn to the Irish political and education system. Thomson clearly demonstrates that Burns's radicalism sets him apart as Scotland's greatest poet but at the same time, he shows his independence of Burns as he turns 'The Twa Dogs' on its head by allowing his version of Luath to reveal the bitter reality of poverty and the class envy that inevitably accompanies it. The fact that this discussion is undertaken by two dogs heightens the poet's concern that Enlightenment philosophy can be dangerous when it falls into the hands of the uneducated; as Luath points out, both the aristocracy and the masses themselves will be sacrificed in the cause of their bourgeois leaders, motivated by greed and desire for their own advancement. This poem, perhaps more than any other, demonstrates Thomson's proficiency in tapping into Scottish labouring-class models and using the Scottish vernacular language of his North of Ireland community to investigate the tensions running through labouring-class politics during the period of the Irish Rebellion.

As his *oeuvre* matured, Samuel Thomson maintained a fine balance between desire for reform and respect for virtuous individual action emanating from all classes. This has, doubtless, complicated his position in any one canonical paradigm. His work vacillates between progression and regression, sometimes biting and satiric, and elsewhere sensitive and emotional. Though he was often critical of the governing classes and in sympathy with the plight of the poor, he also emphasized the importance of individual virtue and personal reform, exhorting 'individuals [to] REFORM THEMSELVES,/And represent them, each the *virtuous man*' (Thomson, 1799, p. 221). He stresses that the poet must take a nuanced view by simultaneously rejecting false pride in poverty and recognizing its full horror, but also by refusing to condone the overthrow of one class to make way for the tyranny of another. Thomson's vision of the Irish labouring-class poet embraced opportunities of self-improvement through education and a network of moral acquaintances, demonstrating a clear preference for 'congenial' conversation over male ribaldry. When hopes of political reform slipped from his grasp, such a literary community enabled Thomson to take refuge in fraternal protection, in the words of Alexander Pope quoted to Thomson by his friend James Orr, 'the feast of reason and the flow of the soul' (Orr, 2012, p. 154).

Notes

1. 'And many a one for another's cause gets body and bones well thrashed'. Thomson, 1793, pp. 26–31.

Bibliography

Burke, Tim (2003) '"But tho' I'm Irish all without, I'm ev'ry item Scotch within": Poetry and self-fashioning in 1790's Ulster', *John Clare Society Journal*, 22, 35–49.
Corkery, Daniel (1991–2002) 'From: *Synge and Irish Literature* (1931)', in *The Field Day Anthology of Irish Literature*, 5 vols, gen. ed. Seamus Deane (Derry: Field Day Publications), 2, pp. 1008–13.
Day, A., P. McWilliams and N. Dobson, eds. (1994) *Ordnance Survey Memoirs of Ireland: Volume Twenty-Six, Parishes of Co. Antrim X 1830–1, 1833–5, 1839–40* (Belfast: The Institute of Irish Studies).
Dowling, William C. (1991) *The Epistolary Moment: The Poetics of the Eighteenth-Century Verse Epistle* (New Jersey: Princeton University Press).
Glass, James (1797) 'Verses by the Rev. James Glass, A.M in answer to those addressed to him by Mr Samuel Thomson of Carngranny', *Northern Star*, 10–14 April.
Hewitt, John (1974) *Rhyming Weavers and Other Country Poets of Antrim and Down* (Belfast: Blackstaff Press).
Keegan, Bridget (2004) 'Romantic Labouring-Class Pastoralism as Eco-Queer Camp', *Romanticism on the Net*, 36–7.
Kinsley, James, ed. (1968) *The Poems and Songs of Robert Burns*, 3 vols (Oxford: Clarendon Press).
McBride, Ian (1997) '"When Ulster Joined Ireland": anti-popery, Presbyterian radicalism and Irish Republicanism in the 1790s', *Past and Present*, 157, 63–93.
Orr, Jennifer, ed. (2012) *The Correspondence of Samuel Thomson* (Dublin: Four Courts).
Pope, Alexander (1965) *The Poems of Alexander Pope*, ed. John Butt (London: Methuen).
Robinson, Philip (1986) 'Hanging Ropes and Buried Secrets', *Ulster Folklife*, 32, 3–15.
———. and Ernest M. Scott, eds. (1992) *The Country Rhymes of Samuel Thomson, the Bard of Carngranny 1766–1816*, in *The Folk Poets of Ulster*, 3 vols, eds. J. R. R. Adams and Philip Robinson (Bangor: Pretani Press), 3.
Spenser, Edmund (1912) *The Poetical Works of Edmund Spenser*, ed. J. C. Smith and E. De Selincourt (London: Oxford University Press).
Thomson, Samuel (1792) 'The Contented Shepherd', *Northern Star*, 26–30 May.
———. As 'Carngranny' (1792) 'The Simmer Fair in the manner of Burns', *Northern Star*, 1 September.
———. (1793) *Poems on Different Subjects, Partly in the Scots Dialect* (Belfast: for the author).
———. As 'Carngranny' (1793) 'The Bard's Farewell', *Northern Star*, 31 July–3 August.
———. As 'Spur' and 'Carngranny' (1797) 'Epigram to a Rank Aristocrat', *Northern Star*, 15–19 May.
———. (1799) *New Poems on a Variety of Different Subjects. Partly in the Scottish Dialect* (Belfast: Doherty & Simms).
———. (1806) *Simple Poems on a Few Subjects* (Belfast: Smyth & Lyons).

4
Sociable or Solitary? John Clare, Robert Bloomfield, Community and Isolation

John Goodridge

On 19 March 1826, John Clare wrote to Alaric Watts, a literary editor, responding delicately to what had evidently been an offer to choose a gift of books:

> I can hardly have the face to state as you desire me what books I like as I do not wish to intrude on the kindness of any one or else I have long desired to see the Poems of 'Miss Landon' which I have not been able to do as yet Montgomerys too are strangers to me excepting some things in periodicals which only made me desire to become acquainted with the rest the reading of no poem ever left such an impression on my fondness for poetry as his 'Common Lot' did which I met with about 10 years ago in a little volume called the 'Beautys of Poetry' (Clare, 1985, p. 368)

The 'little volume' was *The Parnassian Garland, Or, Beauties of Modern Poetry, from the Works of the Most Distinguished Poets of the Present Age* (1807), published in London and edited by John Evans, LL. D., and 'Designed for the Use of Schools and the Admirers of Poetry in general'. It may be 'little' but it is a surprisingly compendious anthology of short, often sententious poems, and would have enabled Clare to sample virtually all his most prominent contemporaries (he mentions two of them here: Letitia Elizabeth Landon, known as 'L.E.L.', and James Montgomery) and some of his forbears, including the labouring-class poets Thomas Dermody, Ann Yearsley, and Robert and Nathaniel Bloomfield. Two poems each by Charlotte Smith and S. T. Coleridge are interleaved with each other, one of several Yearsley poems sits between Robert Southey and W. L. Bowles, and indeed the sense one gets of this evidently popular sourcebook, at least from this distance, is of a levelled and democratic literary landscape.

Appropriately, then, the poem that sticks in Clare's memory from the anthology, Montgomery's 'The Common Lot', begins as follows:

> ONCE in the flight of ages past
> There liv'd a Man – and *who* was He?
> Mortal! howe'er thy lot be cast,
> That Man resembl'd thee!
>
> Unknown the region of his birth,
>   The land in which he died unknown;
> His name hath perish'd from the Earth,
>   This truth survives alone –
>
> That joy, and grief, and hope, and fear,
>   Alternate triumph'd in his breast;
> His bliss and woe, a smile, a tear!
>   Oblivion hides the rest.
>
> (ll. 1–12)

Montgomery was working a theme familiar from Thomas Gray's *Elegy in a Country Churchyard*, but instead of following Gray by making the anonymous soul's posthumous obscurity a matter for consolatory piety, he develops a more triumphalist consolation in the idea of a humanity of common feeling, and the universal significance of the unostentatious, anonymous subject whose memory may ultimately endure and prove more resistant than mere individualism.

It should not surprise us that this caught Clare's eye, since as a writer he in many ways shares this ideal of common values. For example he foreshadows Virginia Woolf's feminist resistance to the power of the first-person pronoun 'I', the 'dark bar' across the page, as she calls it, which for Woolf mars the work of the modern male fiction writer (Woolf, 1977, p. 95).[1] Writing to his friend Eliza Emmerson in March 1830 about grammar and gossip, Clare personifies the first-person pronoun as a 'presumption ambitious swaggering little fellow':

> Had I not recieved your letter to remind me of my errors I should not have been with you in the shape of a letter untill the day after tomorrow for I was indulging in the gossip you desired of me & wishing to make it more commendable by variety I determined to speak in parables & that in past moods & tenses for I am growing out of myself into many existences & wish to become more entertaining in other genders for that little personal pronoun 'I' is such a presumption

ambitious swaggering little fellow that he thinks himself qualified for all company all places & all employments go where you will there he is swaggering & bouncing in the pulpit the parliment the bench aye every where even in this my letter he has intruded 5 several times already who can tell me where he is not or one of his family thats his brother or from how many pen points he is at this moment dropping into his ambitions on humble ex[is]tances he is a sort of Deity over the rest of the alphabet being here there & everywhere <at one & the same time> he is a mighty vapour in grammar (Clare, 1985, p. 504)

Clare's rodomontade on the 'swaggering little fellow' fills the whole letter. The self-confident 'I' of the first-person pronoun is for Clare, as it is for Woolf, a denizen of a male establishment ('the pulpit the parliment the bench') which the writer is careful to distance himself/herself from, wishing to become 'more entertaining in other genders', and 'growing out of myself into many existences'. Those familiar with Clare's life story may find this last aspiration troubling, since seven years after he wrote it he would find himself in long-term residential treatment for a condition which seems to have involved multiple subjective identities, among other 'mad' behaviours. Conversely, some of Clare's more cryptic statements from the later asylum period might well be read as exercises in resisting the burden of individualism, at least in authorship: 'I'm John Clare now. I was Byron and Shakespeare formerly. At different times you know I'm different people – that is the same person with different names' (Tibble and Tibble, 1972, pp. 372–3). This could be read as a survival technique *in extremis*, but it follows a lifelong pattern of questioning and resisting the idea of a fixed personal identity, and a healthy suspicion of those who most loudly and publicly assert theirs.

The 'sociable' Clare of these two topics needs to be stressed, partly because there is another, quite different John Clare, well captured in the pun the *Guardian* newspaper used as heading for an article I wrote about the Clare copyright dispute some years ago: 'Poor Clare' (Goodridge, 2000). This Clare, of whom I have often written myself – for example with Kelsey Thornton in our essay 'John Clare: the trespasser' (Goodridge and Thornton, 1994) – is a more individualistic, unsocialized, even antisocial figure, a member of what he himself would call 'the awkward squad', literally meaning a soldier punished for marching out of step (*OED*, 'squad', n.1, 1(b));[2] an isolated outsider, vulnerable to the whims of the powerful, and transgressive by necessity if not always by choice. He is a mumbling loner suspected by his community of madness or worse, and reciprocally suspicious of humanity in general; at bay in his middle years, latterly sometimes bitterly misanthropic or misogynistic in outlook; always fond of tobacco and drinking, and having a habit in his cups, as Roger Sales wryly puts it, of growing 'abusive and radical just before he slid under a table' (1983, p. 96; see also Sales, 2002). 'Poor Clare' is understood to be a victim, from the earliest accounts, such as those of some of the asylum visitors, and the Frederick Martin biography of 1865. Martin himself was an outsider in London literary life and his affecting though for aught we know entirely imaginary account of Clare being dragged, weeping, from the bosom of his family in the dying days of 1841 and 'thrust into the gaol for the insane' for what the biographer angrily calls the 'new crime' of 'having written poetry' (Martin, 1865, pp. 291–2), helped to establish a paradigm of Clare as a martyr and a rebel, the ultimate victimized literary outsider. For many of Clare's readers and admirers the poet retains the glamour of his outsider status, and in some ways he continues to resist easy absorption into the tourist, leisure, ecological, educational and literary critical industries which have recently begun to lay serious claim to his legacy.

* * *

Both the Clares I have described are recognizable: he was capable of being both an intensely sociable and a deeply enigmatic and shy man, whose sense of 'community' was ambivalent; he understood the difficulties as well as the strengths inherent in communities, and the pleasures as well as the horrors of isolation; and his writing reflects this ambiguity and complexity. I want to explore in the remainder of this essay one of Clare's more important intertextual relationships, which I think casts light on this question of his sociability versus his solitariness. Perhaps more than any other writer of his era, Robert Bloomfield (1760–1823) captured *both* the intense loneliness and the sociability of rural life in the era of enclosure. And Clare's response to him was of a different order to his feeling for any other poet, living or dead: quite simply, he revered him, and described him in superlative terms. 'He is in my opinion our best Pastoral Poet', he writes in a letter to Allan Cunningham, a year after Bloomfield's death. 'His "Broken Crutch", "Richard and Kate", &c. are inimitable and above praise.' In a letter to Bloomfield's friend Thomas Inskip, a few weeks earlier, he had described him as 'the most original poet of the age & the greatest Pastoral Poet England ever gave birth to' (Clare-Cunningham, 9 September 1824 and Clare-Inskip, 10 August 1824, in Clare, 1985, pp. 299–303).[3]

In one of Clare's first extant letters, dated April 1819, he told Edward Drury that he already had three volumes of Bloomfield, and offered to exchange these for a 'Pocket' edition that included *The Banks of Wye*, which he had not yet seen. By October he was still seeking the missing *Banks*, having seen 'all his Works but the above'; he also tells Isaiah Knowles Holland that he knows Bloomfield 'is coming out again this Winter but what Poem I don't know' (Clare, 1985, pp. 6–7, 17). Bloomfield is mentioned in Octavius Gilchrist's showcasing account of Clare, published in the *London Magazine* for January 1820 as 'Some Account of John Clare, An Agricultural Labourer and Poet': 'Beyond his Bible he had read nothing but a few odd volumes, the very titles of some of which he had forgotten, and others, which he remembered, were so utterly worthless, that I should shame to mention the names. A single volume of Pope, however, with the Wild Flowers of Bloomfield' (Gilchrist, 1820). Although the whole piece is designed to emphasize the artless and bookless 'natural genius' of the 'Northamptonshire peasant', Bloomfield's third volume is allowed in, along with key canonical works of morality and poetry, the Bible and Pope, though Clare is rationed to a 'single volume' of Pope's highly-crafted verses, whilst Bloomfield's most artless title is singled out, 'Wild Flowers' (a name that may have given Clare the idea of making a flower reference in his preferred choice of title for his final volume, 'The Midsummer Cushion'). We have seen that in fact he already owned *three* volumes of Bloomfield.

Immediate and persistent critical comparisons were made between Clare and Bloomfield, as two comparably successful and successive labouring-class peasant poets, Clare being seen in some senses as Bloomfield's natural successor in the 'peasant poet' stakes. Notwithstanding the burden that this comparison would become, Clare felt a very powerful affinity to this poet of the previous generation. And Bloomfield himself, though chronically ailing by the time Clare came on the scene, reached out an exceptionally welcoming hand to the younger poet, prompted by an early gift of Clare's first volume from Edward Drury. This is the first of two extant letters he wrote to Clare:

Shefford, Bedfordshire, July 25. 1820

To Mr Clare

Brother Bard, and fellow labourer,

Some weeks past Mr Drury of Stamford sent me your Vollm and I have only been prevented from answering by ill health, which began in January and seems to threaten a longer continuance. I am however very glad to have lived to have seen your poems: They have given me and my family an uncommon pleasure, and they will have the same effect on all kindred minds and that's enough; for, as for writing rhimes for Clods and sticks and expecting them to read them, I never found any fun in that in all my life, and I have past your age 24 years. I am delighted with your 'address to the Lark', Summer Morning', and 'Evening' &c &c. In fact I had better not turn critic in my first letter, but say the truth, that nothing upon the great theatre of what is calld the world (our English world) can give me half the pleasure I feel at seeing a man start up from the humble walks of life and show himself to be what I think you are. – What that is, Ask a higher power, – for though learning is not to be contemn'd it did not give you this.

I must write to Mr Drury, and Mr Claydon, but not now. – I am far from well – have just been walking amidst the most luxuriant crops with my eldest Daughter with and two Sons, but find myself tired.

Let nothing prevent you from writing, for though I cannot further your interest I can feel an interest in it, and I assure you I do.

I am heartily tired, (not of my subject) and must beg you to accept my congratulations and my wishes for your health, which I find after all is one of the most essential blessings of life.

Yours Sir, Most Cordially
Robt Bloomfield.

PS I have written this on 'my Old Oak Table'! and I think you know what I meen?

(Bloomfield, 1820)

I quote this in full to show how decisively Bloomfield acted, even in the fog of late-life illness and exhaustion, to offer praise for Clare's first volume and 'pass the baton' to him. Bloomfield, as the recent full edition of his correspondence shows, was a man who could express intense feelings in his personal correspondence, and the penultimate paragraph above, in particular, stands out in its intensity. There is an impassioned, rallying tone in the phrase 'Let nothing prevent you', and Bloomfield cleverly signals, by distinguishing between two meanings of the word 'interest', that there may be valuable forms of solidarity beyond the confines of the patronly 'interest' that both these poets found difficult to handle. And in a mentorial gesture, Bloomfield in his postscript nudges the younger poet to look again at the poem 'To My Old Oak Table', an important autobiographical text in which Bloomfield had read the table's 'Old Heart of Oak' as both a sympathetic witness and a comforting presence through the trials and triumphs of the poet's life, literally and metaphorically a support for poetry writing, the job that 'nothing' must now be allowed to prevent Clare from doing.

Clare's reply has not survived, but two letters he wrote to other correspondents on 12 September express his pride and pleasure in Bloomfield's attentions (Clare, 1985, pp. 92–5). In one of them, Clare passed on Bloomfield's address, and we know Bloomfield greatly desired to meet him, but in fact they never met, and the story of their close (but not close enough) encounters is as tantalizing as that of Clare and Keats. Clare's best opportunity to visit Bloomfield in Shefford came on his return journey from London in June 1822. But he was in no state to do so, as he freely admits:

> on monday morning I got to helpstone but how I can hardly tell for I was so 'reeling ripe' that when I got to peterbro I askd the name of the place & when it was told me I took it to be a hoax & coud hardly be convincd to the contrary . . . my heart achd as I lost sight of London at the thought of being forcd away perhaps for ever from the merriest set of fellows I ever met with . . . I passd poor Bloomfield for twas no use stopping in the state I was in & had I been sober I dont think my inclination woud have gone far then to persuade me (Clare, 1985, p. 243)

Here, one sort of companionship has driven out another. Clare's second trip to London came as he emerged from a difficult spring. The visit lasted three and a half weeks, being cut short by the news of the imminent birth of (as it would prove) his daughter Eliza. He had enjoyed a riotous time with his friends, including members of the *London Magazine* circle, the painter Edward Rippingille and John Taylor's porter Thomas Bennion, the merry set of fellows whose companionship left Clare on the coach home in the condition of Trinculo, recalled here in his quotation from *The Tempest*, and his admission that in leaving the party, 'my heart achd', as once had that of an erstwhile fellow drinker with several of Clare's new companions, John Keats.[4]

Clare would be plentifully reminded of the opportunity he had lost. Thomas Inskip, Bloomfield's Shefford neighbour, who befriended both men, would still be remonstrating with Clare about it in an unpublished letter written to him in the asylum, twenty-four years later, in which he recalled his own participation in the spree:

> Many vicissitudes have attended my [?move]ments through life since we last met in Saint John Street and [?talk]ed away the hours with the Grape and the Laurel, – with Poetry and Wine till into the ninth Heaven we soared off up fleet street and rang at Taylor & Hesseys Bell while St Bridget's Clock blabbed that three times one makes three! – poor Taylor who sat up to let you in (I recollect) had been wiling away the tedium nursing his wrath and devoting it to your moral instruction when he got you safe in, whilst I returning was left to laugh at your dilemma and seek new adventures the rising sun blushed to behold me entering the doorway of my home. – But, Lord was not it a glorious Evening – . . . I always regretted that your promise solemnly made to me to come and pay us a visit at Shefford was never put into execution, and none of us regretted it more than Bloomfield – You ought to have come, it was very malicious of you or of fortune that preven[ted] you. – I do beseech you in future never omit the chance of seeing a Poet! – The true Poet is not an every day production and there was that in the natures of Clare and Bloomfield after seeing each other would have made them both Clairvoyant ever after. – How often have we talked of you and how often did he yearn to see you. (Inskip, 1846)

This gives an interesting picture of both the pleasure in companionship that these two labouring-class men (Inskip was a watchmaker) had shared, and the yearning that lay behind Bloomfield's first letter to Clare, to know more about this new figure, to get to know a new labouring-class poet of talent who might take things forward and give hope to an ailing fellow poet. Having moved from uproarious reminiscence to the plain scolding he is unable, even at this late stage in both their lives, to hold back from, Inskip turns his ticking-off into a plea which airs this sense of yearning: the plea for Clare never to miss a chance of meeting a poet. The point is not that Clare is likely to meet very many poets in Northampton Asylum where he now resides, but that such comings together are immensely precious, given the 'vicissitudes' of fortune Inskip has witnessed in Bloomfield's end, Clare's incarceration, and his own difficulties in life. What is suggested by these exchanges and reminiscences, in both positive and negative ways, is the sense of vulnerability that these labouring-class writers felt, and a consequent need to band together and value each other – and of course the pleasures that they were able to experience when they did find themselves in each others' company. (Ironically, many of Inskip's surviving letters to Clare in the asylum consist of excuses for not yet having visited him there, though he did make it to Northampton eventually.)

A month before the second London trip, Bloomfield had sent Clare the last of the two surviving letters:

Shefford, Beds, May 3d. 1822

Neighbour John,

If we were still nearer neighbours I would see you, and thank you personally for the two vollums of your poems sent me so long ago. I write with such labour and difficulty that I cannot venture to praise or discriminate like a critic, but must only say that you have given us great pleasure.

I beg your acceptance of my just publishd little vollumn; and, sick and ill as I continually feel, I can join you heartily in your exclamation –

'What is Life?'

With best regards and wishes

I am yours sincerely

Robt. Bloomfield
(Bloomfield, 1822)

The volume he had enclosed with this letter will have been *May Day with the Muses* (1822): a copy, inscribed 'From the author, 3 May 1822', is still in Clare's library. Clare had prompted Taylor on 3 September 1821: 'you'll remember Bloomfield when the books struck off', i.e. to send Bloomfield a copy of Clare's second collection, *The Village Minstrel*, on publication, and Bloomfield now reciprocated with a copy of what would be his own final collection (Clare, 1985, p. 213). He draws Clare closer through the epithet 'neighbour John' and the wish that they were nearer neighbours, as Clare had recently wished Helpston and London closer together.[5] Unable in his illness to muster a proper critical response to *The Village Minstrel*, Bloomfield acknowledges the 'great pleasure' Clare has given 'us' (the plural is a good reminder that in these circles in this period, poems would be read aloud and shared between family and friends, as Clare himself read poems out to his parents). Just as Bloomfield had reminded Clare in the earlier letter of his poem about finding a stable touchstone (or touchwood) in a fragile world, 'To My Old Oak Table'; now, faced with his own mortality, he acknowledges the pith and point of Clare's early poem of existential uncertainty, 'What is Life?', with its description of death as a 'long & lingering Sleep the weary crave' (l.23; Clare, 1989, I, p. 393). Again, these transactions suggest the importance of solidarity and reciprocity, and the exchange of ideas, affection and admiration within the community of labouring-class poets.

May Day with the Muses, however, may have been a step too far for this shared sense of labouring-class solidarity in the face of adversity. On 11 May, evidently not yet having received Bloomfield's parcel of 3rd, Clare wrote to James Hessey: 'what think you of my friend Bloomfields "Mayday" &c &c Ive not seen it yet but a friend of mine at Milton says its "A Mayday of Messrs Baldwin Craddock & Joy" & I am not without my suspicions as to that being the case by what I keep hearing of it' (Clare, 1985, pp. 239–40). Mark Storey identifies the source of Clare's suspicions as his friend Joseph Henderson, who had written to Clare four days earlier, darkly describing 'those [Muses] of Messrs Cradock & Joy tricked out in all the Scool-Boy-Book elegence of a wooden cut *Picture*' (Clare, 1985, p. 240n). Henderson's sceptical response and belief that the collection was a cynical cashing-in operation by Bloomfield's publishers may have been triggered by the framing fiction of *May Day with the Muses*. In the tradition of *The Canterbury Tales* it nests its poems, which are principally narrative, within the framework of a friendly competition to tell the best story in verse. However this framework rests on the pleasing fantasy of a benevolently paternalistic landlord who, on a whim, decides to waive a year's rent for the best competitor. This may have hit a raw nerve with Henderson, an independent and intelligent man who, in his professional capacity as a servant at Milton Hall, will have had to negotiate regularly with a real grandee, his employer Earl Fitzwilliam. The collection has been vigorously defended in recent years by John Lucas, who reads it as Bloomfield's 'most sustained vision of "amity and social love"', seeing it as having 'something . . . of the village pageant' tradition, and importantly both reaching back to late-eighteenth-century texts of rural lament like Goldsmith's 'The Deserted Village', and forward to Tennyson's 'medley' poems and the successful later nineteenth-century traditions of verse dialogue and monologue that followed. Lucas notes that Clare uses Bloomfield's fictitious location of Oakley Hall in his own narrative poem 'Valentine Eve' which 'can hardly be a coincidence', though he sees the latter as being closer to Bloomfield's 'The Broken Crutch' than to the stories of *May Day* itself (Lucas, 1994, pp. 66–7; Lucas, 2006, p. 123; see also White, 2007, pp. 121–46). I have said that Bloomfield captured both the loneliness and the sociability of rural life, and we shall find both phenomena, the loneliness of 'The Widow to Her Hourglass' and the wonderfully boozy, Clarean sociability of 'The Horkey', in the narrative poems. (Though Lucas (2006, p. 131) has noted more restrained drinking in *May Day*, and the prominence of the tale 'The Drunken Father' which was reprinted as a pamphlet by the temperance advocates who were clearly starting to get a grip on the culture by the late stages of Bloomfield's career (Bloomfield, 1880)).

Bloomfield could also bring together in his poetry, ironically, dramatically or simply in contrast, ideas of community and isolation. His first and most famous poem, *The Farmer's Boy* (1800), is a far less blandly reassuring depiction of rural life than almost any critic has observed, although Ian Haywood's important 2011 essay on the poet, following on from his work on violence in the Romantic period, shows for the first time just how thoroughly, sometimes shockingly imbued the poem is with the fearful, tough realities of rural life in the 1790s. In the poem Bloomfield looks back with fondness to a rural childhood that he remembers as having been in many ways idyllic, the more so, no doubt, in contrast to the harsh city life and work he was immersed in when he composed it, and the tone is often one of appreciative love of the rural world. But this does not mean that everything witnessed by the poet or experienced by his persona, Giles, is pleasant or happy. The skipping firstling lambs of Spring are horrifically stopped by the butcher's 'knife that plunges through their throats' ('Spring', l. 352); the mingling of master and men at the Summer harvest festival is acknowledged to be just a fond memory, for nowadays tyranny has gained sufficient strength to 'violate the feelings of the poor' and 'leave them distanc'd in the mad'ning race' ('Summer', ll. 336–7). In the 'Autumn' section, the 'mad girl' collects twigs to whip the 'hovering Demons from her brow' and sleeps out in the pigsty rather than face her, presumably abusive, fellow humans ('Autumn', ll. 123–39). And later in the same season (ll. 191–252), in a passage which captures Bloomfield's delicate awareness of the urge for sociable companionship to offset the loneliness of rural work, the poet describes a moment of hospitality that goes dramatically sour. Giles is sent to guard the growing corn, 'from morn till set[t]ing sun' (l. 198) from the predations of the birds. This was perhaps the loneliest of all jobs, as M. K. Ashby's account of her father Joseph's early life poignantly suggests:

> He had a wooden [bird-scaring] clapper, but if he saw no-one for hours he took to shouting so as to hear a human voice. This method had another convenience; you couldn't cry while you shouted. (1979, p. 24)

Expecting a visit from his 'playmates young and gay' (l. 217) Bloomfield's Giles makes a shelter from wind and rain in 'some sequester'd nook embank'd around' (l. 205), builds a little fire, crops a branch of sloes to toast and builds turf seats for his imagined guests. When they fail to arrive he grows angry; the fields seem like a prison, disappointment 'untunes the soul' (l. 228). Bloomfield follows his master, James Thomson, when he then invites the reader to 'look up' from 'the poor bird-boy with his roasted sloes' (l. 232) to the greater wrong of actual imprisonment, which leads to praise for the prison reformer John Howard (l. 238).[6]

An anecdote, a small incident, has led to the greater idea that the loneliness of rural life becomes as destructive as physical incarceration. Clare is equally aware of the misery of loneliness, fear and boredom in the bird-scarer boy's experience. In his own Bloomfieldian seasonal poem, *The Shepherd's Calendar* (1827) he gives his perspective on the same phenomenon:

> The boy that scareth from the spirey wheat
> The mellancholy crow – quakes while he weaves
> Beneath the ivey tree a hut & seat
> Of rustling flags & sedges tyd in sheaves
> Or from nigh stubble shocks a shelter thieves
> There he doth dithering sit [. . .]
> He wishes in his heart twas summer time again
> & oft hell clamber up a sweeing tree
> To see the scarlet hunter hurry bye
> & feign woud in the merry uproar be
> But sullen labour hath its tethering tye
>
> ('November', ll. 46–51, 54–8, in Clare, 1996a, I, pp. 146–7)[7]

The boy 'quakes' from cold rather than fear (he is reported to be 'dithering', i.e. shivering, four lines later), but the close proximity of the words 'scareth' and 'mellancholly' give a sense of anxiety to his quaking demeanour. What he does is exactly what Bloomfield's 'Giles' does: he builds a makeshift shelter, trying to make some kind of homely comfort for himself in a hostile working environment. Clare follows Bloomfield in showing how the bird-scaring boy must win a seat and a 'home' for himself from the November cold, and can only do so by breaking rules and laws, as others would have to break them. Clare's boy 'thieves' the 'stubble shocks' of straw for his shelter, and, slightly later, 'steals' an hour of leisure in his working day to enjoy his hard-won comfort. The shared assumption of the two poems is that the bird-scarer must achieve for himself the comfort, homeliness and sociability everyone needs, and must do so in the teeth of a hostile world that extracts his labour but offers little comfort to his body or spirit.

Robert Bloomfield died on 19 August 1823, aged 56. His passing drew powerful praise from Clare. This, however, was written a year later, and although the evidence suggests that his death affected Clare profoundly, initially it was just one of a series of bereavements he suffered at this time, including the death of Octavius Gilchrist in June and the loss of the daughter born to Patty that same month. These events contributed to the darkness of mood in this period, which led up to the period of 'high nervous debility' in the winter of 1823 and the spring of 1824. Clare appears, in fact, to have had something very like what we would call a nervous breakdown, emerging from it via a brief spiritual flirtation with the 'Ranters' or 'Primitive Methodists', and a long third trip to London, lasting eleven weeks, during which he was treated by Dr Darling, the physician who had also treated Keats.

Undoubtedly Bloomfield's death contributed something to this crisis, but the first evidence we have of Clare's response (the record may be incomplete) comes as he emerges from the worst of this dark period. It was prompted by a letter from Thomas Inskip, sent in June 1824, recalling their meeting in London on Clare's second trip there,[8] and beginning his long process of reproaching Clare for having failed to visit Bloomfield (I quoted a later example of this earlier):

Dear Clare,
    You will probably feel surprised at hearing from a Person named Inskip, and might be at a loss to know who he was, without being first reminded that he spent a very happy Evening with you in London, when you promised to call on your return home and see poor Bloomfield; my intimacy with that kindhearted Man makes me most sincerely regret you did not fulfill your promise, particularly so,

as I know such a meeting would have been no small pleasure to both, the esteem between both I can vouch for, being mutual; Why did not you come Clare? Your personal acquaintance with Bloomfield would have added a few happy days to your Life and dispersed the gloom from as many of his own; rest assured he fully expected you, and felt a disappointment which you will find best described in his 'Farmers Boys,; look for the poor Bird Boy & you will feel how well.

Inskip points a finger to precisely the passage which, as we saw, most intensely reflects Bloomfield's sense of a need for companionship, and of loneliness and disappointment. This then leads him into an indignant speech about the general neglect Bloomfield suffered in his last years:

> You will doubtless have heard of his Death and most likely of the sale of his effects which took place a few days since, and I doubt not but you will feel not only as a Man, but as a Poet for the loss of a Brother Will it be possible to smother your indignation at knowing so kind, so good a Man, – so great an ornament to his Country was suffered to live and die in indigence, and that his dear Children are permitted to be the Heirs of his Poverty! (Inskip, 1824)[9]

Because this letter was mis-delivered and delayed, and because Clare was in London from May to July, he did not reply until 10 August. He had by then written a triple-sonnet to Bloomfield, and had given the poet's passing some reflection:

> I have often thought of our London Evening & I have often thought of writing to you – poor Bloomfield I deeply regret now its too late I had made up my resolution to see him this summer but if he had been alive I shoud have been dissapointed by this coldblooded lethargy of a disease what it is I cannot tell it even affects my senses very much by times – I heard of Bloomfields death & it shockd my feelings poor fellow you say right when you exclaim 'who would be a poet' I sincerely lovd the man & I admire his Genius & readily (nay gladly) acknowledge his superiority as a Poet in my opinion he is the most original poet of the age & the greatest Pastoral Poet England ever gave birth too I am no Critic but I always feel & Judge for myself I shall never forget the pleasures which I felt in first reading his poems little did I think then that I shoud live to become so near an acquaintance with the Enthusiastic Giles & miss the gratification of seeing him at last – I am grievd to hear of his family misfortunes. (Clare, 1985, pp. 300–1).

Clare interestingly characterizes Bloomfield here as 'Enthusiastic' Giles, his adjective associating Bloomfield's energy and passion with the spiritual passion of his recent friends the Ranters (*OED*, 'enthusiastic', *adj.* and *n.*, definitions 1 and 2). But he goes on to say that he is unsatisfied with the triple-sonnet he has written to Bloomfield's memory. Indeed the whole process of memorializing Bloomfield seems to have become difficult for him. He pressed his friend Henry Cary to include Bloomfield in his 'Lives of the Poets' (Clare, 1985, p. 304), and planned his own biography of the poet.[10] He tried to help Joseph Weston, who was editing Bloomfield's *Remains*, and in doing so came up with a fresh reason for having missed Bloomfield ('my purse got too near the bottom for a stoppage on the road & as it was too great a distance to walk home'), but was unhappy when Weston wanted to omit the first sonnet (see Weston, 1825; Clare, 1985, pp. 321–4; Weston and Hannah Bloomfield, 1825).

One understands Weston's position: the first sonnet is weaker than the other two, which work effectively as a pair.[11] It could be argued, in fact, that Clare's best memorial to Bloomfield was his own continuing poetic endeavours: *The Shepherd's Calendar* (and its planned accompaniment, *Village Stories)*; the enclosure elegies; the Northborough sonnets; *The Midsummer Cushion*. All these landmarks in Clare's mature work owe something to Bloomfield's example and inspiration. In terms of more formal responses, the sonnet-sequence is eclipsed by the rousing comments Clare makes about Bloomfield in his letters to Inskip, Cunningham and Cary in August and September 1824 and to Weston in March 1825.[12] His spirited letter to his 'Brother Bard and Fellow Labourer' Allan Cunningham of 9 September 1824, enclosing the autograph of 'our English Theocritus, Bloomfield', has rightly been prominent in discussions of Bloomfield's influence.[13] In it Clare compares Bloomfield favourably to Crabbe, lashes out at Byron for having sneered at the Bloomfield brothers in *English Bards and Scotch Reviewers*, and concludes by asserting solidarity between labouring-class poets, making a virtue of their proud, outsider status and freedom from the taint of a classical education. It is a *tour de force* of defensive bravado:

> I should suppose, friend Allan, that 'The Ettrick Shepherd,' 'The Nithsdale Mason,' and 'The Northamptonshire Peasant,' are looked upon as intruders and stray cattle in the fields of the Muses (forgive the classification), and I have no doubt but our reception in the Pinfold of his lordship's 'English bards' would have been as far short of a compliment as Bloomfield's. Well, never mind, we will do our best, and as we never went to Oxford or Cambridge, we have no Latin and Greek

to boast of, and no bad translations to hazard (whatever our poems may be), and that's one comfort on our side. (Clare, 1985, pp. 302–3)

This stirring letter appropriately reflects the fact that one of Bloomfield's special contributions to Clare's poetry and self-creation as a poet was his powerful sense of community and its value, both in his poetry and through the reaching-out gestures I have catalogued here. But in terms of how Clare assimilated and internalized Bloomfield's legacy of poetry and literary companionship, there is an equally interesting, if quieter response in a little known poem among the Knight transcripts of the 1840s, 'Song' ('The rushbeds touched the boiling spring'). It is short and worth quoting in full:

1

The rushbeds touched the boiling spring
    And dipped and bowed and dipped again
The nodding flower would wabbling hing
    Till it could scarce get back again
How pleasant lay the daisey plain
    How twisting sweet the woodbine grew
Around the white thorn in the lane
    Bedecked with gems of droppled dew

2

Here Bloomfield lay beside the brook
    His memory haunts the silver flood
Musing upon the open book
    In happy and poetic mood
His fancies left on every place
    The landscape seems his waking dream
Where Hannah shewed her rosey face
    'And leap't across the infant stream'

3

The rush tufts touched the boiling sand
    Then wabbling nodded up anew
Then danced at every winds command
    And dipped to peirce the water through
The twisted woodbine was in flower

And pale among the thorn leaves grew
Here Bloomfield rested many an hour
While bees they sipped the morning dew

4

The little spring it boiled away
And dancing rose the silver sand
For ever boiling night and day
And never made an idle stand
The wild flowers nodded on the brink
And made its wrinkles on the stream
Where Bloomfield often lay to think
And listless spend his summer dream

(Clare, 1984, I, pp. 527–8)[14]

Whilst riparian or river poetry is a recognized genre,[15] we need a distinctive term for Clare's poetry of pools and ponds and the springs, streams, rills and rivulets that flow through his poetry. His sonnet-sequence to Bloomfield had incorporated some of this watery imagery, in phrases such as 'quiet brooks' and 'valley streams' (contrasted to the 'tide of fashion' which is 'a stream too strong'),[16] and had set 'Giles' among the flowing waters. But this poem moves beyond what was by now the rather clichéd habit of using Bloomfield's famous persona from *The Farmer's Boy* as a shorthand term for the poet himself, giving Bloomfield's own name instead (with its fortuitously embedded images of *Bloom*ing flowers and *field*s, my emphases) in order to re-imagine him as a presence in the landscape. The poem also makes a reference to 'Hannah'. One reason for this is suggested by Clare's Oxford editors, who note that this was the name of Bloomfield's daughter. Clare may perhaps have intended to enfold into the poem a little homage to Hannah Bloomfield, whose charming letter to him of 10 March 1825 thanking him for his sonnets to her father he would have remembered. In it she deals with his failure to visit her father with far more grace than Inskip could muster, shifting some of the blame towards Inskip himself: 'You can never know how much he regretted not seeing you at Shefford. He had set his heart upon that pleasure, and attributed his disappointment to Mr Inskips meeting you in London, and giving you such an account of his health &c as made you think a visit then would be ill-timed. – in short he was displeased with him for monopolising you.'

But an even more obvious reason for the name 'Hannah' in the poem is that it alludes to Bloomfield's short poem 'Rosy Hannah', from *Rural Tales* (1801):

I

A spring, o'erhung with many a flower,
    The grey sand dancing in its bed,
Embank'd beneath a Hawthorn bower
    Sent forth its waters near my head:
A rosy Lass approach'd my view;
    I caught her blue eye's modest beam:
The stranger nodded 'how d'ye do!'
    And leap'd across the infant stream.

II

The water heedless pass'd away:
    With me her glowing image stay'd:
I strove, from that auspicious day,
    To meet and bless the lovely Maid.
I met her where beneath our feet
    Through downy Moss the wild Thyme grew;
Nor moss elastic, flow'rs though sweet,
    Match'd Hannah's cheek of rosy hue.

III

I met her where the dark Woods wave,
    And shaded verdure skirts the plain;
And when the pale Moon rising gave
    New glories to her clouded train.
From her sweet cot upon the Moor
    Our plighted vows to Heaven are flown;
Truth made me welcome at the door,
    And Rosy Hannah is my own.

                      (Bloomfield, 1809, II, pp. 115–16;
                           first pub. in Bloomfield, 1802)

The distinction between 'art' verse and 'folk' song seems redundant in these kinds of poems, which write the folk idiom easily into poetry and, equally effortlessly, express sexual desire and experience in a way that avoids both coy euphemism and the kind of frankness that got Clare into trouble with his patrons in 1820–1.[17] The imagery of flower-bedecked springs and flowing water, wild thyme, dark woods and the pale moon carry out this work very well for Bloomfield. These poems also illustrate the limitations of 'echo hunting' as a means of measuring influence. Clare quotes a line from 'Rosy Hannah', but the influence of Bloomfield follows a far more subtle and flexible path than this. Clare's poem recreates the environment and the loving spirit of 'Rosy Hannah', as well as following its stanza form and metre, and yet makes something quite fresh. Bloomfield, seemingly present as the lover in 'Rosy Hannah', is also a companionable presence in Clare's poem, but one who is somehow written or formed into the landscape itself. His 'memory haunts the silver flood'; the 'landscape seems his waking dream'. Poet and place, poem and person are perfectly fused, and in this way Clare's most beloved poetic companion is kept in memory and adequately memorialized at last. As in Bloomfield's 'Rosy Hannah', the stream becomes a stream of memory, for while the 'water heedless pass'd away; / With me her glowing image stay'd'. The life-giving element of running water is used by Clare in a subtle alchemy, to preserve and keep in mind his fellow poet of rural solidarity and isolation.

* * *

Briefly to conclude, then: Clare's writing embodies an intense sense of the importance and precious fragility of a 'community'; most centrally, the community of the village he grew up in, whose culture and ecology he celebrated throughout his writing life. Other communities included those of his 'brother bards', the *London Magazine* circle, the imaginary literary communities of Isaac Walton's 'circle' and of Thomas Chatterton's 'Rowley world', with their all-welcoming poets and deep-pocketed patrons, and the imagined village communities that stretch back through the work of some of the poets he most admired, Bloomfield prominent among them. Yet his sense of community is invariably edged with an unblinking awareness of its limits. To comprehend Clare adequately we need to read both his complex representations of community and his alert sense of isolation; his sociability and his solitariness.

Acknowledgement

This essay draws on material from my forthcoming study for Cambridge University Press, *John Clare and Community*. I am grateful to Heyes for kindly allowing me to quote from his transcriptions of unpublished letters to Clare from Bloomfield, Gilchrist, Preston, Weston and Hannah Bloomfield.

Notes

1. Hermione Lee appropriately entitles the final chapter of her biography of Woolf 'Anon' (1997, esp. p. 750).
2. Clare recalls that in the militia, 'I once got into the awkard squad not for my own fault but that of others which shows that bad company is not very commendable' (1996, p. 96). He also uses the term in relation to punctuation, 'that awkward squad of pointings called commas colons semicolons &c &' (1985, p. 491).
3. For more on Inskip see Williams, 2001 and Hoskins, 2004.
4. On this trip see Clare, 1996, pp. 136–49, and Bate, 2003, pp. 239–46. Clare's echo of the first line of 'Ode to a Nightingale' may be unconscious.
5. 'I wish I livd nearer you at least I wish London w[ould] creep within 20 miles of helpstone I dont wish helpstone to shift its station' (Clare, 1985, p. 230).
6. Compare James Thomson, 'Winter', ll. 359-88 (Thomson, 1984, pp. 138–9 and 235 note), where Thomson praises the Jail Committee of 1729.
7. In the Northborough sonnet 'He waits all day beside his little flock' (Clare, 2003, pp. 272–3), Clare describes the same pattern of boredom and anxious loneliness in the shepherd boy who 'asks the passing stranger whats o clock' (l. 2), 'mutters storys to himself' (l. 5), tries to find a warm spot in the hedge and climbs a tree to see the hunters pass, before anxiously busying himself with work in fear of the master's appearance.
8. Bate, 2003, pp. 191–2, states that Clare met Inskip on his third trip to London, but in fact the two men met on the second trip of 1822, confirmed by Hannah Bloomfield's letter to Clare of 10 March 1825 (quoted in the text).
9. Clare was aware of the death; the latest he could have learned about it is dateable by a verse-letter sent to him by his correspondent Edward Baily Preston on 1 February 1824: 'Since last I wrote poor Giles alas! / Has shook the sand from lifes frail glass' (Preston, 1824).
10. 'Began an Enquirey into the Life of Bloomfield with the intention of writing one & a critisism on his genius & writings', Journal entry for 12 October 1824, Clare, 1983, p. 190; see also entry for 13 March 1825, p. 229.
11. 'To the Memory of Bloomfield', Clare, 1998, IV, pp. 181–4. See Chirico's reading of the poem (2007, pp. 54–61).
12. Clare, 1985, pp. 299–304, 321–4.
13. See especially Ward, 2005, who reproduces Cunningham's reply of 23 September and covering letter of 23 October (postage was delayed for want of a payment frank). Cunningham values Clare's comments on class and education, and ends on a note of brotherly encouragement, urging him to 'Keep up your heart and sing only when you feel the internal impulse and you will add something to our Poetry more lasting than any of the Peasant bards of Old England have done yet.'

14. Clare had also written Bloomfield into the fabric of one of his early poems, 'To an Oaten Reed': 'Sweet pipe awakend on the lowly hill / Where pastoral Bloomfield touchd his 'chanting strain'.
15. See especially Keegan, 2008, pp. 98–121.
16. On the significance for Clare of the term 'fashion' see Ward, 2002.
17. See Bate, 2003, pp. 164–5, for the difficulties Clare had with his patrons over the comic bawdy poem 'My Mary', one of 'some two or three poems' which 'might be expunged, in order to make room for others of riper and purer growth', as Lord Radstock primly and pompously puts it.

Bibliography

Ashby, M. K. (1979) *Joseph Ashby of Tysoe 1859–1919: A Study of English Village Life* (London: Merlin Press).
Bate, Jonathan (2003) *John Clare: A Biography* (London: Picador).
Bloomfield, Robert (1802) *Rural Tales, Ballads and Songs* (London: Vernor and Hood, and Longman and Rees).
——. (1809) *The Poems of Robert Bloomfield*, stereotype edition (London: The Author, Vernor, Hood and Sharpe).
——. (1820) letter to John Clare dated 25 July, British Library, manuscript Egerton 2245, ff. 186 r/v, 187r.
——. (1822) letter to John Clare dated 3 May, from a private collection.
——. (1880) *The Drunken Father: A Ballad* (London: National Temperance Publication Depot).
——. (2010) *The Letters of Robert Bloomfield and His Circle*, ed. Tim Fulford and Lynda Pratt, assoc. ed. John Goodridge, Romantic Circles (online publication): www.rc.umd.edu/editions/bloomfield_letters.
Chirico, Paul (2007) *John Clare and the Imagination of the Reader* (Basingstoke: Palgrave Macmillan).
Clare, John (1983) *The Natural History Prose Writings of John Clare*, ed. Margaret Grainger (Oxford: Clarendon Press).
——. (1984) *The Later Poems of John Clare 1837–1864*, ed. Eric Robinson, David Powell, assoc. ed. Margaret Grainger (Oxford: Clarendon Press).
——. (1985) *The Letters of John Clare*, ed. Mark Storey (Oxford: Clarendon Press).
——. (1989) *The Early Poems of John Clare 1804–1822*, ed. Eric Robinson, David Powell, assoc. ed. Margaret Grainger (Oxford: Clarendon Press).
——. (1996) *By Himself*, ed. Eric Robinson and David Powell (Ashington and Manchester: Mid-Northumberland Arts Group and Carcanet).
——. (1996a) *Poems of the Middle Period 1822–1837*, vols. I and II, ed. Eric Robinson, David Powell, and P. M. S. Dawson (Oxford: Clarendon Press).
——. (1998) *Poems of the Middle Period 1822–1837*, vols. III and IV, ed. Eric Robinson, David Powell, and P. M. S. Dawson (Oxford: Clarendon Press).
——. (2003) *Poems of the Middle Period 1822–1837*, vol. V, ed. Eric Robinson, David Powell, and P. M. S. Dawson (Oxford: Clarendon Press).
[Gilchrist, Octavius] (1820) 'Some Account of John Clare, an Agricultural Labourer and Poet', *London Magazine*, I, no. 1, pp. 7–11.
Goodridge, John (2000) 'Poor Clare', *Guardian*, 22 July 2000, review section, 3: www.guardian.co.uk/books/2000/jul/22/poetry.books.

——. and Bridget Keegan, eds. (2012) *Robert Bloomfield: The Inestimable Blessing of Letters* (Romantic Circles Praxis Series) www.rc.umd.edu/praxis/bloomfield.

——. and Kelsey Thornton (1994) 'John Clare: the trespasser', in *John Clare in Context*, ed. Hugh Haughton, Adam Phillips and Geoffrey Summerfield (Cambridge: Cambridge University Press), pp. 87–129.

Haywood, Ian (2011) 'The Infection of Robert Bloomfield: Terrorizing The Farmer's Boy', in *Robert Bloomfield*, ed. John Goodridge and Bridget Keegan (Romantic Circles Praxis Series) www.rc.umd.edu/praxis/bloomfield.

Hoskins, Philip (2004) 'Thomas Inskip: A Valediction for Robert Bloomfield', *Robert Bloomfield Society Newsletter*, 8, pp. 3–7.

Inskip, Thomas (1846) Letter to John Clare dated 5 October 1846, Northamptonshire Central Library, Clare manuscript 54, ff. 1–2.

Keegan, Bridget (2008) *British Labouring-Class Nature Poetry, 1730–1837* (Basingstoke: Palgrave Macmillan).

Lee, Hermione (1997) *Virginia Woolf* (London: Vintage).

Lucas, John (1994) 'Bloomfield and Clare', in *The Independent Spirit: John Clare and The Self-Taught Tradition*, ed. John Goodridge (Helpston: The John Clare Society), pp. 54–68.

——. (2006) 'Hospitality and the Rural Tradition: Bloomfield's *May Day with the Muses*' in *Robert Bloomfield: Lyric, Class and the Romantic Canon*, ed. Simon White, John Goodridge and Bridget Keegan (Lewisburg, PA: Bucknell University Press), pp. 113–41.

Martin, Frederick (1865), *The Life of John Clare* (London and Cambridge: Macmillan).

Preston, Edward Bailey (1824), letter to Clare dated 1 February, British Library, manuscript Egerton 2246, ff. 280–1.

Sales, Roger (1983) *English Literature in History, 1780–1830: Pastoral and Politics* (London: Hutchinson).

——. (2002) *John Clare: A Literary Life* (Basingstoke: Palgrave – now Palgrave Macmillan).

Thomson, James (1984) *The Seasons and The Castle of Indolence*, ed. James Sambrook (Oxford: Clarendon Press).

Tibble, J. W. and Anne (1972) *John Clare, a Life* (London: Michael Joseph).

Ward, Sam (2002) 'Clare in Fashion', *John Clare Society Journal*, 21, 33–51.

——. (2005) 'Brother Bards: John Clare & Allan Cunningham on Bloomfield', *Robert Bloomfield Society Newsletter*, 10, 6–12.

Weston, Joseph (1825) Letter to Clare dated 3 March 1825, British Library, manuscript Egerton 2246, f. 463r.

——. and Hannah Bloomfield (1825) Letter to Clare dated 10 March 1825, British Library, manuscript Egerton 2246, ff. 465–6.

White, Simon (2007) *Robert Bloomfield, Romanticism and the Poetry of Community* (Aldershot: Ashgate).

——. John Goodridge and Bridget Keegan, eds. (2006) *Robert Bloomfield: Lyric, Class and the Romantic Canon* (Lewisburg, PA: Bucknell University Press).

Williams, John (2001) 'Displacing Romanticism: Anna Seward, Joseph Weston and the Unschooled Sons of Genius', in *Placing and Displacing Romanticism*, ed. Peter Kitson (Aldershot: Ashgate), pp. 146–56.

Woolf, Virginia (1977) *A Room of One's Own* (London: Grafton).

5
John Clare and the Triumph of Little Things

Mina Gorji

John Clare is a great poet of little things. He was drawn to the minor – the tiny, the seemingly insignificant. His poetry celebrates small spaces and littlest creatures – the grasshopper, the bee, the mouse, the drop of dew, nitches, hollows, nests:

> The oddling bush close sheltered hedge new plashed
> Of which springs early liking makes a guest
> First with a shade of green though winter dashed
> There full as soon bumbarrels make a nest
> Of mosses grey with cobwebs closely tied
> & warm & rich as feather bed within
> With little hole on its contrary side
> That pathway peepers may no knowledge win
> Of what her little oval nest contains
> Ten eggs & often twelve with dusts of red
> Soft frittered & full soon the little lanes
> Screen the young crowd & hear the twittring song
> Of the old birds who call them to be fed
> While down the hedge they hang & hide along
>
> (John Clare, 'Bumbarrel's Nest'
> (1832–7), 2003, p. 219)

Clare is a poet who, as Kathleen Jamie noted in a 2005 interview, attends, and the quality of his attention is particular. 'Bumbarrell's Nest' is a poem of subtle perception and immediacy. The materials of the nest are carefully noted: the mosses are 'grey' and 'closely tied' with 'cobwebs' – a detail which brings home a sense of delicacy. Clare is not writing to the eye alone, but also to the other senses: touch is called with the phrase 'warm & rich as feather bed', which in registering temperature and texture gives a sense of direct and tactile encounter. The phrase 'feather bed' domesticates and familiarizes the nest, and, together with the word 'rich', suggests a certain luxuriance, so that its humble materials, 'mosses' and 'cobwebs', associated with neglect and mess, are transformed. More than an accurate natural historical observation, the sonnet dramatizes a small-scale encounter and creates a sense of tender intimacy in its sounds and verbal textures. The poem is built up of delicate sound patterns that create structures of attention and emphasis. '[C]lose' (l.1) is a keyword, evoking a close-up perspective and familiarity as it resounds in 'closely' (l.5) and spreads on assonantally through the run of long *o* sounds, in 'hole' (l.7), 'no' (l.8), and into the little 'oval' (l.9) nest. The eggs are delicately described, 'with dusts of red / soft frittered', and the repeated *t* sound in 'dusts soft frittered' echoes the *t* from 'little' in the previous line.

Scale matters in this poem. The littleness of the bird's world is emphasized through repetition, with the word 'little' recurring three times in five lines.[1] The first time it appears, in line 7, it is emphasized by the run of preceding short *i* sounds in *rich . . . within, / with*. This cluster of sounds creates a pinched-in feeling, giving the effect of contraction at the heart of the sonnet, picked up again in *little, frittered* and *twittring* on lines 9, 11 and 12. 'Little' introduces a sense of tenderness, since it conveys 'an implication of endearment or depreciation, or of tender feeling' (*OED* 3). It is one of a number of words that suggest littleness that accumulate through the poem. Another is 'oddling', a Northamptonshire dialect term for 'solitary' that also suggested smallness, 'one differing from the rest of the family . . . generally applied to the smallest' (Glossary, Clare, 2003, p. 684). The word carries a suggestion of this small scale meaning in its *–ling* suffix, a 'termination' which, as Johnson observed in his *Dictionary*, notes diminution. 'Soft frittered' also suggests littleness; where fritter conveys the sense 'to break into small particles or fragments' (*OED* 2), and 'soft' suggests delicacy. The poem's diminutives contribute to the sense of intimacy, a distinctive feature of Clare's poetics of littleness.

This essay considers why Clare was drawn to little things and traces the significance of littleness in his writing and in his time. Exploring the forms and values of smallness in Clare's poetry, it investigates his distinctive and particular engagements with little things and considers how this illuminates and engages with wider questions about literary and social classification in the period. What values were attributed to the minute in Clare's lifetime? What was the cultural significance of noticing tiny details and small things? And what did it mean for a 'peasant poet' to notice and celebrate them in verse? Which poetic forms were most congenial to little observations? Reading Clare's poetics of littleness in social and historical as well as literary contexts enriches its dimensions of meaning. His minute attentions challenge socially coded hierarchies of value and attention. Equally, attending to the forms and meanings of smallness in Clare's poetry opens up wider questions about the canon. The idea of a canon is often understood and defined in terms of 'greatness' – great works and great poets. The cultural values that shaped what was canonical in the early nineteenth century were based on the values and the status of a social elite, relegating to the margins the voices of those who did not qualify as sufficiently literary (Norbrook, 1993; Guillory, 1993, p. 5). This essay considers how Clare negotiated a place in the canon, not by claiming greatness, but by cultivating a poetics of littleness.

Clare's little poetic was, in part, a play with readerly expectations. Small things were expected from the lowly and mean. In Clare's time, *little* had currency as a social signifier, now lost; it was a term for low rank: 'Of persons: Not distinguished, inferior in rank or condition' (*OED* 8b). The word 'small', similarly, carried this sense, 'Of persons: Low or inferior in rank or position; of little importance, authority, or influence; common, ordinary' (*OED* IV, 16a). Writing about little things, Clare was choosing subjects that would have seemed fitting to his own social stature. Other poets from humble backgrounds were also drawn to the small scale. When Robert Burns, whom Clare admired, introduced his Kilmarnock poems, he described them as 'trifles' (a word which conveyed connotations of smallness and insignificance (*OED* 2a, 3)) (Preface, 1786, p. iii). These verses were written, he explained, 'To amuse himself with the little creations of his own fancy, amid the toil and fatigues of a laborious life' (1786, p. iv). Many of the poems that followed were concerned with 'wee' things: a 'wee mousie', wee dogs, a 'wee modest crimson tipped flower'. Burns had an eye for detail and a minuteness of observation which brought an intimacy to his writing, a sense of the homely and familiar. He often used the diminutive suffix -*ie* (as in *housie, mousie, musie, wifie*) to mark the small scale of his subjects and also his affection for them, since the Scottish diminutive marked familiarity as well as size. The *Glossary* appended to the volume introduces English readers to several Scotch words for little things: *Caup*, a small, wooden dish with two lugs, or handles; *Cog*, or coggie, a small wooden dish without handles; *Luggie*, a small, wooden dish with one handle; *Risk*, to make a noise like the breaking of small roots with the plough; *Smytrie*, a numerous collection of small individuals; *Taet*, a small quantity; *Wiel*, a small whirlpool (Burns, 1786, Glossary). For Burns, attention to little things signalled a commitment to the familiar and local, as well as his own performance of modesty. The humble wee subject might have seemed fitting for the 'Ploughman Poet', but it also marked him as a man of tender sensibility. The capacity to feel for the tiniest creature and to notice the smallest detail, as we shall see, could also be interpreted as a sign of refinement.

Robert Bloomfield was another humble poet drawn to the small scale. Hazlitt noted that Bloomfield's 'excellence is confined to a minute and often interesting description of individual objects in nature', and the word 'confined' suggests that this is a limitation (Hazlitt, 1932, p. 243). In the opening lines of *The Farmer's Boy*, which Clare admired, Bloomfield deliberately and modestly turned to little things:

> The roaring cataract, the snow-topt hill,
> Inspiring awe, till breath itself stand still:
> Nature's sublimer scenes ne'er charmed mine eyes,
> Nor Science led me through the boundless skies;
> From meaner objects far my raptures flow:
> O point these raptures! bid my bosom glow!
> . . .
> Live, trifling incidents, and grace my song,
> That to the humblest menial belong:
> To him whose drudgery unheeded goes,
> His joys unreckon'd as his cares or woes;
> Though joys and cares in every path are sown,
> And youthful minds have feelings of their own,
> Quick springing sorrows, transient as the dew,
> Delights from trifles, trifles ever new.
>
> (Bloomfield, 1800, p. 4)

In these lines, Bloomfield seems to offer an apology for his mean attentions, suggesting an association between his own humble status and the 'trifles' he celebrates. The word 'meaner' finds an echo in 'menial', used a few lines later, so that the choice of 'mean' objects as the focus of his poetry becomes associated with the poet's own 'menial' social status. This connection was registered in sense as well as sound. The word 'mean' denoted, 'Petty, insignificant, unimportant; inconsiderable' (*OED* 3b), and, like 'small' and 'little', it also had a currency as a term of social rank, 'Of low social status; spec. not of the nobility or gentry'

(*OED* II, 2a.). Bloomfield, like Burns, sets out his modest ambitions in terms of the small scale. He introduces a poem that is very definitely not aimed at sublimity or grandeur, does not celebrate great things, but turns, instead, to trifles. And yet in doing so, he, like Burns, was presenting a performance of modesty that was also an assertion of value. 'Trifles' suggested small and insignificant things, but the word also had a strong association in the period with the genteel. The capacity to attend to trifles was a sign of having leisure and refinement. It was, as Freya Johnston has observed, 'a paradox' of refinement 'that little things are held to be at once valuable and worthless: though nothing in themselves, it is a mark of sophistication to be able to make much of them' (2005, p. 153). Attending to little things might seem appropriately modest for a lowly, humble poet who did not aim for grandeur or elevation, but it also functioned as a 'mark of sophistication'.

Trifles mattered to Clare. And, like Burns and Bloomfield, he both celebrated little things in verse and presented his own writing in diminutive terms. He often referred to his poems as 'trifles' in manuscripts and letters (Storey, 1973, pp. 29, 30, 186). The subtitle he gave an early manuscript volume was 'A collection of trifles in verse'. Contemporary critics also described Clare's poems in diminutive terms. In an 1820 essay published in the January issue of *The London Magazine*, for instance, Octavius Gilchrist praised Clare's minute attentions:

> It would be presumptuous in me, having seen but two or three short poems, to pronounce that Clare's genius is not framed for sustained or lofty flights; it is enough for me to acknowledge, that the few little pieces which I have seen want the proofs of his capacity for such: but the most fastidious critic will allow, that the above little poem ['To a Primrose'] evinces minute observation of nature, delicacy of feeling, and fidelity of description; and that poetry affords few trifles of greater promise composed at so early an age and under equal disadvantages. (Storey, 1973, p. 40)

These comments seem to diminish Clare, presenting him as a minor poet – one whose talents were small scale, and who was drawn to tiny subjects, little forms, and 'trifles'. Although Gilchrist admits that it would be 'presumptuous' to assume that Clare was not 'framed for 'sustained or lofty flights', what he goes on to say of his writing seems to confirm this view. The word 'lofty' suggests 'elevated in style or sentiment; sublime, grandiose' (*OED* 2c) and it also suggested social rank, 'exalted in dignity, rank, character, or quality' (*OED* 2b). So it perhaps seemed fitting that a writer of humble station who composed under such 'disadvantages' should be unable to achieve the 'lofty' style and must confine himself to little things. His 'minute observation' might also have seemed appropriate. While the capacity to generalize was a mark of the educated, and abstraction was identified with sublimity and a high style, particularity was often associated with lowness in the late eighteenth and early nineteenth century (Schorr, 1987, pp. 16–18). And yet hierarchies of social rank did not correspond so simply with hierarchies of literary style in the period. Praising Clare in these terms, Gilchrist was not simply belittling his poems, but also elevating them, by using a language associated with cultural prestige. Clare's 'minute observation', his ability to perceive subtle and fine distinctions, was considered an attribute of persons of refinement and high social standing. The word 'minute' suggested both smallness of scale (*OED* 1) and also fineness and subtlety (*OED* 3). Another current sense of 'minute' particular was 'exacting; discriminating. Of an observation, investigation, record, etc.: very precise or particular; characterized by attention to very small matters or details' (*OED* 5). Such 'attention' was thought to be a sign of gentility. Likewise, the word 'delicacy' also had social inflections in the period. The following statement, from Hugh Blair's influential *Lectures on Rhetoric and Belles Lettres* makes clear the common association of delicacy with social refinement:

> DELICACY of Taste . . . implies those finer organs or powers, which enable us to discover beauties that lie hid from a vulgar eye . . . a person of delicate Taste both feels strongly and feels accurately. He sees distinctions and differences, where others see none; the most latent beauty does not escape him; and he is sensible of the smallest blemish. (Blair, 1785, i, pp. 30–1)

The ability to notice the 'smallest blemish' and to make tiny distinctions, to discriminate, is hidden from the 'vulgar'.

That a peasant poet might be possessed of delicacy surprised some of Clare's contemporaries. Introducing Clare's second volume, *The Village Minstrel*, in 1821, his editor, John Taylor remarked that his poems exhibited 'a degree of refinement, and elegant sensibility, which many persons can hardly believe a poor uneducated clown could have possessed' (Storey, 1973, p. 137).[2] One of Burns's early critics noted similar surprise: 'it is truly wonderful that we find so much tenderness, and even so much elegance, in the writings of this uninstructed and unpolished rustic' (Low, 1996, p. 15). Like 'delicacy', 'elegance' was understood to be a mark of the polite and genteel, but the word also had a more lively association with smallness than it does today. Writing in the 1820s, William Hazlitt, whom Clare met in London at their publisher John Taylor's *London Magazine* dinners, explored this association of elegance with littleness in an essay 'On Depth and Superficiality', published in *The Plain Speaker* (1826). He described elegance as *'the pleasurable* in little things . . . beauty or pleasure in little or slight impressions' (Hazlitt, 1931, p. 357). Smallness had a complex social and cultural significance in the early nineteenth century, part of a vocabulary of politeness. By writing about little things with delicacy and attention Clare performs modesty but also asserts his own particular refinement. He is alive to 'little or slight impressions' – the texture of a leaf, the dimpling of droplets, the wind crimpling and wrinkling the surface of the water, the rustle of grasses – and registers these tiny perceptions in the sounds and rhythms of poetry.

Clare was drawn to small poetic forms. He was a prolific writer of sonnets, and these are among the finest examples of his 'delicacy' and 'minute observation of nature'. Seamus Heaney, one of Clare's modern admirers, has noted the correspondence between small subject and form. Clare's 'unmistakable signature', Heaney explains, 'is written in most distinctively and sounded forth most spontaneously in the scores of fourteen-line poems which he wrote about small incidents involving the flora and fauna of rural Northamptonshire' (1994, pp. 132, 142). Clare's sonnets are spaces in which 'small incidents' are recorded, and in which small realities are celebrated in all their particularity:

> Black grows the southern sky betokening rain
> & humming hive bees homeward hurry bye
> They feel the change – so let us shun the grain
> & take the broad road while our feet are dry
> Aye there some dropples moistened in my face
> & pattered on my hat – tis coming nigh
> Lets look about & find a sheltering place
> The little things around like you & I
> Are hurrying through the grass to shun the shower
> Here stoops an ash tree – hark the wind gets high
> But never mind this Ivy for an hour
> Rain as it may will keep us dryly here
> That little wren knows well his sheltering bower
> Nor leaves his dry house though we come so near
>
> ('A Sudden Shower', 1998b, p. 262)

The sonnet form nicely corresponds with the small space described, the 'sheltering bower' in which 'you & I' and the 'little wren' take shelter. Here, as in many of his poems, Clare takes pleasure in little things (insects, birds) and in little impressions – the bees sensing that the weather is about to change, the moistness of 'dropples' (a variant of the diminutive 'droplets') on his face. Noticing the tiny changes in the natural world that preceded a rain shower reveals the kind of sensitivity that might have been expected from a rustic labourer: almanacs such as *The Shepherd of Banbury's Rules* (Campbell, 1744) give examples of this kind of detailed attention. But in this sonnet Clare offers more than a simple prognostication. His observations give the reader unfamiliar with this landscape an intimate sense of place. The poem does not just describe, it dramatizes experience in its sounds and patterns, registering tiniest perceptions in its acoustic texture. Describing water drops hitting a hat, the consonance of 'at' in 'pattered' and 'hat' conveys a sense in sound of the thing described. The alliterative cluster of *h* sounds jam up in the line, 'And humming hive bees homeward hurry bye', suggesting mimetically the frantic hurry of bees sensing rain. There is an intimacy of tone and perspective here that is distinctive and contributes to the 'little poetic'. Just as a grand or sublime style can be conveyed in the sounds and rhythms and diction of verse, so too can a feeling of intimate smallness.

'A Sudden Shower' is a poem of tender detail, akin to the 'precision of intimacy' Henry Mackenzie identified in some of Burns's diminutive addresses (Low, 1996, p. 69). In Clare's poem, however, there is a sense of equality between man and wee beastie. The poem sustains an intimate conversational cadence in which Clare expresses his kinship with little things. He does not write from an elevated perspective or register, looking down at the little creatures beneath him, but is at one with the world of 'little things' – all seek alike a shelter from the rain. Clare draws attention to the correspondence between 'little things' and 'you and I', drawing the reader into a space and relationship of intimacy. The line 'little things around like you & I' is formally emphasized, as the final line of the sonnet's octave. However rather than a shift into a different mode in the sestet, as might be expected, the line runs on, 'Are hurrying through the grass to shun the shower'. This surprising enjambment suggests the disruption described: there was, after all, a break in sense after the first four lines; where the rhyme pattern was completed, so too the sense, and a new clause began in the fifth line, 'Ay there some dropples'.

This poem is also unusual in structure, in that like many of Clare's sonnets, it builds upon a familiar pattern and modifies. Here, the rhyme scheme, *abab cbcb dbdede* is a variation on the Spenserian sonnet: however it repeats the *b* rhyme through the octet and then sounds it again in the second line of the sestet, so that when we reach the twelfth line, where we would expect a rhyme with 'high' in line 10, we are surprised by the new rhyme sound, 'here'. This shift in rhyme serves to emphasize the deictic function of the word 'here', grounding the poem in a particular place. The sonnet's final word, and rhyme, 'near' is also key – articulating the sense of intimacy and closeness which has been built up and suggested through the poem. There is a feeling of delicate enclosure built into the sound patterns of the sestet, where the first word of line 10, 'here', is picked up and repeated by the rhyme on line 12, 'here', and the word 'rain' recalls the earlier rhyme word 'rain' on line 1. The repetition of the spatial position of the word 'little' as the second word of line 13, as it was in line 8, creates a further sense of enclosed patterning. These intricate repeated structures suggest in the form of the poem that feeling of enclosed shelter discovered by Clare and the 'little things'. The sonnet becomes, in Clare's hands, an example of a 'small form that can fit itself to the perceptual reality of other small, living forms: sympathy of scale becomes a means to empathy of sensation' (Lodge, 2013, p. 15).

We find this empathetic mimetic use of the form again in another Clare sonnet about little things first published in *The Stamford Champion* in 1830, 'Sedge Birds Nest':

> Fixed in a white thorn bush its summer guest
> So low een grass oer topt its tallest twig
> A sedge bird built its little benty nest
> Close by the meadow pool & wooden brig
> Where schoolboys every morn & eve did pass
> In robbing birds & cunning deeply skilled
> Searching each bush & taller clump of grass
> Where ere was liklihood of bird to build
> Yet did she hide her habitation long
> & keep her little brood from dangers eye
> Hidden as secret as a crickets song
> Till they well fledged oer widest pools could flye
> Proving that providence is often bye
> To guard the simplest of her charge from wrong

(1998b, p. 153)

Here, Clare invites a miniature perspective early in the poem, bringing us 'low' down in the second line to where the nest is hidden, lower than the grass. The cluster of *t* sounds in *built its little benty nest* suggests in sound the dense clustering of materials that form the nest. The word 'benty' describes the structure of the nest, woven out of reedy grasses (known as bent). The line is framed by two lines that rhyme last words – *twig* and *brig*, but also first words – the long *o* in *So* (l.2) is picked up in *Close* (l.4), creating a half-rhyme that adds to a sense of enclosure around the 'little benty nest', described in line 3. Clare crafts and adapts the sonnet structure to create a sense of secrecy around the little nest, which is well hidden, and is described as 'hidden as secret as a cricket's song' (l.11). This line itself is enclosed, surrounded by lines rhyming *eye/flye*, a pattern which suggests a sense of concealment. The word 'secret' is emphasized rhythmically after the metrical inversion 'Hidden as', with its stress/double unstressed pattern giving weight to the stressed word 'secret' that follows. The poem creates in its structure a sense of the enclosed and hidden little space it describes. Once again, Clare artfully adapts a canonical form. This is a variation on a Shakespearean sonnet, with the rhyme at lines 12 and 13 rather than 13 and 14, to close the poem. By sounding the couplet rhyme before the end of the poem, on line 13, Clare again suggests the enclosure of the nest he describes in the weave of the sonnet's form – so that the rhyme functions spatially to suggest concealment, rather than rhetorically to conclude the argument of the poem, as in a Shakespearean sonnet.

Choosing to celebrate little things in sonnet form was apt since, as Natalie Houston has observed, discussions of the sonnet 'frequently focused on its small size' (1999, p. 245). In his sonnet on the sonnet Wordsworth described the form in terms of small spaces: a narrow room, a scanty plot of ground, the inside of a foxglove bell (Gill, 2010, p. 235). Clare also presented the sonnet in diminutive terms in his own sonnet on a sonnet, 'Sonnet to∗∗∗' ('I walked with poesy'), describing 'the sonnets little garden home' (1998b, p. 357, l.7). In his seminal study, John Barrell has suggested that this poem registers a sense of frustration at 'the limitations imposed on him by living in Helpston: the form of the sonnet is identified with the "bounds" of a landscape, and it restricts him' (1972, p. 166). But Clare's preoccupation with tiny enclosed forms and spaces – bowers, nests, cowslip bells, sonnets – can also be understood in terms of his affection for the local and the small-scale; they are protective and nurturing rather than constricting. The sonnet's 'little garden home' offered Clare a form congenial to the little subjects that made up his familiar world, a form in which he could celebrate the intimate encounter with tiny things.

Clare was not alone in casting little things and minute observations in the sonnet. The form had particular appeal for later Victorian writers who sought to describe little things. Valentine Cunningham has suggested that it became a poetic version of a new technology of miniaturization, the photograph. He describes the equivalence between 'the photograph, the small picture' and 'the sonnet, the small poem', both of which delight in the small image (2011, p. 175). Others found delight and correspondences in even smaller forms. William Sharp, in his popular anthology *Sonnets of this Century* (1886), in which Clare's poems were included, described the sonnet as a 'microscope' which, in the hands of the naturalist 'discloses many beautiful things which, if embedded in some greater mass, might have been but faintly visible and incoherent' (xxviii). And yet Clare's sonnets do not miniaturize, nor do they have the quality of the microscopic; they do not enlarge and magnify, but celebrate the smallness at its own scale and express tender feelings and empathy with their little subjects without distortion. Nor do they present static images like a photograph; instead, they catch at movements and processes, tiny changes, sounds:

> The small wind whispers thro the leafless hedge
> Most sharp & chill while the light snowey flakes
> Rests on each twig & spike of witherd sedge
> Resembling scatterd feathers – vainly breaks
> The pale split sunbeam thro the frowning cloud,
> On winters frowns below – from day to day
> Unmelted still he spreads his hoary shroud
> In dithering pride on the pale travellers way
> Who croodling, hastens from the storm behind
> Fast gathering deep & black – again to find
> His cottage fire & corners sheltering bounds
> Where haply such uncomfortable days
> Makes musical the woodsaps frizzling sounds
> & hoarse loud bellows puffing up the blaze
>
> ('Winter' (1820), 1989, p. 492)

Little sounds frame this early sonnet, which opens with the 'small wind' and closes with the comforting music of the frizzling wood sap and bellows. The opening diminutives draw the reader into this tiny local world: 'small' is an unusual description for the wind – we might expect gentle or light – but here the word gives an unexpected physical dimension to the wind, and, together with 'whispers' suggests a sense of familiar intimacy. The wind's sound is caught in the run of *i* sounds running through *whispers, chill, twig, wither'd*. But where *wither'd* and *chill* are discomforting, and this sense is drawn out by 'frowning cloud', and 'hoary shroud' that follow, the final four lines of the sonnet bring us inside a cosy and intimate space. Clare is once again inviting a correspondence between subject and poetic form, where the phrase 'sheltering bounds' suggests the comfort derived from the enclosed architecture of the sonnet.

Recording small sounds in his sonnets, Clare was being true to the form. In the introduction to *Sonnets of the Century*, Sharp noted that the word 'sonnet' derived from a diminutive for sound: 'It is generally agreed that "sonnet" is an abbreviation of the Italian *sonetto*, a short strain (literally, a little sound), that word being the diminutive of *suono* = sound' (1886, p. xxvii). In 'First Signs of Spring', a Clare sonnet which Sharp included in his anthology, little sounds and little things are once again recorded with accuracy and immediacy:

> The hazel blooms in threads of crimson hue
> Peep through the swelling buds & look for spring
> Ere yet a white thorn leaf appears in view
> Or march finds throstles pleased enough to sing
> On the old touch wood tree wood peckers cling
> A moment & their harsh toned notes renew
> In happier mood the stockdove claps his wing
> The squirrel sputters up the powdered oak
> With tail cocked oer his head & ears erect
> Startled to hear the woodmans understroke
> & with the courage that his fears collect
> He hisses fierce half malice & half glee
> Leaping from branch to branch about the tree
> In winters foliage moss & lickens drest
>
> (Clare, 'First Sign of Spring' (1832?),
> 1998b, p. 296)

Here, once again, the sonnet structure does not develop a rhetorical argument, it seems more loosely expressive – so that the form provides a short unit of descriptive verse to capture observations. It is the quality of attention that distinguishes Clare: he notices precise details, the delicate 'threads of crimson hue' that streak the blossom buds, the 'harsh-toned' sounds of the woodpecker and the clap of the stockdove's wings. Even the jerky erratic movements of the squirrel are caught in the run of *s* and *t* sounds from 'sputters up' to 'startled' two lines later, catching at the quality of the squirrel's movement and surprise – this is what we might describe as an image in and of sound. Clare's sonnets about little things create, in their precise, minute detail, and in their sound patterns, structures of intimacy. The association between little things, precise observation and intimacy is explored in his great elegy for a lost home, 'The Flitting'. The poem is full of little things lovingly described: 'little footpaths' (l.39); a 'little arch' across a brook (l.42); 'moss . . . a small unnoticed trifling thing' (ll.81, 83); 'little pebbles' (l.93); 'little flowers' (l.134); 'little lambtoe bunches' (l.137); 'may-blooms with its little threads' (l.141); 'molehills little lap' (l.178); 'little "shepherd's purse"' (a weed) (l.187), the 'firstlings of his little flock' (l.148). Clare describes how 'every trifle' makes the place 'dear' to him (l.200). Enumerating these little things, Clare recreates the sense of familiar intimacy with a place that he has lost:

> I love the muse that in her hand
> Bears wreaths of native poesy
> Who walks nor skips the pasture brook
> In scorn – but by the drinking horse
> Leans oer its little brig to look
> How far the sallows lean accross
>
> & feels a rapture in her breast
> Upon their root-fringed grains to mark
> A hermit morehens sedgy nest
> Just like a naiads summer bark
> She counts the eggs she cannot reach
> Admires the spot & loves it well
> & yearns so natures lessons teach
> Amid such neighbourhoods to dwell
>
> I love the muse who sits her down
> Upon the molehills little lap
> Who feels no fear to stain her gown
> & pauses by the hedgerow gap
>
> ('The Flitting', 1998a,
> pp. 479–91, ll.163–80)

For Clare, counting and marking particulars is a sign of love: noticing details such as the 'root-fringed grains' and the materials of the 'morehens sedgy nest' evokes a sense of intimacy with the landscape of his childhood. So too does the repeated use of the word 'little' to describe that landscape. The first use of the word in the poem occurs on line 39, as Clare remembers fondly the 'little footpaths' of his old home, now lost; its 'little arch' over a bridge appears three lines later. He associates this attention to little things with a childish way of looking, 'I dwell on trifles like a child.' Clare's attention to little things is not simply an assertion of his refinement and a riposte to a culture in which peasants were not expected to have refined and delicate perceptions, it was also an expression of familiarity and love, a celebration of the local.

'The Flitting' is Clare's poetic manifesto for little things. Like Emily Dickinson, Clare drew on the Bible's championing of the small and persecuted, and like her he made great claims for the small in his writing. Earlier in the poem, the shepherd poet David appears, champion of the little:

> Some sing the pomps of chivalry
> As legends of the ancient time
> Where gold & pearls & mystery
> Are shadows painted for sublime
> But passions of sublimity
> Belong to plain & simpler things
> & David underneath a tree
> Sought when a shepherd Salems springs
>
> Where moss did into cushions spring
> Forming a seat of velvet hue
> A small unnoticed trifling thing
> To all but heavens hailing dew
> & Davids crown hath passed away
> Yet poesy breathes his shepherd skill
> His palace lost – & to this day
> The little moss is blooming still
> (ll.73–88)

The figure of David provides Clare with a model for a small but powerful lyric voice. The shepherd's song has none of the grand style or regal pomp, but sounds a humbler, simpler music, a lyric smallness. These lines were added to a later drafting of the poem (an earlier version ended at line 64, on the word 'heir'). Doing so, Clare inflects the poem's little things with power which has a biblical authority; the meek shall inherit the earth. Here, David represents the triumph of the small: the story of David and Goliath is a parable of the little and the powerless overcoming the giant and mighty. It is only the little moss, a 'small unnoticed trifling thing' that survives. The concluding lines of 'The Flitting' celebrate the triumph of 'little things' – pebbles, moss, little lambtoe bunches, may-blooms – over 'grandeur', 'pomp' and the 'high flown':

> Time looks on pomp with careless moods
> Or killing apathys disdain
> – So where old marble citys stood
> Poor persecuted weeds remain
> She feels a love for little things
> That very few can feel beside
> & still the grass eternal springs
> Where castles stood & grandeur died
>
> (ll.209–16)

Writing of the appeal of little things in *A Philosophical Enquiry into the Origin of Our Ideas of the Sublime and the Beautiful*, Edmund Burke argued that it was their fragility that made them beautiful: 'An appearance of *delicacy*, and even of fragility, is almost essential' to beauty. 'It is', he claimed, 'the flowery species, so remarkable for its weakness and momentary duration, that gives us the liveliest idea of beauty, and elegance' (Burke, 1990, pp. 105–6). Clare loved little things, but for him they were not of 'momentary duration'; they were lasting and enduring.

Clare's preoccupation with littleness was part of a wider interest in the little in nineteenth-century poetry. He is often placed on the margins of the canon, or confined to a minor tradition of labouring-class writing; it is illuminating to see his poetry in relation to and looking forward to a later nineteenth-century poetry of little things. Tennyson, for example, was famous for his attention to detail in nature, and although they shared space in anthologies and annuals of the time, such as *Friendship's Offering*, they have been largely kept apart in literary criticism and history. Discussing the Victorian taste for little things, Cunningham, one exception to this critical tendency, brings Clare and Tennyson together. He has suggested that it was in part a desire for the beautiful, in the Burkean sense, that 'powered our poets' zest for the tininesses they packed their poems with: the snowflakes, the raindrops, little flowers, leaves, petals, fruit and nuts, little birds and tiny creatures of Clare and

Tennyson, of Hopkins and Hardy . . . nature's lovely miniatures' (2011, p. 169). For Clare, however, littleness had more complex meanings. In celebrating small things, he celebrated the triumph and value of the lowly and humble. In doing so with minute particularity he asserted and demonstrated his refined sensibility, and created and expressed a familiar intimacy with the world around him, what Edmund Blunden has described as an 'unparalleled intimacy' with the English landscape (Storey, 1973, p. 370).

By the later nineteenth-century, littleness seems to have lost its particular connotations for labouring-class writing. Clare's poetry of little things found its place in several anthologies of sonnets and lyric in the Victorian period, in keepsakes and annuals alongside other poets from all ranks, without mention of his class or birth.[3] No longer represented as the 'Peasant poet', he is simply 'John Clare'. Yet the language of scale continues to shape how we understand and interpret the literary canon and how we place and distinguish poets within it. When Elizabeth Bishop described herself, in a letter to Robert Lowell, as a 'minor female Wordsworth', she was being modest, and also drawing attention to her own diminutive tendencies, her liking for the small and detailed (Bishop, 1994, p. 222). Like Bishop, Clare described both himself and his poetry in diminutive terms. Writing to his friend and fellow poet James Montgomery on 13 January 1828, he explained: 'all I aspire to is that I may win a nitch among the minor bards in the memory of my country' (Storey, 1973, p. 412). The word 'nitch' is a Northamptonshire dialect term for 'a slight break, notch, or incision hole or incision'. Here, the sense of slightness, or smallness suggested both by 'nitch' and 'minor' marks a prevailing concern with littleness in Clare's writing. Like Bishop, he is a poet who attends to the small-scale, the seemingly 'minor'. What seems like a modest claim here – aspiring to a little 'nitch' in the canon, registers a poetics of smallness that was conscious and deliberate and artful. Indeed, it is arguably Clare's ability to describe little things with intimate precision that has ensured his place in the canon. The great can diminish and fall, but, as Clare explained, in an essay on 'Popularity in Authorship', first published in *The European Magazine* in 1825, the little endures:

> The trumpeting clamour of public praise is not to be relied on as the creditor for the future to draw acceptances from; present fame is not the perpetual almanack to time's fame; they often disclaim all kindred to each other. The quiet progress of a name gaining ground by gentle degrees in the world's esteem is the best living shadow of

fame: fashionable popularity changes like the summer clouds, while the simplest trifle, and the meanest thing in nature, is the same now as it shall continue to be till the world's end (Clare, 1951, p. 260).

Notes

1. Clare often repeated the word 'little' in his poetry, as the linguist Barbara M. H. Strang has noted (see Appendix I, in Clare, 1982, pp. 150–73). She comments on his fondness for 'families of related or antithetical words', 'interlinked clusters' around the semantic field of '"the concealed, the great in small" e.g., little, hid(den)' (p. 167).
2. In an earlier essay on Clare in *The London Magazine* he had praised his 'elegance and tenderness of expression' (Storey, 1973, p. 160).
3. For example, Sharp, 1886; Caine, 1882; Main, 1880; Waddington, 1882 and Dennis, 1873.

Bibliography

Barrell, John (1972) *The Idea of Landscape and the Sense of Place* (Cambridge: Cambridge University Press).
Bishop, Elizabeth (1994) *One Art, Elizabeth Bishop, Letters*, ed. Robert Giroux (New York: Farrar, Straus and Giroux).
Blair, Hugh (1785) *Lectures on Rhetoric and Belles Lettres*, 3 vols, 2nd edn, corrected (London: W. Strahan and T. Cadell).
Bloomfield, Robert (1800) *The Farmer's Boy* (London: Vernor and Hood).
Burke, Edmund (1990) *A Philosophical Enquiry into the Origin of Our Ideas of the Sublime and the Beautiful*, ed. J. T. Boulton (Oxford: Oxford University Press, 1990).
Burns, Robert (1786) *Poems Chiefly in the Scottish Dialect* (Kilmarnock: John Wilson).
Caine, T. Hall (1882) *Sonnets of Three Centuries: A Selection* (London: Elliot Stock).
Campbell, John (1744) *The Shepherd of Banbury's Rules* (London: W. Bickerton).
Clare, John (1951) *The Prose of John Clare*, ed. J. W. Tibble and Anne Tibble (London: Routledge & Kegan Paul).
——. (1982) *Rural Muse Poems by John Clare*, ed. R. K. R Thornton (Ashington: Mid Northumberland Arts Group with Carcanet).
——. (1989) *The Early Poems of John Clare, 1804–1822*, 2 vols, ed. Eric Robinson and David Powell (Oxford: Oxford University Press).
——. (1998a) *Poems of the Middle Period III*, ed. Eric Robinson, David Powell and P. M. S. Dawson (Oxford: Oxford University Press).
——. (1998b) *Poems of the Middle Period IV*, ed. Eric Robinson, David Powell and P. M. S. Dawson (Oxford: Oxford University Press).
——. (2003) *Poems of the Middle Period V*, ed. Eric Robinson, David Powell and P. M. S. Dawson (Oxford: Oxford University Press).
——. (1985) *The Letters of John Clare*, ed. Mark Storey (Oxford: Oxford University Press).

Cunningham, Valentine (2011) *Victorian Poetry Now: Poets, Poems, Poetics* (Oxford: Oxford University Press).
Dennis, John (1873) *English Sonnets: A Selection* (London: Henry S. King & Co).
Gill, Stephen, ed. (2010) *The Oxford Authors: Wordsworth* (Oxford: Oxford University Press).
Guillory, John (1993) *Cultural Capital: The Problem of Literary Canon Formation* (Chicago and London: University of Chicago Press).
Hazlitt, William (1931) 'On Depth and Superficiality', in *The Complete Works of William Hazlitt in Twenty-One Volumes*, ed. P. P. Howe (London: J. M. Dent), xii, pp. 346–60.
———. (1932) 'Preface and Critical List of Authors from Select British Poets', in *The Complete Works of William Hazlitt in Twenty-One Volumes*, ed. P. P. Howe (London: J. M. Dent), ix, pp. 231–46.
Heaney, Seamus (1994) 'John Clare: A Bicentenary Lecture', in *John Clare in Context*, ed. H. Haughton, A. Phillips, G. Summerfield (Cambridge: Cambridge University Press), pp. 130–47.
Houston, Natalie M. (1999) 'Valuable by Design: Material Features and Cultural Value in Nineteenth-Century Sonnet Anthologies', *Victorian Poetry*, 37 (1999), 243–72.
Jamie, Kathleen (2005) 'In the nature of things', *Guardian*, 18 June: www.guardian.co.uk/books/2005/jun/18/featuresreviews.guardianreview15.
Johnston, Freya (2005) *Samuel Johnson and the Art of Sinking* (Oxford: Oxford University Press).
Lodge, Sara (2013, forthcoming) 'Contested Bounds: John Clare, John Keats and the Sonnet', *Studies in Romanticism*.
Low, Donald A., ed. (1996) *Robert Burns: The Critical Heritage* (London: Routledge).
Main, David M. (1880) *Treasury of English Sonnets* (Edinburgh and London: Blackwood).
Norbrook, David (1993) 'Introduction', in *Anthology of Renaissance Literature*, ed. David Norbrook and Henry Woodhuysen (Harmondsworth: Penguin).
Schorr, Naomi (1987), *Reading in Detail: Aesthetics and the Feminine* (London and New York: Methuen).
Sharp, William (1886) *Sonnets of the Century* (London: Scott).
Storey, Mark, ed. (1973) *John Clare: The Critical Heritage* (London and Boston: Routledge and Kegan Paul).
Waddington, Samuel (1882) *English Sonnets by Poets of the Past* (London: Bell).

6
'No more than as an atom 'mid the vast profound': Conceptions of Time in the Poetry of William Cowper, William Wordsworth, and Ann Yearsley

Kerri Andrews

> There are in our existence spots of time,
> Which with distinct pre-eminence retain
> A renovating Virtue, whence, depressed
> By false opinion and contentious thought,
> Or aught of heavier and more deadly weight
> In trivial occupations, and the round
> Of ordinary intercourse, our minds
> Are nourished and invisibly repaired
> (Wordsworth, 2008 [1805], XI, ll.258–73)

This quotation, from Book XI of the 1805 *Prelude*, has become one of Wordsworth's most famous passages, one which links ideas of memory, imagination and place with the nature of time. The concept of specific points resonating beyond the limits of linear time, nourishing the past, present and future poetic self, is an enduring legacy of Wordsworth's project in this poem. I have selected this quotation because of its importance in the Romantic canon; but, as I will argue throughout this essay, Wordsworth was not the first to draw together these concepts: twenty years earlier William Cowper published *The Task*, one of the central concerns of which was the connection between time and memory, and within which past and present exist simultaneously. Equidistant between Cowper and Wordsworth, sits Ann Yearsley, the 'Bristol milkmaid poet', who sought to further explore these complex issues in her rather shorter poem, 'Soliloquy', written in 1795 and published in 1796 as part of Yearsley's final volume of poetry, *The Rural Lyre*. Wordsworth's concern with the relationship between the individual and experience, between time and the development of the poetic self, can therefore be seen as a natural extension of ideas which emerged in the late eighteenth century; ideas given full form by writers like Cowper, and developed by writers like Yearsley, before their adoption as key tenets of what would come to be recognized as a 'Romantic' movement. I should at this point note that when using the words 'Romantic' or 'Romanticism' I am referring to the widespread shift in thinking about poetry and poetics that occurred at the end of the eighteenth century, which was developed during the nineteenth century, and which has come to be associated most frequently with Wordsworth and Samuel Taylor Coleridge. But, as I wish to argue in this essay, the frequent association of 'Romanticism' with the members of the 'Lake' or 'Cockney' schools of poetry has limited our understanding of the ways in which poetic concerns changed or shifted during this period.[1] Furthermore, I will suggest, the reintegration of labouring-class writers like Ann Yearsley into the Romantic canon can help us come to a more complex and nuanced understanding of concepts we now consider fundamental to Romanticism.

In many ways Yearsley's writing has already secured something like canonical status, at least in comparison to the works of other labouring-class poets. The story of Yearsley's tempestuous patronage by Hannah More, the famous playwright, poet and Christian moralist, has ensured that some interest at least continues to be shown towards Yearsley. But that interest has not extended to her later poetry, nor to the people with whom Yearsley associated in the later stages of her career. Whilst her difficult relationships with More and a number of other Bluestockings, including the 'Queen of the Blues', Elizabeth Montagu, have been well documented,[2] very little has been written about the literary networks in which Yearsley was involved in the late 1790s. Newly-discovered documentary evidence shows that she was in fact associating with some of the most radical figures of the day, many of whom would become heavily involved in the formation of what would come to be called 'Romanticism'.[3] Through men such as William Godwin, Thomas Beddoes, Joseph Cottle and Robert Southey, Yearsley was connected with Coleridge and Wordsworth. Given the extensive overlapping of their circles, it is most unlikely that Wordsworth was not aware of Yearsley's later, more philosophical poetry, of which 'Soliloquy' is perhaps the most striking example.

I

It is fitting that, for a poem so concerned with the nature and effects of time, we should know exactly when, and how, 'Soliloquy' came to be written. It was, Yearsley's subtitle indicates, 'Begun from the circumstance of the moment, and prolonged as the images of memory arose in the mind of the author, February 27, 1795' (Yearsley, 2003, p. 45). Yearsley then gives details of this 'circumstance', a dialogue between the poet and her son:

> *Author to her son.*   Go you to bed, my boy.
> *Son.*   Do you write to-night?
> *Author.*   I do.
> *Son.* (laying his watch on the table).   See, how late!
> *Author.*   No matter – You can sleep.
>
> (Yearsley, 2003, p. 45)

This preface locates the poem firmly in the present as a production arising from chance events combining suddenly to create a profound impression on the mind of the poet. It is significant that this chance event is a domestic encounter, one that we can assume has occurred many times in the past through the tone of Yearsley's son's question, 'Do you write to-night?' This is not the first time he has seen his mother up late, writing. It is important too that what changes everything in this encounter (it can be assumed that it was not this poem, being the production 'of the moment', that the author originally sat down to write), is the son's watch, which has been laid down on the table. As J. M. S. Tompkins has noted, the watch is 'a pleasant sign of comparative prosperity' (1938, p. 88), given that 'timepieces were luxuries among the rural poor' until the nineteenth century (Waldron, 1996, p. 246). It is especially so in Yearsley's case as her literary career began shortly after she and her family were discovered starving in a barn during the harsh winter of 1783–4, a story that was widely broadcast by Yearsley's first patron, More. Ten years and several publications later, Yearsley was able to buy her son a luxury item, a watch; its appearance in this poem is an explicit statement about Yearsley's change in status. It is perhaps also significant that the second book of Cowper's *The Task*, one of two books in the poem which shares common ground with Yearsley's poem, is entitled 'The Time-piece'. Yearsley's preface therefore draws attention not only to the poem's domestic, but also perhaps its intellectual origins, as well as the poet's class status. It is not difficult to imagine Yearsley's satisfaction in being able to demonstrate the quality of life that her labours have now brought to her family.

But perhaps of greatest importance to this poem is its origins in 'the moment', a 'moment' which is 'prolonged' by the perception of 'memories' provoked by the watch and what it stands for. The peculiar

98 *Class and the Canon*

nature of the present in Romantic-period poetry has prompted some intriguing and provocative observations from Heather McHugh:

> One could say that the construction of the present has always been attended by [a] dilemma, based as it is on two contrary models: that of the perishing and that of the perpetual. On the one hand, the present can figure as a tiny spot at the intersection of the past and future (two vectors, having, like all vectors, direction and magnitude, of which a point has neither). In this construction of time, the present's point is as hard to announce as to occupy: as soon as it's had or said, it's gone, just another one of many moments, each disappearing, each under the sway of momentariness. But on the other hand the present, far from being hard to occupy, is hard to escape – we're always in it, never in the past or the future. This construction of the present makes a moment not momentary but momentous. (McHugh, 2002, p. 169)

That McHugh is writing here of Wordsworth and *The Prelude* is suggestive of the ways in which the representation of time in 'Soliloquy' presages the concerns that poetry would seek to address in the very near future. Indeed, the idea that 'the present makes a moment not momentary but momentous' is central to the way in which Yearsley's poem conceptualizes time. The watch 'toils', and later acts as a 'tell-tale' of man's 'doings', but cannot actually represent what time *is* (Yearsley, 2003, ll.1 and 59). Time is much more than the mere act of measurement – it is given meaning for Yearsley in Berkeleian terms, by what the mind perceives and experiences. This can be seen in the poem's opening lines:

> How patiently toils on this little watch!
> My veins beat to its motion. Ye who sing
> Of atoms, rest, and motion, say, why Time
> Sets in this toy a larum to my heart.
>
> (Yearsley, 2003, ll.1–4)

In these four lines we have two different ways of quantifying time – the watch, and the poet's veins – and they are initially in sync, the poet's veins 'beating' to the watch's 'motion', bringing together time as perceived in the body, and time as measured through mechanical, man-made means. Yet the apparent unity between body and machine, indicated by the 'veins' beating 'to the motion' of the watch is undercut by the metre which runs in opposition to the sense. The first hint is given by the juddering of 'patiently' as it interrupts the rhythmic structure established by the iambic metre. The line settles again into iambs with 'this little watch' only to be disrupted by the requirement to place stress on the word 'beat' in the following line. The effect is akin to a palpitation: the heart, and the poem, have gained an extra 'beat' where one was not expected. This rhythmical disruption serves to underscore the difficulty of measuring time according to the pulse which, being organic and human, is subject to emotional disturbance, unlike the 'patiently toiling' watch. But that disturbance is carefully controlled, as demonstrated by the deliberate positioning of the commas in the third line, disrupting the rhythm in a different way by forcing the reader to linger on 'rest' before they can proceed to the word 'motion', placing the two in tension. Yearsley's verse 'skips a beat' here not because of emotional excess, but as a result of poetic skill: her poetry is governed by principles of science, not feeling.

This is of interest because at this point in the poem Yearsley includes a note stating that 'Mechanical philosophy is that which undertakes to account for the phenomena of nature from the principles of mechanics, taking in the consideration of motion, rest, figure, size, &c. This is also called the corpuscular philosophy' (Yearsley, 1796, p. 43n). Marie Boas Hall has defined the principles of the theory of mechanical philosophy thus: 'the nature of any compound depended on the size and shape of the component parts, corpuscles or primitive concretions; the size and shape of the spaces between the parts; and, most important of all, the motion at any given moment of the parts' (Hall, 1981, p. 469). Proponents of this theory, including Robert Boyle, held that by measuring observable features of things, such as 'the size and shape of the component parts', the world could be understood. Yearsley therefore places her poetry within this larger intellectual debate, but these ideas, she suggests, are insufficient, as the very concept of measurement is itself inadequate:

> O sacred Time! thy moment goes not down
> But I go with it! Sixty coming hours
> Are with us poor expectants of more price
> Than sixty years sunk to oblivion.
>
> (Yearsley, 2003, ll.5–8)

The significance of spans of measured time – the moment, sixty hours, sixty years – cannot be satisfactorily measured, and thereby given meaning, by Mechanical Philosophy. Instead, time acquires meaning in this poem through the thoughts that are provoked – the memories and reflections that occur to the poet as a result of looking at the watch on the table. This point is explicitly made by Yearsley when she refers to 'Memory' as Time's 'willing slave', which has 'silent fascinating pow'r' for the poet, for whom it will be 'Forever sacred to my pensive mind' (ll.9–12). Time and memory are intimately and inextricably linked.

But the power of Memory is revealed to be greater still in the next verse paragraph. Through the act of invoking 'Mild Contemplation', Yearsley is able not only to break down the boundaries between past and present, but also those between life and death:

> Hail, much rever'd in death!
> Thou knew'st to chart the moral world, and bend
> The springs of thought to wisdom: thou wert wont
> In life to smile, when wilder than the bard
> On Cambria's height I struck the lyre: my sigh,
> Made harsh and inharmonious by despair,
> Thou taught'st to break with melody. This hour,
> Led on by Contemplation, I behold
> Thine eyes that beam'd benevolence, thy heart
> Once rich with fine regard.
>
> (Yearsley, 2003 [1796], ll.16–25)

Mary Waldron has suggested that at this point Yearsley may be addressing James Shiells, a loyal supporter of hers for more than a decade, who had recently died at the age of sixty-six, as Yearsley's own poem of lament indicates.[4] Given that she is here writing of a man whose death she clearly laments, it is of interest that this passage describes how Yearsley has been taught by Shiells to control her 'despair', and thereby to turn it into something more elegant, and, perhaps, more marketable. Instead of the 'harsh and inharmonious' outpourings of emotion, Yearsley learns here that 'melody' is created in the pauses for breath, through carefully placed and structured 'breaks', which will render her emotions beautiful. Such breaks are usually associated with an overflow of emotion, as a natural physiological consequence of too much feeling, but here the poetic speaker is being taught to introduce these breaks in a controlled, and therefore unnatural, manner. Despair, as a result of these pleasing pauses, is reconstructed as a commodity. The irony, to which this passage is alert, is that when the poetic speaker responded naturally to despair, running 'wilder than the bard' across the mountains, she was ridiculous – her behaviour caused her mentor to 'smile' at her folly. By learning to contain her emotions in the apparently-natural rhythms of iambic metre, blended with appropriately melodic emotional 'breaks', she can be seen as both sympathetic and marketable, and is in a position to be taken seriously as a poet.

It is not just the power of emotion that is being referenced here, however. Yearsley conjures an intriguing image of the speaker, 'Led on by Contemplation', who is again able to 'behold / Thine eyes', and 'thy heart', breaking down the boundaries that would usually separate past and present. For a moment, the power of memory means that they exist together in a 'momentous' moment. Yet this moment is not infinite – it is 'This hour' – a finite period of time in which the magic of memory is able to transcend linear time. Indeed, it can be suggested that it is only whilst the speaker is in the act of remembering that this is possible – once the memory has run its course, the moment will pass, and the distinctions between past and present will be restored. That this state is temporary is indicated by the tense of the passage; whilst the speaker 'beholds' in the present tense, what they are looking at is already past. 'Thou taught'st', Yearsley writes of the addressee, 'thou wert wont', the 'eyes' that the speaker is here beholding 'beam'd benevolence', and the heart that was 'Once rich with fine regard', is no longer. Indeed, as the moment slips from the speaker's grasp, she exclaims 'Ah me! that heart / 'Mid this inhospitable scene was mine!' (Yearsley, 2003, ll.25–6). Although this memory is undoubtedly powerful, it is not sufficiently so to bring the person wholly into being once again, or to escape the imagined landscape of unwelcoming 'barren rock' where the poet is 'ship-wreck'd'. Instead it is an echo that emerges, an echo that is already fading as the inevitability of loss and death reclaim the 'eyes' and 'heart' through the use of the past tense.

In contrast, the act of remembering for Cowper brings the past sharply into view, complete with 'all its pleasures and its pains'. All that is needed is 'A kindred melody' for the 'cells / Where mem'ry slept' to be 'forced open', and the poet can 'retrace / (As in a map the voyager his course) / The windings of [his] way through many years' (Cowper, 1785, pp. 231–2). But for all the clarity, Cowper's remembrances are tainted with bitterness and regret:

> Short as in retrospect the journey seems,
> It seem'd not always short; the rugged path
> And prospect oft so dreary and forlorn
> Moved many a sigh at its disheart'ning length.

> Yet feeling present evils, while the past
> Faintly impress the mind, or not at all,
> How readily we wish time spent revoked,
> That we might try the ground again, where once
> (Through inexperience as we now perceive)
> We miss'd that happiness we might have found.
>
> (Cowper, 1785, VI, p. 232)

As Cowper conceives the relationship between past and present, it is not possible to entirely leave the present moment, the place of experience, in order to enjoy memories from a time before that experience. Where Yearsley was able to recall at least the shade of James Shiells, Cowper is unable to bring back anything from the dead, save fruitless grief at their passing:

> But not to understand a treasure's worth
> 'Till time has stol'n away the slighted good,
> Is cause of half the poverty we feel,
> And makes the world the wilderness it is.
>
> (Cowper, 1785, VI, pp. 233–4)

This final line is expressive of the same sort of bleakness found in Yearsley's poem, with its 'inhospitable' scenes, barrenness and ship wrecks. In Cowper's poem the only source of comfort seems to come from the movement from the specific to the general, from the 'I' of the first lines of this section, to 'we' and 'they'; from a personal grief caused by memory and experience, to a comment on a more general human condition. Only when the recollection is at an end does the speaker resume his use of 'I'.

This is one of the most striking differences between Cowper and Yearsley, and ultimately Wordsworth; for the two later poets it is the individual, not the general, experience of memory that has particular power. This is true even when recollection leads to unsettling thoughts. Wordsworth, having explored one of the 'spots of time', a moment 'worthy of all gratitude' (2008 [1805], XI, l.275), finds its power transient:

> The days gone by
> Come back upon me from the dawn almost
> Of life: the hiding-places of my power
> Seem open; I approach, and then they close;

> I see by glimpses now; when age comes on,
> May scarcely see at all, and I would give,
> While yet we may, as far as words can give,
> A substance and a life to what I feel:
> I would enshrine the spirit of the past
> For future restoration.
>
> (Wordsworth, 2008 [1805], XI, ll.334–43)

The idea that these 'spots of time' are 'hiding-places' of the poet's power, places that 'seem open' but 'close' when the poet approaches to make use of them, is an intriguing one, and is suggestive again of the unquantifiable nature of time – these 'spots' are both here and not here, in the present but also in the past – much as the figure of James Shiells is for Yearsley. And though Wordsworth expresses an anxiety about the effects of temporal distance in accessing these 'hiding-places' of power, he does not shrink from this aspect of memory.

This is not to say that the power of memory is not troubling to Wordsworth or Yearsley. Indeed, for Yearsley's speaker, the process of being 'Led on by Contemplation' to recall a powerful memory threatens to overwhelm her entirely. Wordsworth, in contrast, when reflecting on his father's death, finds solace in Nature, and, by implication, in the ordinary passage of time:

> Thou wilt not languish here, O Friend, for whom
> I travel in these dim uncertain ways;
> Thou wilt assist me as a pilgrim gone
> In quest of highest truth. Behold me then
> Once more in Nature's presence, thus restored
> Or otherwise, and strengthened once again
> (With memory left of what had escaped)
> To habits of devoutest sympathy.
>
> (Wordsworth, 2008 [1805], XI, ll.390–7)

Wordsworth trusts here both in the recuperative powers of Nature, once he is returned to 'Nature's presence', and in the healing power of memory. The act of recollecting his father, who has gone on 'In quest of highest truth' to an afterlife, will help and strengthen the poet to return 'To habits of devoutest sympathy'. In contrast, the act of remembering her mentor appears to lead for Yearsley to the demolition of this tenet of Christian belief. Where Wordsworth finds solace and healing in memory, Yearsley finds desolation and despair as she contemplates the eternal and unchanging nature of the universe:

> Couldst thou declare how long the storms of fate
> Shall beat around me, when I may repose,
> Or be as thou art! I have read the code
> Of statutes form'd by man for future worlds;
> And found his plan, so pompously display'd,
> One lot of heterogeneous fragment. Man
> Adores in fancy, violates in fact,
> Laws serving his frail being. Yon pale moon
> Forsakes the mountain top, to bring us round
> Her renovated splendour; nature works
> Obedient and unseen forever: we
> May meet in spheres remote – If not, farewel![5]
>
> (Yearsley, 2003, ll.27–38)

As Wordsworth seeks 'assistance' from his father's shade, so too does Yearsley from Shiells's. But though there is a sense of optimism at this point in *The Prelude* about the life to come and the power of memory in giving consolation, in Yearsley's poem there is already a feeling that there are no answers to the questions that are being asked. Not only can Shiells not tell Yearsley how long she must endure 'the storms of fate', but, by the end of the passage, the blasphemous notion that there is no heaven at all is being seriously considered. The speaker concedes 'we / May meet in spheres remote', but the combination of the conditional tense and the dismissal of the teachings of the Bible, this 'code / Of statutes form'd by man for future worlds', indicates the level of doubt being expressed. The teachings of the New Testament are nothing more than 'pompous' 'Laws serving' man's 'frail being', containing nothing that can explain the nature of the universe.

In this conviction Yearsley echoes Cowper. Despite repeated avowals of his Christian faith, Cowper's poem nonetheless expresses serious doubts about the role of humanity in interpreting God's will:

> The pastor, either vain
> By nature, or by flatt'ry made so, taught
> To gaze at his own splendor, and t' exalt
> Absurdly, not his office, but himself;
>
> (1785, II, p. 73)

This pastor 'discredits much/The brightest truths that man has ever seen', leaving people with nothing to anchor them in a belief in a world beyond their own. Similarly, Yearsley's speaker discovers only the incomprehensible and the infinite, and is left to 'Conjecture without end!' (2003, l.54) It is interesting that Yearsley places more trust in Shiells's ability to guide here, even after death, than she does in the teachings of the Bible, which she rejects with cynical language that echoes Cowper. As a result, Yearsley experiences what Geoffrey Hartman has termed 'the deistic Abstract Void' which is 'a breeding place for terrible conceptions' not only in *The Task* and in Yearsley's poem, but also in the darker episodes of *The Prelude* (1964, p. 233).[6]

Central to the expression of these doubts about Christian theology is the way in which time is conceptualized. At the beginning of Yearsley's poem mechanized time and time measured by the beating of the 'veins' are brought together, revealing the inadequacy of measuring time at all when it can only acquire meaning through memory and experience. But in this section of the poem, the speaker contemplates how she will perceive time when she dies, forcing the reader to consider how time can be understood when there are no more memories, when the individual mind is no longer able to perceive or experience. It is appropriate, then, that it is the image of the 'pale moon' that leads to such questioning, as the lunar cycle is one of the oldest ways developed by human beings for reckoning and recording the passage of time. But instead of the moon's motions giving meaning to time, they open the way to eternity, to a time beyond measure, beyond the capacity of the human mind to comprehend, where 'nature works / Obedient and unseen forever'. And it is into this unchanging, neverending time that the speaker sees herself disappearing. Still addressing Shiells, Yearsley writes:

>   The change
> Fulfill'd in thee may chill me; ev'ry thought
> Oblit'rate; vision, fancy forms, be doom'd
> To sink, like beaming glory in the west;
> Whilst space contracts on my weak eye, and heav'ns,
> By human artists coloured, fade away,
> As life goes gently from my beating heart.
> Grant this could be – the import were no more
> Than as an atom 'mid the vast profound
> Impell'd, not swerving from the whole. Suppose,
> This frame dissolving, to the busy winds

> My ashes fled dividing: shall I know
> To mourn?
>
> (Yearsley, 2003, ll.41–53)

The poet returns here to perhaps the most fundamental way in which humans measure time, the beating of the heart – earlier it was only the 'veins' that 'beat to the motion' of time, but in the moment of death, it is the heart itself that marks the passage of the last moments. But just as before when Yearsley described the 'veins', this passage is also carefully constructed. The complex syntax of 'Suppose, / This frame dissolving, to the busy winds / My ashes fled dividing', created by the placing of the punctuation, serves to subtly bring 'dissolving' and 'dividing' into a delicate balance not only metrically, but syntactically. The demonstration of such control enables poetry to be presented as a means to preserve memory and identity, to enable the reader to relive a particular 'spot of time' each time they read the poem. The poem, unlike the human heart, or the watch, is not subject to the limits of physiology or mechanics, but is, for all intents and purposes, eternal. So too, therefore, are the memories, and the moments, that it records.

II

Although 'Soliloquy' demonstrates Yearsley's considerable control over poetic form and metre, there is a bleakness in its representation of the universe which contrasts strikingly with the approach taken in her second poem about James Shiells. Where Yearsley's speaker in 'Soliloquy' is apparently overwhelmed by the smallness of human life in relation to the universe, the speaker in 'To the Memory of James Shiells, Esq.' finds comfort in contemplating the origins of the cosmos:

> The ancient Chaos struck me as a void
>   Dreary and vast, whence hollow murmurs rose:
> I question'd, if some universe destroy'd
>   Might not its mingled atoms once compose?
> 'Ah think not, Anna!' was thy mild reply,
> 'That back to Time's dark birth thy daring thought shall fly.'
>
> (Yearsley, 1796, p. 85)

This stanza reveals a great deal about Yearsley's imaginative powers, the nature of her relationship with Shiells, and indeed her position in relation to contemporary scientific debates. As in 'Soliloquy', the speaker here initially finds the size of the universe unnerving; it is 'Dreary and vast', a 'void' oxymoronically filled with 'hollow murmurs'. But the speaker's question, 'if some universe destroy'd / Might not its mingled atoms once compose?' reveals that Yearsley's imagination is unusually daring, having the capacity to imagine multiple universes, and suggests that Yearsley's ideas, expressed both here and in 'Soliloquy', were shaped by contemporary scientific theories about the earth and the wider cosmos.

In 1788 James Hutton had formulated his theory that the earth was much older than had previously been thought – millions of years older – and that the earth's crust had been formed and reformed many times over:

> The immense time necessarily required for this total destruction of the land, must not be opposed to that view of future events, which is indicated by the surest facts and most approved principles. Time, which measures every thing in our idea, and is often deficient to our schemes, is to nature endless and as nothing; it cannot limit that by which alone it had existence; and as the natural course of time, which to us seems infinite, cannot be bounded by any operation that may have an end, the progress of things upon this globe, that is, in the course of nature, cannot be limited by time, which must proceed in a continual progression. (Hutton, 1998, p. 7)

The evidence of the earth's strata revealed, for Hutton, that time has no useful meaning – the timescales involved for the reshaping of the earth are so vast as to effectively place 'nature' outside of time. The phrase, 'which to us seems infinite', indicates the subjective nature of time, that it appears eternal only from a human point of view, where meaningful timescales are so much shorter.

Tom Furniss has indicated the importance of the ideas on which Hutton drew, and which he 'reconfigured', to the early Romantic poets including Wordsworth and Coleridge: the 'geological aesthetics of the period . . . impacted on the first generation of Romantic poets despite the fact that they appear not to have read Hutton's work' (Furniss, 2010, p. 307).[7] Whilst Hutton may not have been read directly, his ideas were certainly circulated amongst the early Romantic poets; Furniss notes that Coleridge was exposed to Hutton's theories by Thomas Beddoes (Furniss, 2010, p. 319, n.14). As a friend of Yearsley's, it is entirely plausible that Beddoes was the means by which Yearsley also became acquainted with Hutton, whose ideas can be seen at work in both 'Soliloquy' and 'To the Memory of James Shiells'. It is in the second poem that Yearsley engages most fully with these ideas, and indeed looks beyond them. Hutton may have found evidence to challenge received notions of the origins and nature of the earth by suggesting that it has been reshaped and remade thousands of times over, but Yearsley extends these thoughts to the universal level. In her poem, Yearsley contemplates not just the reshaping of a planet, where 'rocks that had been laid down over millennia on the sea bed, . . . had buckled upwards to form part of a massive mountain range, then had been ground down particle by particle to sea level once more' (Jay, 2009, p. 19), but the rebirth of an entire universe from the ashes, or the 'mingled atoms', of the old. It is a cycle with 'no vestige of beginning, no prospect of an end' (Jay, 2009, p. 19), to borrow a phrase from Hutton, and contemplating it in this manner frees Yearsley's speaker from her fear of the chaotic 'void' that the universe would otherwise appear to be.

Interestingly, though, this is a flight of the imagination that cannot be tolerated by the James Shiells of Yearsley's poem, who recalls the poet back from the brink of such radical thoughts to remind her of what should be her limits. J. M. S. Tompkins has suggested that Yearsley is in this poem 'shaken by this extension of imaginative vision', and that James Shiells is merely 'checking her audacities' to prevent such shocks (1938, p. 87). Mary Waldron argues that Shiells is actually 'striving gently to bring Yearsley back to received belief' (1996, p. 247), but neither theory seems to me to entirely ring true given the sentiments of the stanza that follows:

> I priz'd thee with a more than common love! –
>   Alas! I saw thy faculties decay:
> I saw for thee the hours too swiftly move –
>   Age mark'd the sum thy Friendship mourn'd to pay.
> I could not snatch thee from the arm of Time,
> Or keep thy weary soul from her immortal clime!
>
> (Yearsley, 1796, p. 85)

In this stanza it is almost as if the poetic speaker is herself outside of time, in the same way that Hutton conceives 'nature' as being outside of time from a human's point of view. Shiells claims that 'Time's dark birth' is a matter too great for Yearsley to contemplate – her 'daring thought' cannot reach that far, he suggests – but it is Shiells whose thought is incapable of grasping the effects of Time upon himself. Yearsley is not 'shaken' by the turn of her imagination, but by the failure of Shiells's imagination to follow her, a consequence, it is suggested, of his increasing age. For Shiells, 'the hours too swiftly move' for him to be able to follow his protégée, something that is poignantly reversed when death comes for Shiells; then it is Yearsley who is unable to follow him.

Yet this does not cause the poet to despair, as it does in 'Soliloquy'. Where that poem rejected any consolation from Christian teachings and showed little faith in the existence of an afterlife, 'To the Memory' seems to suggest there is some form of life after death:

> Faithful to truth, by angels' friendship blest,
>   With them approach, and gild this lonely vale;
> Behold thy moral virtues in my breast –
>   Thy fewer foibles vanish'd on the gale!
> Behold how Fancy soothes! – Oh! what is life
> But visionary bliss, with Reason still at strife?[8]
>
>   (Yearsley, 1796, p. 86)

Though the poet mentions the 'friendship' of angels, this is not the route to an afterlife proposed here. An afterlife is available, though, firstly through the holding of the deceased person's 'moral virtues in my breast' – the transmission of values and learning from one person to the next – that enables a person to live on past their death. Indeed, death distils that person's qualities, ensuring that the 'moral virtues' survive whilst the 'fewer foibles' 'vanish on the gale'. Secondly, and perhaps more importantly, poetry itself acts to preserve Shiell's memory – poetry itself becomes an afterlife. It is through Yearsley, then, that Shiells will live on, both in the internalized lessons absorbed by her, and in the poetry written in his honour. In this way are the grand timescales of the macrocosm connected with the rather smaller ones of the human microcosm, linking the regeneration of the earth as described by Hutton with the continuation of human life through the act of remembrance, embodied in the act of writing poetry.

III

This connection across the ages, linking the distant past with the present, is important also in Wordsworth's and Cowper's poetry. But where Yearsley seeks to use her own imagination to explore ideas of time and space, an exploration which does not always provide her with answers or meaning, Wordsworth looks back into human history in order to make sense of the cosmos:

> Three summer days I roamed, when 'twas my chance
> To have before me on the downy Plain
> Lines, circles, mounts, a mystery of shapes
> Such as in many quarters yet survive,
> With intricate profusion figuring o'er
> The untilled ground, the work, as some divine,
> Of infant science, imitative forms
> By which the Druids covertly expressed
> Their knowledge of the heavens, and imaged forth
> The constellations, I was gently charmed,
> Albeit with an antiquarian's dream;
> I saw the bearded Teachers, with white wands
> Uplifted, pointing to the starry sky
> Alternately, and Plain below, while breath
> Of music seemed to guide them, and the Waste
> Was cheared with stillness and a pleasant sound.
>
> This for the past, and things that may be viewed
> Or fancied, in the obscurities of time.
>
> (Wordsworth, 2008 [1805], XII, ll.337–55)

The poet is not alone in asking questions of the world, or indeed the universe, but is part of a line of people stretching back to the beginning of British history. Indeed, the contemplation of these relics, the 'Lines, circles, mounts', the 'mystery of shapes', brings the people who made these marks back to life in the poet's imagination. For Wordsworth, as for Yearsley, it is through imagination and memory that the boundaries of linear time can be broken down, and by which time, and our place within it, are given meaning.

But Wordsworth contemplates the universe through this imagined scene of ancient Druidic ritual, rather than engaging with it directly. This is an unusual move for Wordsworth, who far more frequently figures himself alone in similar episodes in *The Prelude*, including the crossing of the Alps in Book VI. It is an effective move, though – the figures conjured by Wordsworth stand as proxies for the poet, enabling him to distance himself from the frightening scale of the ideas raised here. Their relics are still visible – their legacy still perceivable – they have not disappeared into the vastness of time. As a result, Wordsworth is able to retain a footing in the known past rather than being overwhelmed by the 'Dreariness and vastness' of the universe, as Yearsley seems to be (Yearsley, 1796, p. 85).

Cowper, in contrast, is highly sceptical of the value of looking back to former ages. For him, there is little to be learned, and much to be lost, through seeking to connect the present with ideas of a larger, collective past. For Cowper, meaning can only be found through God, who exists beyond and outside of time:

> All truth is from the sempiternal source
> Of light divine. But Egypt, Greece, and Rome
> Drew from the stream below. More favor'd we
> Drink, when we chuse it, at the fountain head.
> To them it flow'd much mingled and defiled
> With hurtful error, prejudice, and dreams
> Illusive of philosophy, so call'd,
> But falsely.
>
> (Cowper, 1785, II, p. 71)

All that is needed is this 'sempiternal force'. Cowper lists the many questions these ancient philosophers might have asked of themselves, and shows them all to be fruitless as 'Knots worthy of solution, which alone / A Deity could solve' (Cowper, 1785, II, p. 72). All that this history of enquiry and exploration has to offer humanity in terms of meaning is darkness. Only 'Revelation . . . illuminates the path of life' (Cowper, 1785, II, p. 72).

The differences between Cowper, Wordsworth and Yearsley in this area are striking. Where Cowper dismisses the utility of scientific or philosophic enquiry into the past, Wordsworth finds solace in the visible links to human history. But the calmness of Wordsworth's lines, 'This for the past, and things that may be view'd / Or fancied, in the obscurities of time' is different again to Yearsley's desperate command, 'Return, return!' as she urges her imagination to retreat from the contemplation of her own 'ashes fled dividing' into infinity (Yearsley, 2003 [1796], l.52):

> Return, return!
> Nor lose thy strength in phrensy, nor resign
> The form I love. – This watch is down! Ye points,

> Attun'd to motion by the art of man,
> As tell-tales of his doings, can ye mark
> Eternity by measur'd remnants? No. –
> Fallacious in your working, ye would say,
> With us, the life of man is but a day.
>
> (Yearsley, 2003, p. 1796, ll.55–62)

So powerful is the speaker's imagination at this point that she is at risk of dying as a result of this 'phrensy'. The questions being asked are too big, too much for the speaker's mind or body to control; the 'Impatient pow'r / Of thought' could at any point 'fly' into the 'vast profound', disappearing for ever, and taking both 'strength' and 'form' with it. But the command to 'Return, return' is not in itself enough to return the speaker to the present – she still holds her son's watch. Only when that is released does the speaker's voice attain some semblance of its former control. Interestingly, the poetic rhythm does not falter at all here, despite the apparently overwhelming nature of the sensations being experienced as the reverie comes to an end. As before, Yearsley is able to retain control of her verse, maintaining the connection between words and measure, between poetry and time. This coincides with the watch's loss of its previous status, both as symbol of familial prosperity and as a useful object – it is incapable of measuring time in any meaningful way. Once more it becomes a work of man, 'Attun'd to motion by the art of man', rather than being able to understand time, or give it meaning in and of itself. All it can do is measure 'remnants' – the true nature of time has been captured in the extraordinary flights taken by the speaker's imagination, and by the poet's careful control of metre and rhythm.

Sadly, the watch would become a remnant too of Yearsley's prosperity, a relic of better times. Only two years later Yearsley was bankrupt: there would be no more watches, nor indeed any more poetry. But in 'Soliloquy' and 'To the Memory of James Shiells, Esq.', Yearsley had sought to understand her place in the universe, to explore the nature of individual thought and experience. In so doing, she was both building on the work of poets like Cowper and Edward Young, and prefiguring the Romantic sensibility that would very shortly emerge and whose development Yearsley was witnessing at first hand. As a friend of Beddoes – whose Pneumatic Institute was frequented by Coleridge and Robert Southey – and visited by William Godwin when he met with Southey in 1798, Yearsley was closely involved with the networks within which the most famous members of the new generation of poets were developing. The importance of this period, 1796–7, when Yearsley was publishing her final volume of poetry, and Wordsworth and Coleridge were preparing their first, is demonstrated in the conclusion of *The Prelude*: it is *this* moment that Wordsworth chooses to remember:

> Whether to me shall be allotted life,
> And with life power to accomplish aught of worth
> Sufficient to excuse me in men's sight
> For having given this Record of myself,
> Is all uncertain: but, beloved Friend,
> When, looking back thou seest, in clearer view
> Than any sweetest sight of yesterday,
> That summer when on Quantock's grassy Hills
> Far ranging, and among the sylvan Coombs,
> Thou in delicious words, with happy heart,
> Didst speak the Vision of that Ancient Man,
> The bright-eyed Mariner, and rueful woes
> Didst utter of the Lady Christabel;
> And I, associate in such labour, walked
> Murmuring of him who, joyous hap! was found,
> After the perils of his moonlight ride
> Near the loud Waterfall; or her who sate
> In misery near the miserable Thorn;
> When thou dost to that summer turn thy thoughts,
> And hast before thee all which then we were,
> To thee, in memory of that happiness
> It will be known, by thee at least, my Friend,
> Felt, that the history of a Poet's mind
> Is labour not unworthy of regard:
> To thee the work shall justify itself.
>
> (Wordsworth, 2008 [1805], XIII, ll.386–410)

The importance of this place and moment to Wordsworth's most eloquent exploration of the relationship between mind and self – the Somerset hills in the summer of 1797 – is suggestive of the links between a nascent Romantic sensibility and Yearsley's philosophical poetry. But so too are the ways in which Yearsley and Wordsworth engage with, and dispute, arguments made by Cowper in *The Task*. Where Cowper retreats from scientific enquiry as a way of finding meaning, both Yearsley's and Wordsworth's poems are closely tied to advances in fields as varied as horology, geology and physics. All three poets find some measure of consolation through memory, though for Cowper this consolation is often blended with pain and regret. For Yearsley and Wordsworth though, the act of remembrance also provides a means of considering the most fundamental questions: the origins of the universe; the nature of thought; the origin of the self as a thinking and experiencing being; and the role of poetry in exploring and preserving such ideas: all were concerns that would occupy writers well into the next century. Having been neglected for nearly two centuries, Yearsley's later poetry ought now to be recognized as a crucial bridge between the work of late eighteenth-century poets, and the new generation of soon-to-be Romantic writers.

Notes

1. Roe (2010) does much to return attention to the west country as the site of the first emergence of the Romantic movement. Also see Labbe (2011). Labbe investigates Smith's interest in 'how memory functions to fulfil one's potential through a creative rewriting' (p. 1), and compares this with Wordsworth's poetics.
2. See Waldron (1996); Stott (2003); Landry (1990); and Demers (1993).
3. See Andrews (2009) and forthcoming.
4. Shiells had attempted to intervene on Yearsley's behalf when her first patronage relationship, with Hannah More, collapsed spectacularly and publicly in 1785 as a result of a dispute over Yearsley's earnings. More took the decision, with her friend Elizabeth Montagu, to place Yearsley's money in a trust fund, giving no legal assurances that Yearsley's children would receive the money on their mother's death. Yearsley objected, and More took offence. Shiells would prove a regular subscriber to Yearsley's poetry, and he also helped promote and distribute her poetry. In addition, Yearsley enjoyed a warm friendship with his painter daughter, Sarah Shiells – the friendship is commemorated by Yearsley in a poem to Sarah's artistic abilities, and by Sarah Shiells in a portrait of Yearsley. See 'Ode to Miss Shiells, on her Art of Painting' (Yearsley, 1787); Sarah Shiells's portrait of Yearsley was made available to the public in May 1787 by subscription.
5. There is little information about Yearsley's denominational affiliations. She is described by More in 1784 as having been 'given' by her mother 'an early tincture of religion', but no further details are offered. Yearsley's later associates included the Baptist Joseph Cottle and, probably, Coleridge who was at this point a Unitarian. There is no evidence regarding Yearsley's religious beliefs in 1796, beyond what can be gleaned in her published writings.
6. See also Hartman (1987).
7. See also Heringman (2004).
8. For more information about the role of 'Fancy' in Romantic poetry, see Robinson (2006).

Bibliography

Andrews, Kerri (2009) 'A recently discovered letter from Ann Yearsley to Joseph Cottle', *Notes and Queries*, 56:2, 388–90.
——. (forthcoming) *Ann Yearsley and Hannah More, Patronage, and Poetry: the Story of a Literary Relationship* (London: Pickering & Chatto).
Cowper, William (1785), *The Task* (London: J. Johnson).
Demers, Patricia (1993) '"For Mine's a Stubborn and a savage will": "Lactilla" (Ann Yearsley) and "Stella" (Hannah More) Reconsidered', *Huntington Library Quarterly*, 56, 135–50.
Furniss, Tom (2010) 'A Romantic Geology: James Hutton's 1788 *Theory of the Earth*', *Romanticism*, 16:3, 305–21.
Hall, Marie Boas (1981) *The Mechanical Philosophy* (New York: Arno Press).
Hartman Geoffrey (1964) *Wordsworth's Poetry, 1787–1814* (New Haven and London: Yale University Press).
——. (1987) *The Unremarkable Wordsworth* (London: Methuen).
Heringman, Noah (2004) *Romantic Rocks, Aesthetic Geology* (Ithaca and London: Cornell University Press).
Hutton, James (1998 [1788]) *Theory of the Earth; or an Investigation of the Laws Observable in the Composition, Dissolution, and Restoration of Land upon the Globe* (Kessinger Publishing: n.p.).
Jay, Mike (2009) *The Atmosphere of Heaven: The Unnatural Experiments of Dr Beddoes and his Sons of Genius* (New Haven and London: Yale University Press).
Labbe, Jacqueline M. (2011) *Writing Romanticism: Charlotte Smith and William Wordsworth, 1784–1807* (Basingstoke: Palgrave Macmillan).
Landry, Donna (1990) *The Muses of Resistance: Labouring-Class Women's Poetry in Britiain, 1739–1796* (Cambridge: Cambridge University Press).
McHugh, Heather (2002) 'Presence and Passage: A Poet's Wordsworth', *Modern Language Quarterly*, 63:2, 167–96.
Robinson, Jeffrey C. (2006) *Unfettering Poetry: The Fancy in British Romanticism* (Basingstoke: Palgrave Macmillan).
Roe, Nicholas, ed. (2010) *English Romantic Writers and the West Country* (Basingstoke: Palgrave Macmillan).
Stott, Anne (2003) *Hannah More: the First Victorian* (Oxford: Oxford University Press).
Tompkins, J. M. S. (1938) *The Polite Marriage* (Cambridge: Cambridge University Press).
Waldron, Mary (1996) *Lactilla, Milkwoman of Clifton: the Life and Writings of Ann Yearsley, 1753–1806* (Athens, GA: University of Georgia Press).
Wordsworth, William (2008) *The Major Works, including* The Prelude, ed. Stephen Gill (Oxford: Oxford University Press).
Yearsley, Ann (2003) *Selected Poems*, ed. Tim Burke (Cheltenham: The Cyder Press).
——. (1787) *Poems on Several Occasions* (London: G. G. and J. Robinson).
——. (1796) *The Rural Lyre* (London: G. G. and J. Robinson).

7
The Pen and the Hammer: Thomas Carlyle, Ebenezer Elliott, and the 'active poet'

Marcus Waithe

A university-educated man of letters, whose social connections in London were decidedly aristocratic, Thomas Carlyle is not generally thought of as a 'labouring-class' writer. The reality is that his origins were decidedly humble. Born in a modest 'arched house' in the unprepossessing village of Ecclefechan, Carlyle spent his early life in the Calvinistic labouring and farming community of the West of Scotland.[1] He was the son of James Carlyle, a poor man who began his working life as a jobbing stonemason, before becoming a local builder, and then a farmer. Rather than focus on the question of class, critics have tended to concentrate on the religious and aesthetic legacy of this background. Ian Campbell identifies the strict Calvinism of Carlyle's father as the source of his lifelong doubts about the value of poetic expression, while David DeLaura observes that 'Poetry is a revealing test-case of Carlyle's uneasiness with virtually all contemporary creative work' (Campbell, 1974, p. 7; DeLaura, 2004, p. 32). My contention is that Carlyle's inherited anxiety about 'eloquence' was not simply a product of narrow doctrine. In his youth, he had been a fervent champion of Burns, Goethe and Schiller; and while in the grip of this idealist phase, he applied the term 'poet' as a mark of philosophical distinction. The rule-breaking mechanisms of poetry were even considered useful, in peeling back the 'sham' of appearances to unveil the 'real' (Carlyle, 1898, pp. 176–7).

What makes Carlyle repudiate these early enthusiasms is hard to determine; but the death of his father marks a clear watershed. Henceforth, he would be haunted by the possibility of a broken inheritance, a fate he understood primarily in occupational terms. The fear was that the worlds of manual craft and letters were incommensurable, and that in consequence he could carry nothing forward from the life of his father. At the same time, Carlyle manifests an exaggerated – and possibly compensatory – concern for the value of 'work' in the abstract. This was the notorious 'Gospel of Labour', first expressed across the pages of *Past and Present* (1843), and proposed in more extreme terms in *Latter-Day Pamphlets* (1850).[2] Instead of construing that emphasis on physical work as evidence of an abandonment of poetry, I shall focus on Carlyle's concurrent efforts to make poetry acceptable. This means looking beyond the prohibitive legacy of James Carlyle's religious conviction, and showing how his example as a mason inspired an attempt to include literature within the compass of 'work'.[3] In the memory of his father, Carlyle found the resources not just to close the gap between the literary life and the mason's trade, but to imagine what a 'refurbished' poetry might be. The new literature that emerges is initially characterized as 'craft', and is linked to artisanal notions of apprenticeship and workmanship. It is then reconceived as a mode of 'action' in the world. In the last part of this essay, I consider the culmination of these approaches in Carlyle's approving review of Ebenezer Elliott's *Corn Law Rhymes* (1831), a work heralded by him as the production of a 'true' poet, whose 'labouring' credentials were sufficient to heal the rift between eloquence and 'real work'.

I am concerned, then, with a writer whose inherited sense of occupational worth was destabilized by a consciousness of *not doing* physical labour, and whose sympathy for the value in specifically manual exertion ran counter to his existing professional commitments. The nuances of this position were not well appreciated by Carlyle's contemporaries, even those who knew him well. John Stuart Mill made no reference to the social background of his erstwhile friend when lambasting him for suggesting an equivalence between 'such work ... as is done by writers' and 'real labour', 'the exhausting, stiffening, stupefying toil of many kinds of agricultural and manufacturing labours' (Mill, 1996, p. 91). Unlike William Gladstone, who enjoyed posing as a woodman on his estate at Hawarden, or William Morris, who wore a workman's smock, Carlyle's remedy did not entail dabbling in working-class identity as an alien element. On the contrary, it meant reconnecting with abandoned origins, recovering something lost not just from the culture, but from his own life.

The phenomenon of Chartist poetry, and the rise of the autodidact or working-class intellectual, has rightly received critical attention in recent years.[4] This essay differs, in exploring a version of class that has broken away from the corresponding social reality. As such, it considers a predicament more familiar in the twentieth-century context of 'the grammar-school boy' than in the nineteenth century.[5] If Chartist poetry sought to project a 'voice of labour', then I am interested in Carlyle as a writer who desired, but lacked, an equivalent voice.

I. Books and buildings

Immediately after his father died in 1832, Carlyle began work on a kind of private obituary. Already coming to terms with his arrival in the literary world, and with the social 'anarchy' he had witnessed on recent visits to London, he was now being changed – or rather returned to his origins – by the act of recalling the paternal presence in words. Critics wishing to identify the source of Carlyle's 'anti-intellectualism' tend to neglect the warring loyalties expressed across this document.[6] Though published posthumously as part of *Reminiscences* (1881), the recollections of James Carlyle were carefully composed and considered, and they evince a particular interpretation of the differences between father and son. The author is in the process of convincing himself, and perhaps also a ghostly auditor, that the gulf between them is bridgeable. The first part of this task involves expressing gratitude to his father for funding his education. He is led to speculate, 'Nay, am not I also the humble James Carlyle's work?' (Carlyle, 2009, p. 3). The thinking is that whatever the father made cannot be wholly alien to him, so that we should admit the possibility of a worker in flesh, as well as a builder in stone.[7] Less easy to contain is the recollection that 'Poetry, Fiction in general, he had universally seen treated as not only idle, but *false* and *criminal*' (Carlyle, 2009, p. 10). Carlyle freely admits that his father was unaffected by his own 'noisy and enthusiastic' attention to the poetry of Burns (p. 9). The approach, as before, is to find identity amidst difference: father and son are seen to have taken different – but ultimately compatible – approaches to 'the Wisdom of Reality'. Harmony is restored through the precarious re-description of this common ground as 'Poetry': 'The Poetry *he* liked (he did not call it Poetry) was Truth'. Ultimately, his father's hostility to it could not be disguised, and Carlyle resorts to pleading the mitigating influences of environment and a defective education (p. 10).

In the process of honouring his father's memory, Carlyle was still willing to register flashpoints of dispute, and even to discard the stricter implications of the paternal creed. His own youthful appreciation of poetry, for instance, is set against his father's perverse intransigence in the matter, his 'most entire and open contempt for all idle tattle' (Carlyle, 2009, p. 6). The narrative perspective in this case is complex: while sympathy is extended to both parties, one cannot help noticing that the position of the father is also convergent with the mature prejudices of the son. Carlyle would increasingly characterize himself along the same lines: as an opponent of eloquence, a kind of anti-Burns never distracted from 'virtuous industry' by 'rich men's banquets' (1828, pp. 314–15). In these recollections, Carlyle gives Burns credit for his 'poetry', but only at the cost of a guilty internalization, a reproduction of James Carlyle's scorn for undirected speech. Something similar happens when the older Carlyle is drafted into a paternal role by requests for advice from aspiring writers. He wrote to C. A. Ward, for instance, that literature was 'the questionable enterprise of unfolding whatever gifts may be in you in the shape of mere Spoken or Written *Words*'.[8] It is a task he contrasts with '*work* in this world'.

Puritanical suspicion of rhetoric was not merely a negative response to creative endeavour; in Carlyle, it prompted constructive thoughts of an alternative. This was suggested by James Carlyle's life as a mason, and epitomized by the thought that 'a portion of this Planet bears beneficent traces of his strong Hand and strong Head' (Carlyle, 2009, p. 3). What emerges is a reformed 'speech' of substantial acts. Initially, it exacerbates the opposition between poetry and paternal authority. A 'good Building', Carlyle explains, 'will last longer than most Books' (2009, p. 23). In its assumption that a book's value must stand by the longevity of its material form, rather than its dissemination, reception, or reproduction, the comment is oddly circumscribed. At other points, the emphasis on continuity prevails, and Carlyle attributes to this paternal mason the transcendental powers of a poet, '"uniting the Possible with the Necessary" to bring out the Real' (p. 9). '[B]uilding (*walling*)', we learn, 'is an operation that beyond most other manual ones requires incessant consideration, ever-new invention' (p. 24). The rapprochement recedes with the gathering appreciation that stonemasonry is a singular craft, which bears no obvious comparison with 'speech'. Our attention is directed instead to 'small differences' in modes of construction, as between 'Palace-building and Kingdom-founding, or only of delving and ditching' (p. 4).

Such comparative analysis is eventually displaced by an intrusion of parabolic form, delivered by the primal scene in which Carlyle imagines his father undergoing a mundane apotheosis as he embarks on his career as 'William Brown's first Apprentice':

> the two 'slung their tools' (mallets and irons hung in two equipoised masses over the shoulders), and crossed the Hills into Nithsdale, to Auldgarth, where a Bridge was building. (2009, p. 22)

This tale of personal transformation culminates in ritual admission to the secret of a 'noble craft'. But there is significance, too, in the accidental detail: in the 'slung', but instrumental, 'clothing' of these human forms, in the bodily experience of balance and mass that hints at a reconciliation of heft with skill. This manner of 'showing', or doing, is also apparent in the recollection of a summer scene, in which the father is pictured 'diligently, cheerfully labouring with trowel and hammer' (p. 24). The components of the description do not eliminate resistance between the human will and the task, but Carlyle offers no equivalent in ordinary experience for a union of mood with the pliability of tools. James Carlyle was merely a 'hewer' at the bridge, but the tale's symbolic premise is that he would later join the company of those 'cunning hands' who piled it together (p. 22). To function as an appreciative description, this allusion to 'cunning' must evoke a form of 'knowing' purged of the rhetorical 'craft' that contaminates eloquence. It must heal the division that has seen '*kenning* and *can-ning*... become two altogether different words'.[9] In this way, the scene conjures an untroubled home for qualities that the mason shares with the writer. It promises a refuge for the kind of restless, travelling intelligence that lacks an equivalent mandate when employed in the service of letters.

Just at that point when Carlyle is most absorbed in the otherness of this 'substantial' occupation, he confronts us with its present degradation. His father, he explains, 'wisely quitted the Mason trade' to become a farmer, 'when universal Poverty and Vanity made *show* and *cheapness* (here as everywhere) be preferred to Substance' (p. 30). At that moment, the connection between letters and artisanship is restored. Only, they are now seen as partners in degradation. The following year, Carlyle wrote that 'Literature, one's sole craft and staff of life, lies broken in abeyance'.[10] The thought that 'the age of Substance and Solidity is gone' might imply that he saw no prospect of steering a course between the literary and the tangible (Carlyle, 2009, p. 6). In what follows, I adduce evidence to the contrary: though constitutionally prone to despair, Carlyle was in fact consciously developing a language for thinking about literary vocation as manual 'apprenticeship'.

II. Carlyle's 'author-craft'

In a letter to the House of Commons concerning the petition for a copyright law, Carlyle described himself as a 'Writer of books'. In that homely prepositional phrase, he neatly encapsulates the petition's call for legal recognition of authorship as a 'useful labour' that is 'honest' and 'innocent'.[11] Opting for 'writer' over 'poet', he subtly disclaims the unremunerative 'privilege' of sacerdotal or aristocratic authority. The designation emphasizes the manual task of 'one who writes'; and the appended specification, 'of books', refuses priority to the specialist in that line over any other. In this case, the emphasis also had strategic value, for Carlyle was aiming to expose the unfair treatment of authors as compared with other tradesmen.

Better known for claiming that 'The only Sovereigns of the world in these days are the Literary men', and for the self-aggrandising thesis proposed in 'The Hero as Man of Letters' (1840), Carlyle had been convincing himself privately of a more humble, and personally resonant, affinity.[12] It received its most concerted articulation in a footnote to his essay on the 'State of German Literature' (1827). There, Carlyle referred to the 'Singer-guilds' of Nürnberg in which 'poetry was taught and practised like any other handicraft, and this by sober and well-meaning men, chiefly artisans, who could not understand why labour, which manufactured so many things, should not also manufacture another' (1827, p. 32). Significantly, it takes 'artisans' in this account to recognize the false distinctions under which the rest of the world labours. Closer to home, a living example emerges in Carlyle's recollection of a visit paid him in Chelsea by Allan Cunningham, a poet and biographer who had been apprenticed to a stonemason in his youth. Carlyle pointedly records Jane's allusion to their guest's overlapping identity: he is, she notes, 'a genuine Dumfriesshire mason still' (Carlyle, 1898, p. 214). It is a description that improves on the condescending 'portrait' of Cunningham printed the following year in *Fraser's* 'Gallery of Literary Characters': 'Like Ben Jonson', the article states, 'he began with trowel and mallet, which he abandoned for divine poetry', a 'higher department' ('Gallery of Literary Characters', 1832, pp. 248–9). The accompanying sketch is more Carlylean, in showing Cunningham seated next to a pile of books, and holding a mallet against one leg. Rough creases and an open-legged posture lend ambivalence to his 'genteel' attire, while the indistinct lines of his fashionable tie shade into the appearance of a workman's neckerchief.

That year, Carlyle proposed an ambiguous correction of an otherwise flattering term, applied to him by Mill in a letter: instead of appearing to be an 'Artist', he hoped that 'a few years' would see him 'stand forth in his true dimensions, an honest Artisan'.[13] The effect is self-deprecating, but there is pride and a resolution not to be 'placed' in these words. Crucially, it also offers a commentary on Carlyle's stirring resolution to 'write my Books as he built his Houses' (Carlyle, 2009, p. 8). A. Abbott Ikeler observes that Carlyle would admit the 'preaching virtue' of the poet only to have him 'more usefully occupied in "doing" some poem' (1972, p. 9). This insistence on 'doing', I would suggest, is better regarded as a strategy, one that precedes, and to a certain extent persists in parallel with, the more militant conviction of *Latter-Day Pamphlets* that 'Talk, except as the preparation for work, is worth almost nothing' (1850, p. 193).

Carlyle's approval of artisanal identity translates readily into an emphasis on 'craftmanship' [*sic*] in style, a preference that can be traced to the succinct mode of expression favoured by his father, who 'seldom or never spoke except actually to convey an idea'.[14] The sense emerges of a person who is keen to husband words as valuable materials. On sending advice to Edward Strachey, Carlyle recommended that he 'Be *wisely brief*', 'not in phrase only, but still more in *thought*'.[15] The familiar writerly value of concision enters more distinctively artisanal territory when he counsels a sculptural exclusion of the '*un*essential', and then a workmanlike ability to 'Everywhere hit the nail on the *head*, and do not strike at it again!' That year, Carlyle wrote in similar terms to compliment Elizabeth Gaskell on *Mary Barton* (1848), while recommending a future effort to 'reject the *un*essential more and more', and employing an artisanal persona to apply the mechanical force: 'Jem Wilson, too, knows very well that one should *hit the nail on the head*, always; and having riveted it home, go to the next nail, *not* beating on the intermediate spaces, – if we *are* smiths.'[16] Having taken the analogy some distance, Carlyle causes it to dissolve into the identity of 'smith': by now, not just a generic token of authorial attainment, but a claim to shared occupation with those who 'nail' (see Waithe, 2011).

When Carlyle discusses his own work, the medium of words is characterized as a physical substance or texture. As early as 1822, he explained to his brother that 'Grammar in writing is like fingers and arms in a manual trade.'[17] According to that characterization, it becomes an agent or tool required for the fashioning of material otherwise resistant to manipulation. A letter to his father from 1823 advances an intriguing distinction between forms of writing. Observing the shift from literary composition to letter writing, he notes that 'I lay aside my author-craft, and willingly betake me to another sort of writing.'[18] One should not assume that all allusions to 'craft' are meant to invite comparison with a manual standard of excellence. The word is often used in a purely generic sense.[19] Still, the compound term 'author-craft' performs a more specialized function, suggestive of an affinity between the calling of authorship so unfamiliar to Carlyle's father, and the stonemasonry or farming that filled his working life.

Carlyle's re-description of writing depended on attention to its plasticity. In 'The Early Kings of Norway', he explained that 'The Icelanders, in their long winter, had a great habit of writing; and were, and still are, excellent in penmanship.'[20] There seems less room in this for confusion with the generic sense of the word. Penmanship is not work in the abstract, but the manual application of a physical instrument to paper. This is writing, but it is also manifestly a craft.[21] The problem with substantial words is that they must be cut to shape, and *made* to fit. It follows that the sense of physical blockage is strong in Carlyle's accounts of writing. While such complaints are often discussed in the light of his digestive problems (see, for instance, Guest, 2004), it is worth considering an explanation founded in the action of writing itself. In *Past and Present*, he exclaims that 'the very Paper I now write on is made, it seems, partly of plaster-lime well smoothed, and obstructs my writing' (Carlyle, 1843, p. 141). The letter to his brother in which he defends the value of grammatical study contains a passage that contributes to this conception of writing as the subduing of something resistant and obstructive:

> The small worm on the coasts of the Mediterranean perforates a rock of flint by continued application; your fiery tiger would crunch his teeth to pieces on it instantly, and go off howling, without even breaking the surface. For the sake of perseverance, therefore, persevere.[22]

It is here that the correspondence between a reluctant raw material and the role of craftsman is most clear.[23] There is no natural link between the substance and the final product, no built-in telos guaranteeing the emergence of a 'civilized' form. The link is entirely reliant on the agency of a skilled individual who has harnessed perseverance to an apprenticeship in that particular 'trade'.[24]

Carlyle's faith in the alternative value system of *craft* began to ebb in later life. The process of disillusionment, though already implicit in his father's resignation of the mason's trade, was hastened by his experience of life in London. There he complained of poor standards – epitomized by 'villainous [Cock]ney shoes' – and a 'second trade' of 'puffery' that subordinated the doing of work to the necessity that you 'convince the world that thou hast done it'.[25] Increasingly, his conception of 'doing' relied on a demonstration of 'action' and 'force'.[26] Though not usually associated with the artistic sphere, these values inform his distinction between 'idle poets' – 'whose haunts lie in the dilettante line' – and 'the active poets', who 'are incessantly toiling to achieve, and more and more realise' (Carlyle, 1850, p. 261). My attention therefore turns to a parallel strategy of self-representation, which focused less on a quiet internalization of his father's example, than on a public celebration of it, in a different, and resolutely physical guise. Unlike the slow apprenticeship of *craft*, which was increasingly a matter of reminiscence, this approach required compelling expression 'in the moment'. Perhaps because comparison of writing to hard labour was less credible and more outlandish than the cultivation of 'author-craft', Carlyle's first application of this idea was vicarious, and retained a connection with the artisanship whose value would not be seriously challenged until he left Craigenputtock for London in 1834.

III. The pen and the hammer

Soon after his father's death, Carlyle began work on a review essay about 'The Sheffield Radical', Ebenezer Elliot. Published in the *Edinburgh Review* in 1832, it described Elliott as 'a middle-aged Mechanic, at least Poor Man, of Sheffield or the neighbourhood'.[27] The portrait follows of Elliott as a 'quite unmoneyed, russet-coated speaker; nothing or little other than a Sheffield worker in brass and iron' (Carlyle, 1832, p. 138). Carlyle's agenda has been construed by Karen Wolven as a demonstration of literary ability in the uneducated and the poor (1999, p. 238). Respect for his 'peasant father' makes this emphasis credible, as does the pointed, and not wholly sympathetic, observation of the *Westminster Review* that the anonymous 'Author' of *The Village Patriarch* (1829), 'calls his book "A Poor Man's Poem"'.[28] According to that notice, the sole merit of Elliott's earlier volume lay in its status as a social 'thermometer' (*Village Patriarch*, 1829, p. 92). Carlyle did challenge the truism that 'poor men do not write'; but I want to suggest that the appreciation was as much about Elliott's capacity to evoke a refashioning of Carlyle's own expressive possibilities as his ability to inspire other 'working men' (Carlyle, 1832, p. 138). In the wake not only of his father's death, but also Goethe's, Carlyle was looking for examples of literary endeavour to regenerate the resources of his 'dilettante' profession. In Elliott, he found a poet 'who can handle both pen and hammer like a man' (p. 139). He was a poet whose 'voice' could not be confused with 'idle tattle', because of its 'coming from the deep Cyclopean forges, where Labour, in real soot and sweat, beats with his thousand hammers "the red son of the furnace"' (p. 138). Elliott, in short, represented a solution to the central conflict between quiet integrity and guilty speech that runs through *Reminiscences*. As such, he was welcomed as a new hope, 'an intelligible voice from the hitherto Mute and Irrational'. Notwithstanding the earlier assistance given to Elliott by Robert Southey, who had first corresponded with him in 1808, Carlyle's review proved to be a turning-point in the poet's career. Apart from popularizing Elliott's work, its legacy was felt in the appraisals of subsequent writers, who borrowed from Carlyle a determination to attribute the form of the poems to the labouring aspect of the man. In *Household Words*, Dickens reflected that 'His poetry is just such as, knowing his history, we might have expected; and such as, not knowing it, might have bodied forth to us the identical man as we find him' (1851, p. 237). Elliott's reputation as a labouring poet also inspired Gaskell, who included three epigraphs from his works in *Mary Barton*. Most notably, a passage from *The Splendid Village* (1833) is chosen to preface the novel's description of learned weavers who botanize and read Newton's *Principia* (Gaskell, 2006, pp. 37–8). Two biographies appeared the year after Elliott's death, one by January Searle, and the other by the poet's son-in-law, John Watkins. And in 1854, a shorter work appeared by J. W. King. Though Carlyle thought Searle's study 'worth very little', it borrowed many of its descriptive terms from him.[29] Elliott is called 'some grim Cyclop', 'a strong man; a sort of gigantic Titan', in phrases that acknowledge strength without renouncing the poetic realm of mythology and simile (Searle, 1850, pp. 15, 17). King referred similarly to Elliott singing with 'the strength of a Titan', and noted the 'unpoetic element' in which he wrote, keeping 'busts of Shakespeare, Achilles, Ajax, and Napoleon, in the midst of piles of iron and steel' (King, 1854, pp. 4, 17). In this way, Carlyle's review generated a language for talking about 'poetic' virtues that encompassed the virtues of the 'hardworking, practical man' (Searle, 1850, p. 18).

Up to a point, Elliott was happy to play up to this image. In the preface to the edition examined by Carlyle, he responded to the reviews already published in the *New Monthly Magazine* and the *Athenæum*.[30] He makes no effort to confute the 'supposition that they are the work of a mechanic' (Elliott, 1831, p. iv). This was an allusion to Bulwer's assertion in the first of these notices that the poems were 'composed by a common mechanic', but also a reiteration of his own apology in the preface to *The Village Patriarch*, that 'If my composition smell of the workshop, and the mechanic, I cannot help it.'[31] Instead, he enlarges on an argument akin to Gaskell's, that one should not 'wonder, if mechanics write well in these days' (1831, p. iv). Inclusion of a 'Declaration of the Sheffield Mechanic's Anti-Bread-Tax Society' (of which Elliott was the founder) no doubt bolstered the impression of a 'mechanical' origin. And yet Elliott would have been hard-pressed to describe *himself* in these terms, not at least without qualification.[32] Carlyle never actually met the poet, and his testimony is consistent with that fact, being in various respects at odds with the reality of Elliott's life. A letter published in Watkins's biography illustrates the complexity of his social position: 'Do not address me Esquire', Elliott insists, 'I have been a hard-working man all my life, and am now a humble tradesman with a very large family to maintain, and so they call me a big man, because we cannot get into a very small house' (Watkins, 1850, p. 133). Seeking to explain away a 'discrepancy', Elliott only succeeds in drawing attention to it. As an assertion of identity, his words evidently backfire; but they highlight in the process a problem of 'placing' that warrants further attention.

Although Elliott's involvement in Radical politics justifies his reputation as 'the poor man's friend', he was not a poor man himself, but something more like a local businessman, or 'jobbing merchant'.[33] Claiming descent from Border cattle thieves, he described his father as having received a 'first-class commercial education' in Newcastle-upon-Tyne.[34] Alluding to his mother, who was the daughter of a yeoman whose 'ancestors had lived on their fifty or sixty acres of freehold time out of mind', he concludes that 'I have made out my descent, if not from very fine folks, certainly from respectable' (Watkins, 1850, p. 5). His father became the 'nominal proprietor' of the Rotherham foundry of Clay and Co., which seems unlikely to have generated serious income, but did allow Elliott to be sent to school, at least before he was set to work in the paternal foundry 'as a punishment' for truancy (Morris and Hearne, 2002, pp. 16–19; Watkins, 1850, p. 16). While this experience, which lasted until the age of 23, was Elliott's chief claim to being 'a working-man', he was careful to note that 'I am not aware that I ever did so call myself' (Watkins, 1850, p. 26). Given his professed relief in escaping an education that bred feelings of inferiority, a comparison with Dickens's spell in Warren's Blacking Factory seems inappropriate. Watkins nevertheless suggests a similar apprehension of 'disgrace', on pointing out that 'His destination was not that of a common working-man, but of a master – of one whose head sets to work the hands of others' (p. 33).

In short, Elliott's economic position for most of his life was not that of a labourer, but of a 'master', whose exposure to the trade cycle brought ruin and prosperity in equal measure. In a letter to Macvey Napier, written after the review was finished, Carlyle acknowledged the fresh information that his subject was 'now, rather improved in circumstances' and 'keeps some little hardware shop'.[35] However, he thought his name was 'Reuben Elliott', and the prefatory stress on his having been 'bred an actual hammerman or something of the sort' carefully reinstates the factual basis upon which his thesis depended, in presenting a poet who 'by his skill in metallurgy, can beat out a toilsome but a manful living'.[36] Elliott actually gave up being a 'hammerman' in any exclusive sense long before, when he took on the management of his father's foundry (see Brown, 1971, p. 308). After being declared bankrupt in 1816, he moved from Rotherham to Sheffield in 1819, and set up as an iron dealer.[37] No longer directly involved in manufacturing, he entered a lucrative trade in which 'he made 20*l.* a day, sitting in his chair, without seeing the goods'.[38] According to Watkins, he lost one third of his savings in the crash of 1837, leaving him with £6,000 (1850, p. 82). This would imply that around the time of Carlyle's review, Elliott was worth in savings alone the sizable sum of £9,000. Tokens of respectability followed, including frequent listing under various resolutions and petitions published in the local press.[39] In the late 1820s, Elliott was even able to send one of his sons to Peterhouse, Cambridge, after Southey pulled strings at the University (Brown, 1971, p. 308; Seary, 1939). These facts do not contradict Elliott's claims about his origins, and there is no reason why intermittent wealth should impinge on his class position. But they inevitably complicate Carlyle's attribution of poetic qualities to a union in one person of the pen and the hammer, and his insistence on a 'personal battle with Necessity' (1832, p. 138).

It is not just Elliott's social background that eludes Carlyle's descriptive categories: his poetry, too, resists the emphasis on a sinuous materialization. This is not surprising, given the relative lateness of his 'discovery' of a poet whose style and aesthetic identity were formed in the first two decades of the century. Elliott had previously published volumes in 1801 (*The Vernal Walk*), 1810 (*The Soldier and Other Poems*), 1820 (*Peter Faultless to His Brother Simon*) and 1823 (*Love . . . to which is added The Giaour, a Satirical Poem (Addressed to Lord Byron)*). He ascribed his poetic 'conversion' not to work in the foundry, but to the chance revelation of Sowerby's *English Botany* (1790), which led him out into Sheffield's 'near' countryside in search of flowers to paint (see Sowerby, 1870). A largely decorative and derivative poetry was the result, heavily influenced by Romantic conceptions of genius and communion with Nature. In *The Vernal Walk*, 'serpentine rills rejoice' and 'Mountain torrents shine' in Wordsworthian fashion, while an opening address to the sun as the 'unbounded sea of light', evokes the seasonal poetry of James Thomson.[40] Unsurprisingly, given the accompanying pastoral lament for 'POOR DAMON, hapless lover!', the poet is not figured as a 'smith', but as a 'bard of nature', who 'Warbles his rustic song' (Elliott, 1801, pp. 25, 39). As he moved through the phases of his career – from praise of Nature, to literary satire, and then socio-political satire – Elliott's mood darkened.[41] While the shift in priorities is unmistakable, it is a change that occurs without entirely displacing the Romantic legacy: even amidst the apocalyptic warning that 'Rivelin's side is desolate' ('The Tree of Rivelin', in *Corn-Law Rhymes*), he finds room for allusion to 'rock and rill' (1831, p. 54).

Readers familiar with Sheffield would have appreciated that 'The Tree of Rivelin' was no incidental nature poem. Its title and setting implied a challenge to the binary distinction between 'natural sensitivity' and the identity of 'northern, industrial poet' that ran through metropolitan appraisals of Elliott's poetry. A scene of walks not just for Elliott but for many workers engaged in the metal trades, the Rivelin Valley exemplified the way that a pastoral environment on the city's outskirts could co-exist with the active industry of water-powered grindstones (Wolven, 1999, p. 236). Watkins's account is unusually perceptive of the discrepancy between this reality and the 'cyclopean' myth. He dispels the 'burly ironmonger' image, reporting that Elliott was 'of nervous temperament, weak in body', with 'sympathies' that were 'continually vibrating with torture, like the strings of the Æolian harp in a rough wind' (1850, pp. 127–8). Even Searle contradicts some of his earlier testimony in admitting surprise on first meeting Elliott, and finding him 'a man of short stature, instead of the bulky Titan I had pictured him in imagination' (1850, p. 159). In this way, the poet's physical form interrupts a process of authorial fashioning that has stressed 'natural vigour', in Carlyle's phrase, to the exclusion of the physical facts and the 'Romantic' portion of his career (1832, p. 139).

This discrepancy is no more apparent than when Elliot responds to his late reputation as a 'mechanic': 'Is it strange', he asks, 'that my language is fervent with a welding heat, when my thoughts are *passions*, that rush burning from my mind, like white-hot bolts of steel?' (1831, p. vii). Notwithstanding the metallurgical premise, this 'welding heat' is soon reconfigured in Romantic and affective terms. The strongest evidence Carlyle is able to adduce for a 'Vulcanic dialect' comes not from the poetry, but from the earlier part of the same long sentence from the Preface: 'He says . . . his feelings have been *hammered* till they are *cold-short*; so they will no longer bend; "they snap, and fly off," – in the face of the hammerer' (Carlyle, 1832, p. 148). Taken as a whole, the actual sentence begins and ends in the 'heart', and is not about wielding the hammer, but about being hammered.[42] Carlyle's mixture of paraphrase and quotation obscures the declared effect of this treatment, which is that his feelings 'snap – and fly off in sarcasm', as material figure is converted into mordant polemic. The implication is that Elliott's trajectory was more 'conventional' than his admirers were keen to believe. He realizes, rather than reverses, Raymond Williams's analysis of the early nineteenth century as a period when the *'Artist'* and *'artisan'* were parted along lines of 'sensibility' and 'skill' (1968, p. 60).

No single phase of Elliott's career perfectly exhibits the synthesis of labouring subject and muscular style that Carlyle's description encourages. Even in the 'political phase', the references to labour tend to be Shelleyan: less glorifications of manual prowess than opportunities to extend a theme of tyrannical oppression, as in the fourth of six poems called 'Song', which intones the message that 'freedom's foes mock'd labour's groan' (Elliott, 1831, p. 69). Elliott's opposition to the Corn Laws and the 'tax-bribed plough' led him to satirize pastoral convention, and with it the agrarian tradition of labour poetry that sets working rhythm to poetic rhythm.[43] The anti-reaper poem, 'Rogues v. Reason' exclaims 'Your cause is thresh'd – 'tis time! forgive / The husk that casts ye out; / And with your horrid bread-tax live, / Or try to live without.'[44] In these lines, the 'time' of political reform runs counter to the timing of the scythe. Elliott's perspective is that of the master of an enterprise who resents the privileges accorded to rural landowners. His vision relies on the simple equation ventured by his poem 'Reform', that 'They murder'd hope, they fetter'd trade' (1831, p. 75).

Elliott claimed to be an instinctual free-trader, and no doubt his radicalism was encouraged by the example of his father; but it was the failure of his business that clinched the political direction of travel, and it is in this respect that Carlyle most misjudges Elliott.[45] He never countenanced Elliott's radicalism, but he appears not to have appreciated its orientation, its appeal to competition rather than co-operation, its roots not in 'soot' and 'sweat', but in the politics of a trade position.[46] Though genuinely interested in securing the poor man's bread, Elliott made little attempt to distinguish that cause from the business-owner's unbridled capacity to compete with Continental enterprises, breaking with Chartism as soon as it abandoned its opposition to Protection. After the Chartists repudiated Corn-law Repeal, Elliott resigned from the Sheffield Working Men's Association, complaining that the real enemy was landed 'aristocracy' (Watkins, 1850, pp. 130–1). Carlyle projected on to Elliott his own hostility to '"Competition" and "*Laissez-faire*"', seemingly unaware that these were idols to his 'Corn Law Rhymer', not enemies (1832, p. 149). Given the close alignment of working-class politics and free-trade arguments in this period, the confusion is to a certain extent understandable.[47] Nevertheless, its effect was to aggravate the discrepancy between Elliott's actual poetic impetus, and Carlyle's view of it as intrinsically related to the life of the forge.

That Elliott could afford to rent a handsome stone villa in Upperthorpe, and was more iron-dealer than hammer-handler, is not in itself so interesting as what it reveals about Carlyle's need to believe in the possibility of a reconciliation between literature and 'work', and about his method, in deputing the task to an inspired 'mechanic' not obstructed by the 'dead letter' of education (Morris and Hearne, 2002, p. 38). A similarly vicarious approach to a 'solution' was employed later in the century by Ruskin, when he identified Sheffield, and the St George's Museum he founded there, as an arena in which 'workers in iron' could re-form the possibilities of artistic expression through an encounter between local workmanship and the history of European art. In both cases, the pressing concerns of an educated 'patron' were vested in the figure of the artisan, whose fixed social position was re-interpreted as a basis for untrammelled and 'authentic' creative expression.

The irony is that Elliott's 'labouring class' credentials were not in fact more impeccable than those of Carlyle. What Carlyle recognized, of course, was Elliott's lack of professional reliance on activities his father had condemned as 'idle tattle'. By clothing Elliott in the garb of a workingman, whose poetry was hammered out at the forge, he could reserve the possibility of a manually-inflected art, operating at a safe distance from Grub Street. As such, the misrecognition is best understood as a species of wishful thinking: Carlyle desired to find, beyond the craft identity he had been cultivating, the stature of an 'active poet' who could more fully realize a lettered repetition of his father's work on the bridge at Auldgarth. In a final twist, this process of identification eventually unsettles Carlyle's willingness to indulge Elliott as an exception: in the closing remarks of his review, he cannot help asking, 'Whether Rhyme is the only dialect he can write in; whether Rhyme is, after all, the natural or fittest dialect for him?' (1832, p. 165).

Notes

1. Note Devine's observation that while Scottish universities attracted a 'broader social range than Oxford and Cambridge', 'the hard evidence does not entirely support the myth of the "democratic intellect"' (2012, p. 175).

2. See Houghton, 1985, pp. 242–62 and Briggs, 1971.
3. See also Treadwell, 1998. Treadwell's emphasis differs from mine in stressing 'the dangerously Romantic notion that writing displaces or even *replaces* labour' (p. 241).
4. See, for instance, Goodridge, 2003 and 2006; Chase, 2007; Rose, 2001 and Sanders, 2009.
5. On the 'grammar-school boy', see Hoggart, 1958, p. 246. William Barnes is a similar example: I discuss his representations of field labour in Waithe, 2013.
6. See 'Anti-Intellectualism' in Houghton, 1985, pp. 110–36.
7. See Ruskin's 'Traffic', in which he explains that 'you will build with stone well, but with flesh better' (Ruskin, 1903–1912, XVIII, pp. 433–58 (p. 458)).
8. 'To C. A. Ward' (6 July 1854), Carlyle, 2012, para. 2 of 3.
9. The *OED* defines the Scottish and Northern English 'kenning' as '1. Teaching, instruction' and '5. a. Mental cognition; knowledge, cognizance; recognition.'; and 'canning' as 'Being able, ability'.
10. 'To Sarah Austin' (13 June 1833), Carlyle, 2012, para. 4 of 7.
11. 'To The House of Commons' (7 April 1839), Carlyle, ibid, para. 1; para. 4 and para. 8 of 11.
12. Carlyle, 1898, p. 184; Carlyle, 1841, pp. 154–95. See, for instance, Salmon, 2002.
13. 'To John Stuart Mill' (28 August 1832), Carlyle, 2012, para. 2 of 8.
14. Carlyle coined the term 'craftmanship' in *Chartism* (1840, p. 135); Carlyle, 2009, p. 6.
15. 'To Edward Strachey' (20 December 1848), Carlyle, 2012, para. 2 of 2.
16. 'To Elizabeth Gaskell' (8 November 1848), ibid., para. 2 of 3.
17. 'To Alexander Carlyle' (12 January 1822), ibid. para. 1 of 5.
18. 'To James Carlyle' (2 April 1823), ibid. para. 1 of 4.
19. See the *OED*'s note: 'sometimes applied to any business, calling, or profession by which a livelihood is earned' (IV. 6.a.).
20. Carlyle was paraphrasing Dahlmann, 1840–3; see Carlyle, 1838, pp. 201–310.
21. See Henry Thoreau's remark that 'the style is no more than the *stylus*, the pen he writes with' (1975, p. 232).
22. 'To Alexander Carlyle' (12 January 1822), Carlyle, 2012, para. 1 of 5.
23. The heavily revised First Draft of *Past and Present* (British Library ms. 41641) amply confirms Calder's verdict that 'Carlyle was both artisan and artist' (1949, p. 154).
24. Carlyle referred to his literary endeavours as an 'apprenticeship' in a letter to his brother: 'To Alexander Carlyle' (1 March 1820), Carlyle, 2012, para. 2 of 4.
25. 'To Jean Carlyle Aitken' (9 April 1835), Carlyle, 2012, para. 4 of 5; Carlyle, 1898, pp. 208–9.
26. See Houghton, 1985, pp. 196–217.
27. Carlyle, 1898, p. 255; 'To Macvey Napier' (6 February 1832), Carlyle, 2012, para. 4 of 6.
28. '*The Village Patriarch* A Poem', 1829, p. 93. The quotation marks in 'a poor man's poem' suggest that Elliott intended an allusion rather a self-description (Elliott, 1829, p. v).
29. 'To John A. Carlyle' (13 January 1852), Carlyle, 2012, para. 2 of 1.

30. Elliott, 1831. Carlyle also referred to *The Village Patriarch*, of which early editions were published in 1829 and 1831. For an account of the complicated publication history, see Storey in Elliott, 2010, p. 33.
31. Bulwer, 1831, p. 290; Elliott, 1829, p. viii. William Barnes replied similarly to criticism of his decision 'To write in . . . a fast out-wearing speech-form': 'I cannot help it', he confided (1862, p. iii).
32. According to Carlyle, Elliott claimed to be 'one of the lower, little removed above the lowest class' (Carlyle, 1832, p. 138). Elliott actually asked 'is it of no importance what a man of the middle class – hardly raised above the lowest, thinks – when the lowest are beginning to think?' (1829, p. vii).
33. Elliott's closest approach to poverty followed his bankruptcy in 1816, when he was reduced to accepting help from Earl Fitzwilliam (Morris and Hearne, 2002, p. 28). The phrase 'jobbing merchant' was applied by *Holden's Dollar Magazine* ((April 1850) Vol. V, No. IV, p. 225).
34. Elliott recalls his father working 'for a salary of sixty or seventy pounds a year, with house, candle and coal!' (in Watkins, 1850, p. 7).
35. Carlyle wrote to Macvey Napier on 8 April 1832, promising to deliver the review within two weeks (Carlyle, 2012, para. 2 of 3); by 18 May 1832, he was writing to J. S. Mill with the news that 'the Corn Law Rhymer has got his *Article*' (para. 4 of 7); see also, 'To Macvey Napier' (22 June 1832) (para. 2 of 5).
36. J. S. Mill misinformed Carlyle, both as to Elliott's name and occupation (Letter 51, 'To Thomas Carlyle' (29 May 1832) in Mill, 1963, p. 104). Carlyle, 1832, p. 144.
37. Morris and Hearne, 2002, p. 25. Advertisements in the local press indicate the scale of Elliott's operation: one offers 'a constant and complete assortment of IRON and STEEL' (*Sheffield Independent*, 4 February 1832); another offers to let 'four chambers' on Gibraltar Street to a 'Factor or Merchant, in extensive business' (*Sheffield Independent*, 2 June 1831).
38. Letter 'To Mr. Tait' (Watkins, 1850, p. 82). According to King, Elliott set up business on Gilbraltar Street with capital of £150, raised 'by the affectionate generosity of his wife's sisters', 'which accumulated something handsome, it is said a fortune!' (1854, p. 17).
39. See the petitions to Thomas Aline Ward, Esq. to serve as MP for Sheffield (*Sheffield Independent*, 17 September 1831), and to the Master Cutler requesting a mechanics' educational institute (*Sheffield Independent*, 13 October 1832). Elliott was also a special constable (*Sheffield Independent*, 25 April 1829).
40. Elliott, 1801, p. 11, p. 6. Elliott included an extended defence of the Lake Poets in the satirical 'dedication' to Byron that prefaces *The Giaour* (Elliott, 1823, pp. 133–80 (p. 136)).
41. See Elliott, 1820, addressed to 'a living pedant' (p. 3), and the anti-Byronic *The Giaour* (Elliott, 1823).
42. The sentence begins, 'But when suicidal anti-profit laws speak to my heart' (Elliott, 1831, p. vii).
43. 'Drone v. Worker', Elliott, 1831, pp. 55–7. See Jeremy Prynne on 'the exertion of a field-worker . . . who *also* sings, as a comfortable discharge of customary practice' (2007, pp. 11–20). See also an early and unidealized example of this convergence in 'The Thresher's Labour' by Stephen Duck (d. 1756) (Southey, 1831).

44. A correspondent signing himself 'Agricola' countered that 'the agricultural labourer, and the farmer himself, is obliged to live and is satisfied with the very refuse of what their [Sheffield operatives] appetites refuse' (*Sheffield Independent*, 15 June 1833, p. 1); 'Rogues *v*. Reason', Elliott, 1831, p. 61.
45. Elliott reflected that even in youth 'I was a free-trader, though I knew it not' (Watkins, 1850, p. 12).
46. See Searle, 1850, p. 131: 'Elliott was a redoubted champion of competition, and . . . he looked upon communism as fatal to the best interests of man.'
47. Carlyle would have understood Elliott better had he seen the dedication to Jeremy Bentham added to the 1833 edition of *The Splendid Village*, p. 45.

Bibliography

Barnes, William (1862) *Poems of Rural Life in the Dorset Dialect*, third collection (London: John Russell Smith).
Briggs, Asa (1971) 'Samuel Smiles and the Gospel of Labour', in *Victorian People: A Reassessment of Persons and Themes 1851–67* (Harmondsworth: Penguin Books), pp. 124–47.
Brown, Simon (1971) 'Ebenezer Elliott and Robert Southey: Southey's Break with the Quarterly Review', *Review of English Studies*, 22.87, 307–11.
Bulwer, Edward (1831) 'A Letter to Doctor Southey, &c. &c. Poet Laureate, Respecting a Remarkable Poem by a Mechanic, 19 March 1831', *New Monthly Magazine*, XXXI (April), 289–95.
Calder, Grace J. (1949) *The Writing of Past and Present: A Study of Carlyle's Manuscripts* (New Haven: Yale University Press).
Campbell, Ian (1974) *Thomas Carlyle* (London: Hamish Hamilton).
Carlyle, Thomas (1896–99) *Centenary Edition of The Works of Thomas Carlyle*, 30 vols, ed. H. D. Traill (London: Chapman and Hall).
——. (1827) 'State of German Literature', in *Critical and Miscellaneous Essays in Five Volumes*, I, in Carlyle, 1896–99, XXVI, pp. 26–86.
——. (1828) 'Burns', in *Critical and Miscellaneous Essays*, I, in Carlyle, 1896–99, XXVI, pp. 258–318.
——. (1832) 'Corn-Law Rhymes', in *Critical and Miscellaneous Essays*, III, in Carlyle, 1896–99, XXVIII, pp. 136–66.
——. (1838) 'The Early Kings of Norway', in *Critical and Miscellaneous Essays*, in Carlyle, 1896–99, XXX, pp. 201–310.
——. (1840) *Chartism*, in *Critical and Miscellaneous Essays*, IV, in Carlyle, 1896–99, XXIX, pp. 118–204.
——. (1841) *On Heroes, Hero-Worship and the Heroic in History*, in Carlyle, 1896–99, V.
——. (1843) *Past and Present*, in Carlyle, 1896–99, X.
——. (1850) *Latter-Day Pamphlets*, in Carlyle, 1896–99, XX.
——. (1898) *Two Notebooks of Thomas Carlyle from 23rd March 1822 to 16th May 1832*, ed. Charles Eliot Norton (New York: The Grolier Club).
——. (2009) 'James Carlyle', in *Reminiscences*, ed. Ian Campbell and K. J. Fielding (Glasgow: Kennedy & Boyd), pp. 1–33.
——. (2012) *The Carlyle Letters Online*, co-ordinating editor Brett E. Kinser, senior eds. Ian M. Campbell, Aileen Christianson and David R. Sorensen (Duke University Press), carlyleletters.org.

Chase, Malcolm (2007) *Chartism: A New History* (Manchester: Manchester University Press).
Dahlmann, F. C. (1840–3) *Geschicte von Dannemark*, 3 vols (Hamburg).
DeLaura, David (2004) 'Carlyle and the "Insane" Fine Arts', in *The Carlyles at Home & Abroad: Essays in Honour of Kenneth J. Fielding*, ed. David Sorensen and Rodger Tarr (Aldershot: Ashgate), pp. 27–37.
Devine, T. M. (2012) 'A Global Diaspora', in *The Oxford Handbook of Modern Scottish History*, ed. T. M. Devine and Jenny Wormald (Oxford: Oxford University Press), pp. 159–82.
Dickens, Charles (1851) 'Ebenezer Elliott', *Household Words*, II, 232–8.
Elliott, Ebenezer (1801) *The Vernal Walk* (Cambridge: B. Flower).
——. (1810) *The Soldier and Other Poems* (Harlow).
——. (1818) *Night: A Descriptive Poem* (London: Rotherham).
——. (1820) *Peter Faultless to his Brother Simon; Tales of Night, in Rhyme, and Other Poems* (Edinburgh: Archibald Constable & Co.).
——. (1823) *Love, a Poem in Three Parts to which is added, The Giaour, a Satirical Poem (Addressed to Lord Byron)* (London: C. Stocking).
——. (1829) *The Village Patriarch: A Poem* (London: Edward Bull, Holles Street).
——. (1831) *Corn Law Rhymes*, 3rd edn (London: B. Steill).
——. (1833) *The Splendid Village: Corn Law Rhymes, and Other Poems* (London: Benjamin Steill).
——. (2010) *Selected Poetry of Ebenezer Elliott*, ed. Mark Storey (Cranbury, NJ: Associated University Presses).
'Gallery of Literary Characters: No. XXVIII ALLAN CUNNINGHAM, ESQ' (1832) *Fraser's Magazine*, VI (Aug – Dec), 248–9.
Gaskell, Elizabeth (2006) *Mary Barton*, ed. Shirley Foster (Oxford: Oxford University Press).
Goodridge, John, gen. ed. (2003, 2006) *Eighteenth- and Nineteenth-Century English Labouring-Class Poets*, 6 vols (London: Pickering & Chatto).
Guest, Kristen (2004) 'Dyspeptic Reactions: Thomas Carlyle and the Byronic Temper', in *Nervous Reactions: Victorian Recollections of Romanticism*, ed. Joel Faflak and Julian Wright (Albany: SUNY Press), pp. 141–61.
Hoggart, Richard (1958) *The Uses of Literacy: Aspects of Working-Class Life with Special Reference to Publications and Entertainments* (Harmondsworth: Penguin).
Houghton, Walter (1985) *The Victorian Frame of Mind, 1830–1870* (New Haven: Yale University Press).
Ikeler, A. Abbott (1972) *Puritan Temper and Transcendental Faith: Carlyle's Literary Vision* (Columbus: Ohio State University Press).
King, J. W. (1854) *Ebenezer Elliott: A Sketch, with Copious Extracts from his Descriptive Poems* (Sheffield: S. Harrison).
Mill, John Stuart (1996) 'The Negro Question', in *Essays on Equality, Law, and Education*, ed. John Robson, *The Collected Works of John Stuart Mill* (London: Routledge), XXI, pp. 85–95.
——. (1963) *The Earlier Letters of John Stuart Mill, 1812–1848*, ed. Francis E. Mineka (London: Routledge).
Morris, Keith and Ray Hearne (2002) *Ebenezer Elliot: Corn Law Rhymer & Poet of the Poor* (Rotherham: Rotherwood Press).
Prynne, Jeremy (2007) *Field Notes: 'The Solitary Reaper' and Others* (Cambridge: Cambridge University Press).

Rose, Jonathan (2001) *The Intellectual Life of the British Working Classes* (New Haven and London: Yale University Press).

Ruskin, John (1903–12) *The Crown of Wild Olive*, in *The Library Edition of the Works of John Ruskin*, 39 vols, ed. E. T. Cook and Alexander Wedderburn (London: George Allen), XVIII, pp. 433–58.

Salmon, Richard (2002) 'Thomas Carlyle and the Idolatry of the Man of Letters', *Journal of Victorian Culture*, 7, 1–22.

Sanders, Mike (2009) *The Poetry of Chartism: Aesthetics, Politics, History* (Cambridge: Cambridge University Press).

Searle, January (1850) *The Life, Character and Genius of Ebenezer Elliott, the Corn-Law Rhymer* (London: Charles Gilpin).

Seary, E. R. (1939) 'Robert Southey and Ebenezer Elliott: Some New Southey Letters', *Review of English Studies*, 15.60, 412–21.

Southey, Robert (1831) 'An Introductory Essay' in *Attempts in Verse by John Jones, an Old Servant* (London: John Murray), pp. 1–168.

Sowerby, James (1870) *English Botany; or, Colour Figures of British Plants, with their Essential Characters, Synonyms and Places of Growth* (London).

Thoreau, Henry (1975) 'Thomas Carlyle and his Works', in *Early Essays and Miscellanies, The Writings of Henry D. Thoreau* (New Jersey: Princeton University Press), pp. 219–67.

Treadwell, James (1998) '*Sartor Resartus* and the Work of Writing', *Essays in Criticism*, 48, 224–43.

'*The Village Patriarch*: A Poem' (1829) *Westminster Review*, XI (July–October), 92–6.

Waithe, Marcus (2011) 'Hill, Ruskin and Intrinsic Value', in *Geoffrey Hill and his Contexts*, ed. Piers Pennington and Matthew Sperling (Oxford: Peter Lang), pp. 133–49.

——. (forthcoming 2013) 'William Barnes: Views of Field Labour in *Poems of Rural Life*', in *The Oxford Handbook of Victorian Poetry*, ed. Matthew Bevis (Oxford: Oxford University Press).

Watkins, John (1850) *Life, Poetry and Letters of Ebenezer Elliott, The Corn-Law Rhymer* (London: John Mortimer).

Williams, Raymond (1968) *Culture and Society 1780–1950* (Harmondsworth: Penguin).

Wolven, Karen (1999) 'Ebenezer Elliott, The "Corn-Law Rhymer": Poor Men Do Write – The Emergence of Class Identity within a Poetry of Transition', in *Victorian Keats and Romantic Carlyle: The Fusions and Confusions of Literary Periods*, ed. C. C. Barfoot (Amsterdam: Editions Rodopi), pp. 235–46.

8
Samuel Ferguson's Maudlin Jumble

Matthew Campbell

> One thing more before I cease; if I were asked to characterize, as shortly as may be, these poems, I should do so by applying to them the words of Spenser, 'barbarous truth'.
>
> (Yeats, 1886; 1970, p. 87)

The new Irish lyric in English after Thomas Moore gave as many opportunities for Tory fun as it did for radical censure, combining the rude and the refined or the authentic and the counterfeit in a strange synthetic stew. If Erin had a tear and a smile in its eye, the mixing of the modes might also be difficult to pin down: the tear was allied to a subject-matter grounded in political as much as amorous defeat and the smile suggested that amorous or political mischief was never far away. Moore, author of the bestselling *Irish Melodies*, was not just the friend of Byron, but his biographer and co-conspirator in the destruction of the supposedly scandalous journals. He was also the thinly-veiled ventriloquist behind the *Memoirs of Captain Rock* (1824) a text rather closer to Irish mischief than its author's London Whig connections might suggest. One of Moore's successors, the young barrister and unionist antiquarian Samuel Ferguson, writing for an Irish Tory audience, was more willing to accept that the tear was the true expression of Gaelic poetry and music. He would, however, not shirk translating the strangeness of writing from a Catholic culture which retained more than just a memory of its Gaelic past. Not only was it not wholly vanquished, but after the Emancipation of 1829, it was turning its attentions to the Union of 1801 itself. As an educated Protestant with Scottish heritage, Ferguson was separated from the Catholic Irish poetic tradition by both class and religion, but what he sought to do as a translator was deliberately to engage in the creation or recreation of an Irish canon, in which the rude 'peasant' songs of Gaelic would form an integral part of a newly imagined Irish culture. Through this canon, difficulties of class, not to mention religion, nationality and politics, would be elided. The successes of Daniel O'Connell's popular politics in the late-1820s and early '30s were not so much antipathetic background to Ferguson's work as spur. Along with the unionist intellectuals involved in the establishment of the *Dublin University Magazine* in 1833, Ferguson sought to understand the persistence of the culture of a once-pauperized Gaelic Ireland now turning into a mass English-speaking and increasingly English-reading constituency which was enjoying a first partial enfranchisement. By the 1840s its first experiments in democracy were to find, in the nationalism of the Young Irelanders, an ideology developed from the French-inspired republicanism of the United Irishmen of forty years previously. According to Joep Leerssen, one difference between the 1790s and the 1840s was that 'a massive cultural transference took place in Ireland between the Gaelic tradition and the urban English-speaking educated classes' and resulted in 'a complete Gaelic re-orientation of Ireland's public space and public sphere, particularly after Catholic Emancipation'.[1] Leerssen's 'massive cultural transference' or 'complete Gaelic re-orientation' may look slightly counter-intuitive, given the great shift to the English language along with the move to the cities which occurred in these decades. But to take one small example, among the first students enrolled to learn Irish in the newly-formed Ulster Gaelic Society in Belfast in 1830 were the Protestant Trinity unionist Samuel Ferguson and his schoolfriend, later Britain's first Catholic Lord Chancellor under William Gladstone, Thomas O'Hagan.[2] If Leerssen's 'complete Gaelic re-orientation' was given impetus by the participation in the project of the recovery of Gaelic by men concerned to make establishment careers such as Ferguson and O'Hagan, the literary and linguistic interest of that establishment in Gaelic culture was accompanied by a fear that a political transformation might follow the renewed cultural confidence of newly-urban English-speaking and English-reading Catholics. Up to the middle of the 1840s, when Famine was to disperse cultural revival along with a large part of the population of Catholic Ireland, the Unionist fear, as expressed a few years previously in Ferguson's 1833 *Dublin University Magazine* article, 'A Dialogue Between the Head and Heart of an Irish Protestant', was that this combination of political enfranchisement and cultural resurgence might result not just in repeal of the union, but 'a violent separation' (p. 587).

Ferguson's early work served a post-Emancipation unionist readership which needed to understand the new challenge to its supposed ascendancy. He found the grounds for this understanding in the matter of the poetry and song which had been revealed to English-speaking Ireland by antiquarian research. He also found the matter of that poetry to be inextricably bound up in aesthetic questions, and in particular the question of finding adequate forms for the new English versions of this source material. Ferguson wrote in the *Dublin University Magazine* that no matter how modern, and thus inauthentic, the polite measures or prosodic proprieties of Tom Moore appeared to be, his lyrics still shared something with sources which appeared to come not just from a different aesthetic but a different society. Nevertheless, they offered common ground, if not community:

> The contrast between the native songs and the lyrics of Moore, is indeed strangely striking – as strange as uncouthness can present in juxta position [sic] with politeness, but still no more than that which may be admitted to have distinguished the *Merus Hibernicus*, from the modern Irish gentleman. We will look in vain for the chasteness, the appositeness, the antithetical and epigrammatic point, and the measured propriety of prosody, which delight the ear and the judgement, in a song by Thomas Moore, among the rude rhymes which accompanied the same notes two centuries ago; but the stamen and essence of each is interwoven and transfused through the whole texture and complexion of the other – for sentiment is the soul of song, and sentiment is the one imprescriptible property of the common blood of all Irishmen. (Ferguson, 1834, II, pp. 153–4)

Elsewhere Ferguson was wary of the organicism implicit in bringing the 'juxta position' of the uncouth and the polite forward into union, but here he does dally with metaphors of grafting which are allowed one further mix, into the troubled matter of 'common blood'.

To go from stamen to essence looks like a simple rhetorical shift in synonym, but going from texture to complexion seems inevitably here to lead to blood. It is stirred by sentiment: the 'one imprescriptible property of the common blood of all Irishmen' is the tear rather than the smile. Ferguson later asked that his readers 'no longer imagine that humour is the characteristic of the Irish. Their sentiment is pathetic. Desire is the essence of that pathos' (Ferguson, 1834, II, p. 155). Claiming this 'imprescriptible property' of sentiment for his Protestant readership, would enable them to claim the post-Union protestant patriotism for which Ferguson argued with much anguish. In one of its most telling passages, the 1833 'Dialogue' feared that the rewards of loyalism might be no more than the loss of identity within both Ireland and the larger United Kingdom, since the Irish Protestants might end up, 'neither English nor Irish, fish nor flesh, but a peddling colony, a forlorn advanced guard that must conform to every mutinous movement of the praetorian rabble' (p. 591).

To suggest a share in the 'common blood' which has as its property the sentiment expressed in Irish song is thus not quite a prefiguring of an Arnoldian annexation of the imagined Celt into the British racial mix. As the 'Heart' side had earlier averred in the 'Dialogue', 'I know not whence my blood may have been drawn, but it circulates with a swifter liveliness at the name of this country, and I feel and know that I am the heart of an Irishman' (Ferguson, 1833, p. 589). This is more an early-Victorian physiology of blood-stirring patriotism than the racial categories of mid-Victorian anthropology. Eve Patten suggests that Ferguson's part of the *Dublin University Magazine* project from the early 1830s through to the great disruption of intellectual revival by Famine in the latter half of the 1840s, was that of 'the young critic playing to a hard-line unionist gallery' (2004, p. 25), and this might ultimately have been the case. But Ferguson's translating practice and its aesthetic strictures – in particular the terms under which he suggests an English-language culture might thrive in Ireland – were placed in negotiation with the recovery and translation of an Irish-language culture and a respect for its corresponding aesthetic strictures. If the end result was to be an argument for Union, then its considerable sophistication was that it was founded in a literary negotiation prefigured as a sort of poetic power-sharing, in which an intuition of a commonality of culture might be allowed to follow the metaphors of a commonality of the blood of the patriot, whether Irish or British, Catholic or Protestant. Ferguson aspired to forge an imagined community which might mature enough in the United Kingdom to allow a peaceful admission of class, sectarian and linguistic differences.

Finding that the first translating efforts to render anew in English the older Irish poetry were unsatisfactory, he sought recompense in translation of a feudal bardic tradition and its successor in Jacobite lyric, both of which he saw as inherently pious (albeit Catholic) and thus recoverably conservative. But he was also prepared to do service in a late flowering of the sentimental expressiveness of a broadly-conceived British Romanticism. The Irish contribution would be to find, after the example of Robert Burns or William Wordsworth, its own musical museum or lyrical ballads. As Patten has pointed out, this was a matter of civic idealism as much as scholarly conscience or poetic opportunity, a recasting of Irish unionist patriotism in the interests of a new intelligentsia in a post-Union Dublin beginning to re-establish its cultural if not political independence within the United Kingdom. Patten rightly emphasizes the example of eighteenth-century Scotland for Ferguson and his contemporaries as one British example of a public sphere created in the conditions of vibrant print culture (2004, pp. 29–52). Colin Graham goes further, stating that 'Scotland is the site in which Ferguson frequently tests out how to configure Irish difference, and, most importantly, how tactically to place Ireland over against England in order to further his goal of bringing Ireland to the centre of the union, giving it, to twist a phrase, "parity of esteem" within the United Kingdom' (2009, p. 25). Ferguson began his publishing career in *Blackwood's Edinburgh Magazine* and it was to provide one model for the *Dublin University Magazine* as a deliberately Irish-centred unionist forum. After Ossian, and as one of the great corrective voices of poetic authenticity, Burns in particular provided a connection between something working in a register which was not only lower class but in a supposedly lower aesthetic register, namely folk song. But the lyrics of British folk song provided extraordinary imaginative impetus for the development of British Romantic art song and poetry, both from the simplicity of diction and sentiment in lyric (the Wordsworthian 'real language of men') and the strong narrative drive of the ballad.

Ferguson nursed a fancy that Burns was 'in all probability of Irish blood', if only on the grounds that, 'Had he been a foundling, his face alone would have been considered Irish enough for similar surmise' (Ferguson, 1834, II, p. 156). But it was the songs that Burns collected, edited and composed which suggested to Irish poets a successful class encounter between the civilized and the barbarous, enabling them to effect the creative linguistic combination of the synthetic in the institutions of the Scottish public realm. This was a combination now in need of creation in Ireland. In the mid-1840s, Ferguson saw that Burns's acceptance by 'civilizing institutions' could be of benefit for the programme of a strong Irish literary culture. He also wondered why it had as yet to happen:

> Perhaps the main distinction will be found in the use of a language of civilization, and in the presence of civilizing institutions to which the people were attached. The accident of using a barbarous, or a polished language undoubtedly makes the greatest difference . . . Yet for

a long time we have had the language and institutions under which these tastes grew up in Scotland among us here; and the question may reasonably be urged – why have they not here been attended with the like results? (Ferguson, 1845, II, p. 293)

This is one of a number of statements of the question in the 1840s, made by Ferguson's nationalist contemporaries grouped around *The Nation* newspaper, which, as I have discussed elsewhere, look very much like the statements later to be made again in the 1880s and 1890s at the beginning of an Irish revival which had separatist aims (Campbell, 2010). Ferguson's hope in 1845, given the promotion of original Irish writing in an organ of a different political bent from the *Dublin University Magazine*, *The Nation*, was that Irish literary culture was beginning to develop 'like results'. His 1847 'Lament for Thomas Davis', for instance, gains much of its power from the great sense of the loss of one exemplar for incipient 1840s literary revival. The other fact of loss, suggested throughout the 'Lament' in its metaphors of harvest and its failure, as well as its mode of indigenous Irish pastoral elegy, was that of Famine and the turning of revival to economic catastrophe and political upheaval as the 1840s progressed.

Yet even in the spring of 1845, writing just before the first failures of the potato crop, Ferguson saw that Ireland had yet to establish the social and political conditions for the encouragement of a figure like Burns. This was not just the security of recent Scottish history and its 'ten thousand modes of peaceful prosperity, and of respect at home and abroad'. It was also:

that the middle and upper classes of that country were then, as they still are, proudly national, interested in every thing that concerns the interests or reputation of their native land; familiar with its local peculiarities of manners and dialect, and piquing themselves on the perfect sympathy that subsisted between them and the peasantry. If a young Irish farmer of the present day displayed ability, or wrote humorous, pathetic or philosophic verses, he might perhaps look for the worthless laudation of a local newspaper, provided there was a local newspaper of his party within reach; but that he should expect to be taken by the hand and caressed by the gentry of his neighbourhood, that he should hope, even, if he expressed himself with the independence becoming a man of genius, to avoid suspicion and repulse from his neighbours of condition, would be a thing unheard of – a mere suggestion of romance. (Ferguson, 1845, II, p. 293)

Ferguson's suggestion that Scotland provided a culture that nourished labouring-class writing, whereas Ireland did not, is of course unduly predicated on the imagined persistence of feudalism in Scotland. To ally this with a reiteration of the claim for an Irish sense of nationality to equal that of Scotland, as made in the 1833 'Dialogue' by one who might be thought to be loyal to the Union, makes Ferguson's contribution not so much an analysis of a culture in need of new matter and new forms, as a prescription for its remedy. To return to the Hardiman articles of the previous decade, Ferguson had already suggested that the remedy lay in the supposed barbarity of the Gaelic folk song tradition, and the seemingly reckless abandon of its fugitive authors.

Ferguson's various versions of the lyric 'Páistín Fionn' (little fair child or fair girl) are exemplary of his celebration of the mixture of desire and pathos in Irish song, allied to a sense of the thrill of the loose living of those of another epoch, another class. He called that mixture a 'maudlin jumble'. The publishing afterlife of the song meant republication in Ferguson's 1865 *Lays of the Western Gael*, a markedly different narrative version by Douglas Hyde in his 1893 *Love Songs of Connacht*, and a place in Thomas MacDonagh's select anthology of poems of the Irish Mode in *Literature in Ireland* (Ferguson, 1865, pp. 204–6; Hyde, 1893, pp. 49–52; MacDonagh, 1996, pp. 129–30). It is still in the repertoire of the traditional singer, often in macaronic versions. Yeats also published a number of versions of the lyric based on Ferguson's translation. It was first inserted into the 1911 revision of the one-act play *A Pot of Broth* along with the Tramp character's imagined memory of its performance by the lovesick boys of the parish: 'such of them that had any voice at all and not choked with crying, or senseless with the drop of drink they took to comfort them and to keep their wits from going, with the loss of you'. The Tramp relates its composition by a lovesick artisan poet:

> I was standing by the man that made the song, and he writing it with the old bit of a carpenter's pencil, and the tears running down –
>
>> My Paistin Finn is my sole desire,
>> And I am shrunken to skin and bone,
>> For all my heart has had for its hire
>> Is what I can whistle alone and alone.
>>   *Oro, oro!*
>> *To-morrow night I will break down the door.*
>
>> (Yeats, 1952, pp. 99–100)

The lyric eventually came fully into the Yeats canon in 1935, as one of 'Two Songs Rewritten for the Tune's Sake' (Yeats, 1957, pp. 550–1). In 1834, Ferguson's initial introduction of the song didn't promise much, but the terms are the same as those offered by Yeats's Tramp. Ferguson ventured an unmetrical translation of the final stanza and glossed it thus:

> Now, this is the conclusion of as maudlin a jumble of incongruous parts as ever came staggering into the imagination of a man half-drunk, half-desperate; yet it is arranged with a perfect minuteness of verbal propriety. When we call it a maudlin jumble, we do not mean to say that it makes the worse song. We are sure Pastheen Finn thought it all the better for evincing, as it does, the bothered state to which she had reduced her sweetheart; and only wondered, as we do, how, under the united influences of such a quantity of love and drink, he could attend so clearly to the minor details of a subject, the general arrangement of which appears to have so much perplexed him. (1834, II, p. 163)

The stanza which provokes this praise of an aesthetic of incongruity alternating with 'perfect minuteness of verbal propriety' had been translated at first literally from the Irish text given by Hardiman:

> Tréigfead mo chápáid 's mo cháirde gaoil
> U'r tréigfid mé á mhaireann de mhnáibh a' t-saoíghil;
> Ní thréigfead le'm mharthainn tú, ghrádh mo chróidhe!
> Go sínfear á g-cómhra faoí chlár mé.[3]
>
> I shall forsake my friends and my friendly relations,
> And I shall forsake all the other girls in the world;
> But I shall not forsake, during my existence, you, love of my heart,
> Till I be laid in the coffin under the clay!
>
> (Ferguson, 1834, II, p. 163)

In its way, this looks like a stock declaration of undying love. But Ferguson has drawn our attention to 'the minor details' and these appeared in the eventual metrical version of the song published as one of the twenty 'Versions from the Original Irish' appended to the fourth and final article in the series.

These are the last three stanzas as printed in the fourth of the Hardiman articles in November 1834:

> Were I in the town where's mirth and glee,
> Or twixt two barrels of barley bree,
> With my fair Pastheen upon my knee,
> 'Tis I would drink to her pleasantly!
>   Then Oro, come with me, come with me, come with me,
>   Oro, come with me, brown girl sweet!
>   And, oh, I would go through snow and sleet,
>   If you would come with me, my brown girl sweet!
>
> Nine nights I lay in longing and pain,
> Betwixt two bushes, beneath the rain,
> Thinking to see you, love, once again;
> But whistle and call were all in vain –
>   Then, Oro, come with me, etc.
>
> I'll leave my people, both friend and foe,
> From all the girls in the world I'll go,
> But from you sweetheart, oh, never, oh, no,
> 'Till I in the coffin, stretched cold and low!
>   Then Oro, come with me, etc.
>
>   ('Pastheen Finn', in Ferguson, 1834, IV, pp. 535–6)

Ferguson's gloss is in keeping with the precocity of his performance in the Hardiman articles as a whole, and, as he had shown in his 1833 'Dialogue', what he describes as an instinctive desire to 'declare ourselves one of the number of those who can feel for, and sympathise with, the poor Papist' (1834, I, p. 465). If Ferguson at one stage suggests he might feel one with the papist, he eventually holds back from such union, and a romantic feeling for the oppressed, meets its successor, Victorian 'sympathy'. In his understanding of a lyric like 'Páistín Fionn' Ferguson aspires in his Hardiman articles to serve what will become both a romantic and an antiquarian ideal, of the understanding and toleration of difference not unity within the whole culture of Ireland. With remarkable prescience, Ferguson's early *Dublin University Magazine* essays work out in the 1830s a formula for the cessation of antagonism and hostility through tolerance within the United Kingdom.

A 'maudlin jumble' is not a continuous, sympathetic, unified, aesthetic artefact. Whatever the mimetic achievement of the drunken desperation of the lover speaking through a drunkenly desperate lyric, Ferguson can admit that the jumble of incongruous parts is matched by perfect minuteness of verbal propriety. He wonders at the art of the translated balladeer while worrying over his state of mind. Little is hidden or sentimentalized in Ferguson's version: the girl's lover veers from the fantasy of two full barrels of beer and easy sex to the desperation of his nine nights sleeping out alone in the rain, and the eventual imagining of his own ageing and lovestruck death. Those two barrels, two bushes, and nine nights are retained in Yeats's version, which in its eventual revision and publication becomes a lyric attached to an aged libertine, a song from an old man, perhaps a dirty old man. The two barrels, two bushes, and nine nights suggest either some blaspheming on Catholic liturgical numerology (the novena, for instance) or naturalistic particularity: the indigent lyricist really did sleep out for nine nights. The lyric is barely constrained in sentiment, while precise and economical in expression: the pleading of the refrain conveys simple unornamented desire for its peasant object, who despite her fair hair has the sunburnt skin of the worker in the fields: she is a brown girl sweet. Ferguson allows in the characteristic prosodic decorations of direct repetition (brown girl sweet rhymes with itself), and the lyric extravagance of obsessive internal rhyme: 'And oh, I would go, through snow and sleet'.

And he makes certain decisions about translating the Gaelic, both literally and in terms of the considerations of finding adequate English verse form. Take the stanza above with the two barrels of beer. This was Hardiman's 1831 Gaelic 'original':

> Dá mbeinnse insa mbaile i mbí súgra is greann.
> Nó idir dhá bharaille lán de leann;
> Mo shiúirín im aice's mo lámh faoina ceann,
> Is súgach do ólfainn a sláint.
>   Is óró bog liomsa! Bog liomsa! Bog liomsa!
>   Is óró bog liomsa! A chailín dheas dhonn!
>   Is óró bhogfainn, dá mbogfása lion
>   I dtús an phluide go sásta.
>
> (Hardiman, 1831, I, p. 218)

Here is Ferguson's literal translation in the April Hardiman reviews:

> If I were in the town where's mirth and glee,
> Or between two barrels full of ale,
> My little darling near me, and my hand under her head,
> It is pleasantly I'd drink her health.
> Then vourneen come with me – come with me – come with me,
> And vourneen come with me – damsel beautiful, brown;
> And vourneen I would go, if you would go with me!
>
> (Ferguson, 1834, I, pp. 465–6)

If we compare these versions with the eventual English poetic version printed the following November, we can say with Breandán Ó Buachalla that, 'the basis of Ferguson's success was his strict adherence to the line as the basic metrical and semantic unit . . . [in his translating] whatever difference there is being due mainly to metrical exigencies'. Ó Buachalla is clear that 'the 'different phonological and prosodic systems' of Irish and English mean that it is 'well-nigh impossible to render Irish metres into English', but he does allow the success of an effect in another of Ferguson's translations where he 'let the metrical line run free except for the final foot' (1987, pp. 33–4).

That is, in deciding on an eventual English-language poetic version in 1834, Ferguson brings it all back into rhyme. There, the triple feet which introduce four full rhymes – mirth and glee, barley bree, upon my knee, pleasantly – sound strange, even primitive, in English. And the odd word there, bree, is another sort of translation, of beer into whiskey, and Scotch whiskey at that. Burns's 'Scotch Drink', first published in the Kilmarnock edition of his *Poems* in 1786, counsels, 'How easy can the *barley-bree* / cement the quarrel'. Keats picked up the phrasing in his sonnet written in Burns's cottage in Ayr in 1818, finding 'My pulse is warm with thine own barley-bree.'[4] Whether Scots-derived or not, the first line of Ferguson's version of 'Páistín Fionn', to follow Ó Buachalla, is hardly even English, syntactically or prosodically: 'Were I in the town where's mirth and glee': 'were' and 'where' link together a line trying not to break up into English common measure at 'town' – although 'town' does pick up its assonantal music at mid-point later in the stanza, with Pastheen and drink, and then in the refrain, 'brown', 'snow' and 'brown' again. English is carrying an approximation of both the Irish song and its tune, in assonantal, slant and even sight rhymes.

To grasp just how fresh Ferguson's achievement was in his translation of this little lyric, it must be remembered that he had another English version of the song in mind when he made his. It is one to which he was aware his would act as a corrective, or a sort of counter-translation. It is John D'Alton's English version, supplied by Hardiman in the *Irish Minstrelsy*.

> With what rapture I'd quaff it, were I in the hall
> Where feasting – and pledging – and music recall
> Proud days of my country! While she on my breast
> Would recline, my heart's twin one! And hallow the feast.
>   Then Vourneen! fly with me – fly with me – fly with me
>   With thy nut-brown ringlets so artlessly curled;
>   Here is the one that will live and will die with thee,
>   Thy guard and thy guide through the wilds of the world.
>
> (qtd Hardiman, 1831, I, pp. 217–19)

Starting with the word 'quaffed', D'Alton never gives us more than an insipid drawing room version of the stanzas. The whiskey barrels are translated into a civic banquet and the desire until death of Ferguson's version is written as drawing-room pastiche, a series of stock sentiments of regret, memory and immortality, stray angels and all. One particularly unfortunate solecism exchanges the brown skin of the blonde country girl (páistin fionn, fair-haired girl) for a dye-job and a perm: 'nut-brown ringlets so artlessly curled'.

Nothing could be further from the Romantic characteristics of Irish song, as they appeared to Ferguson: 'Desire, despair, and the horrible reality of actual famine – these are the three dread prompters of song', he says. Together they make 'nothing impure, nothing licentious' but rather the 'savage sincerity' which is characteristic of Irish poetry:

> in its association with the despondency of conscious degradation, and the recklessness of desperate content, is partly to be found the origin of that wild, mournful, incondite yet not uncouth sentiment which distinguishes the national songs of Ireland from those of perhaps any other nation of the world.

On the one hand this is an assertion of the utter singularity of Irish song. On the other, it represents the challenge to the English poem, or the poet writing in English who might hazard a translation or version of this savage sincerity given the inherent differences of the English and the Irish:

> We believe that no dissipating continuance of defeat, danger, famine, or misgovernment, could ever, without the infusion of Milesian blood, Hibernicize the English Peasant; and that no stultifying operation of mere security, plenty or laborious regularity could ever, without actual physical transubstantiation, reduce the native Irishman to the stolid standard of the sober Saxon. (Ferguson, 1834, II, pp. 154–5)

If we hear an irony directed at hybridity here, in Ferguson's 'infusion' and 'transubstantiation', he still moves the argument on. In the third article his own savagery is reserved for the long footnote in which the severe problems he notes in D'Alton's versions in Hardiman are, he suggests, even more marked in other contributors:

> Mr D'Alton's perversions are, however, mere petty-larceny travesties compared with the epic grandeur of Mr Curran's heroic declaration of war against the original. This fierce invader of the barrenness of Irish Literature, gives no quarter to the absence of whatever tropes, sentiments or episodes he may conceive best suited to its creditable Saxonisation. War to the knife against all deficiencies is his slogan, and with pruning-hook in one hand and grafting-knife in the other, he hacks, he hews, he notches, buds, mortises, and mangles; sticks in a ramification of metaphors here, claps on a mistletoe-bough of parasite flowers there, and, in a word, so metamorphoses the original, that it (the Roman Vision for instance,) comes out of his hands as unlike itself as an espalier stock that has been once a crab-tree. (1834, III, p. 455n)

Ferguson particularly savours the irony of the English-language half of Hardiman's ur-nationalist project aspiring for full 'Saxonisation'. But with this emphasis on incongruous parts and maudlin jumble as opposed to Hibernicizing the English peasant or Saxonizing the Irish poem, what does the unionist Ferguson think he is doing in his contribution to this debate? While he seems to be both courting and parodying a discourse of impurity and adulteration, there is also a suggestion that his is an altogether more earnest attempt to revert back to some unadulterated, unadulterable, pre-hybrid feudal state, in which the Irish character existed before or beyond its language, culture, religion and class. A new variety must result from the grafting of a maudlin jumble in the process of Saxonization.

The extra complication of course, is that the aesthetic limits placed on the new hybrid form as it crosses over in the process of translation may be at odds with the political aspirations of the critic who describes them. Ferguson, after all, was writing in an organ associated with the landed, Protestant class in Ireland. In the self-same articles he defended property and Union as the honourable result of a victory won by the class from which he came and for which he wrote. He himself was of Ulster-Scottish 'stock', certainly not willing to be grafted on to the aboriginal Irish Catholic masses. Yet through the ironies of his criticism of the nationalist Hardiman he seems to hold out against the aesthetic and antiquarian dangers which Hardiman's practice had unwittingly courted. That is the grafting of the savagely sincere feudal Irish ballad with the polite Whig British lyric, or the intermingling and eventual blending of cultures and classes which might have resulted in the new hybrid poetry of the united (for thirty years or so, by the time of Ferguson's articles) United Kingdom of Great Britain and Ireland. He certainly did not ascribe to the hopes of one originator of English versions of Irish poems, Charlotte Brooke, who wrote well before revolution or Union of the 'nearer acquaintance' between Britain and Ireland that would be achieved by poetry, an acquaintance bearing family resemblances: 'Let them tell her, that the portion of her blood which flows in our veins is rather ennobled than disgraced by the mingling tides that descended from our heroic ancestors' (1789, p. viii). Brooke envisages her act of translation of Irish poems as creating the circumstances for seduction, teasing the Irish muse out of her embowered state. Not that this teasing need then result in the marriage of Ireland and Britain: that is a fact already for Brooke, given the ennobling of British blood through its mingling with the greater antiquity of Irish heroic tradition.

Samuel Ferguson's version of this is perhaps the best remembered part of his Hardiman articles. He does not envisage that his antiquarian project seeks only the high ground of culture, transcending sectarian, class or political conflict. Rather, at the end of the third article, the *Dublin University Magazine* unionist envisages the 'perfect society' of the 'nation' (his terminology) as shown through the conservative principles that the Irish poetry before him shows. But this will not result in a bland union. Before presenting the reader with his version of 'The Fair Hills of Holy Ireland' / 'Uileacan dubh O!', Ferguson swaps the high ground for love of country.

> Alas that a nation glowing with the most enthusiastic courage, moved by the tenderest sympathies, and penetrated by a constitutional piety as devoted as profound, should so long have misapplied these noblest attributes of a high-destined people! What material for an almost perfect society does the national genius not represent? Instinctive piety, to lay the only sure foundation of human morals and immortal hopes; constitutional loyalty, to preserve the civil compact inviolate; legitimate affection, to ensure public virtue and private happiness; endless humour, to quicken social intercourse; and last, and save one attribute, best, indomitable love of country to consolidate the whole.
>
> This sacred loyalty we have reserved for our conclusion, as a green spot of neutral ground, where all parties may meet in kindness, and part in peace. (Ferguson, 1834, III, p. 467)

This is not union or consensus or agreement. Nor is it the forgiving and forgetting which English poems on Irish subjects suggest might be an eminently reasonable solution. Ferguson sees that the parties of Ireland must agree to differ, or in the terms of his later praise of his friend, if political opponent, Thomas Davis: 'Wherever he went, he was surrounded by an atmosphere of good will, which hostile politicians could not enter without mutually conceding "the right to differ", and arguing to do something for the common good' (Ferguson, 1847, p. 197). Nevertheless, as here, for all their kindness given the land over which they claim sovereignty, the parties will *part*.

Ferguson found in Jacobite and Reformation-era Irish poetry a feudal culture well-suited to the Tory readers of the *Dublin University Magazine*: he opens his articles viewing a divided contemporary Ireland, in which his religion had just suffered the trauma of Catholic Emancipation, and his party and class that of the Great Reform Act. Irish poetry presents a simpler, feudal, we might say more Romantic, age. We could easily imagine Walter Scott condoning such sentiments as Ferguson makes, introducing the *ancien régime* of Irish poetry to his Tory readers:

> We will look nearer to the time when those who had high treason in their hearts had arms in their hands . . . when victors and vanquished could afford to seem what they really were, and genuine feeling found utterance undisguised, in the passionate sincerity of exultation or despair. (Ferguson, 1834, I, p. 457)

This passionate sincerity attaches to peasant and aristocrat alike and is manifest in the aesthetic forms of both heroic and lyric. Attending to such shifts in category and keen to seek out 'allegories of union', the contemporary critic may still try to run them together rather too quickly. David Lloyd, for instance, is very good on the way in which the plainness of diction or 'uncouthness' of Ferguson's literal translations finds its way in to the eventual verse translations to become 'an essential part of the verse in rhythm and idiom, reflecting exactly Ferguson's idea of the primitive but powerful sentiments of the Irish race' (1987, p. 84). This may be, like so many of the inventions of Irish poetry in the early nineteenth century, a happy accident as much as conscious artistic design. But primitivism is not entirely the object, given the pressure of epic and heroic models that Ferguson found in the medieval material with which he was to work later in his career, not to mention his more immediately post-Romantic interest in ballad and song.

For Lloyd, Ferguson's sectarian and class politics run easily into the aesthetic theory behind his translations:

> Ferguson's aim was to present a theory of the gradual development of the native Irish loyalties from the immediate clan to the idea of a constitutional monarchy, obliging a transition from investment in the sensuous to investment in the supersensuous. Knowledge thus becomes unifying rather than – as with Hardiman – divisive and sectarian. The ideal of transparent translation repeats this theory . . . it ensures a continuous transition into which no arbitrariness enters [and it] allows for the undisturbed reproduction in English of the essential quality of the Gael, which, for Ferguson, as for Arnold thirty years later, is 'sentimentality'. (1987, p. 84)

This might well describe Brooke's enlightenment project and Arnold's liberal call for the renewed study of Celtic literature. But Ferguson's Romanticism is at odds with such transparently unionist conceptions of translation. The notion of an 'ideal of transparent translation' is borrowed from Robert Welch's praise of Ferguson's English versions, 'remaining absolutely true in as many particulars as possible, to the spirit, tone and rhythm of the originals, and to their curious, if at times chaotic image sequences' (1980, p. 130). Welch's 'absolutely true' is too strong, and may be answered by Lloyd's rather bland dismissal of it as naïve: 'a continuous transition into which no arbitrariness enters'. But most talk of arbitrary signs forestalls much discussion of poetry, and Welch does attend to something of much more interest in the 'originals' themselves. This is their 'chaotic image sequences', or indeed Ferguson's own phrasing: 'as maudlin a jumble of incongruous parts as ever came staggering into the imagination of a man half-drunk, half-desperate'.

What is this romantic aesthetic of the chaotic, the incongruous and the jumbled? In its way it is an aesthetic of taking your mind off the matter in hand, of distractedness, anomaly and anachronism rather than, to borrow an apt musical term, the unison envisaged by Charlotte Brooke's 1789 vision of the British and Gaelic muses walking hand in hand. 1789 is also a date remembered in European history for reasons other than the first translations of Irish poetry. In Ireland's case it was to be nine years before revolution of a sort was to come, and one unintended effect of the 1798 rising in Ireland was Union. Returning to poetry, 1798 was also the year of Wordsworth and Coleridge's *Lyrical Ballads*, and the preface later fixed to that production in the year in which the Union took effect, 1801, would lay down rules of plain and simple diction that Ferguson could not ignore thirty years later. It is facile, perhaps, to elevate such coincidences into the conditions of writing, but writing in 'the real language of men' became an aim for any number of nineteenth-century poets, a liberating aim in particular for those keen to sound regional accents. Wordsworth's preface also offers a description of the metre of poems as a kind of incongruity, a challenge to the sonic mimesis of a poetry in which the sound must seem an echo to the sense. Wordsworth rewrites Pope when he says he hears 'something regular' in metre, and that serves a sort of therapeutic function, since it 'cannot but have great efficacy in tempering and restraining the passion by an intertexture of ordinary feeling, and of feeling not strictly and necessarily connected with the passion'. He heard this most strongly in the 'artless' metre of 'the old ballads' (Wordsworth, 1969, p. 739). The challenge is not only an aesthetics of decorum and appropriateness, but, when applied to the Irish poem (or indeed novel), a challenge to the desire that literary form will effect the necessary connections of hybridization, Hibernicization, Saxonization or indeed union.

For Wordsworth's intertexture of feeling not strictly and necessarily connected with the passion, compare Ferguson introducing his English metrical versions of Irish poems in the last of the Hardiman articles:

> Nothing, however, will perplex him [the translator] more than the reconcilement of measure and sentiment. We do not here allude to the compressed character of Irish versification before noticed; but to the marked difference between the characters of the prosody and the sentiment, rendered still more striking where the original is associated with any of the more ancient melodies. Here, while the

rhythm and music breathe the most plaintive and pathetic sentiment, the accompanying words, in whatever English dress they may be invested, present a contrast of low and ludicrous images as well as of an incondite simplicity of construction the most striking and apparently absurd. In the original this want of adaptation is by no means apparent; but to preserve in English those almost evanescent touches which there counteract the otherwise inevitable absurdity of the piece is next to impossible. True, the words of such songs are invariably less ancient than their music; and from being confined to the peasantry, may well be supposed to have acquired a corresponding uncouthness by frequent interpolations and corruptions of the original text. Poetical art is the greatest desideratum in all; in none, even the most grotesque, is there any lack of poetical feeling. (1834, IV, p. 429)

Ferguson is talking about much more than the conundrum of translating the sounds of poems here. It is a highly sophisticated poetic argument borrowing in equal parts from a Romantic aesthetic of expressiveness, or 'sentiment', and an antiquarian concern for textual history, or the 'incondite simplicity' of the authentic. The rhythm of the Irish lyrics owes much to the melodies for which the lyrics were composed, melodies often much older than the lyrics themselves. By a sort of double archaeological process the translator must convey the Irish language lyric excavated from the past while hinting at the quite separate history of its melody.

Ferguson's contemporary Edward Walsh insisted on 'writing the measure of the translation to the exact song-tune of the original', and his inheritor Thomas MacDonagh recognized the textual differences of 'Irish poems that sing to the same air' (Walsh, 1847, p. 31; MacDonagh, 1996, p. 36). Both suggest that considerations of melody allow both effective translation and an acknowledgement of the histories of textual difference when song and melody may have allied themselves in a number of differing partnerships without fear of accusations of promiscuity. If histories of lyric and melody, like prosody and sentiment may allow marked differences, as Ferguson puts it, then the low and ludicrous in the sentiment can only hint at the plaintive and pathetic mode which they borrow. A Wordsworthian 'intertexture of ordinary feeling' must be conveyed in the English poem. And for all the difficulty of doing that in translation, Ferguson seeks to suggest 'those almost evanescent touches which there counteract the otherwise inevitable absurdity'. The perplexity at 'the reconcilement of measure and sentiment', the 'marked difference' of prosody and sentiment, the counteracting of verbal propriety and peasant feeling: nothing could be further than an 'ideal of transparent translation'. Sect, class and imagined ethnic difference all agree to differ. While the English version seeks to convey the jumble of the peasant original, to mark its difference albeit in English, the hope is that when English and Irish part, as they must, it will be in peace.

Notes

1. Leerssen, 2002, p. 13. See also Ó Ciosáin, 1997, in particular his final chapter, where he calls for a more nuanced account of this shift from an oral or manuscript Irish-language culture to an English-language print and popular culture: 'to write about the "Irish language" or "the English language in the nineteenth century", is to write the history of ideas rather the culture, a history in which people become the more or less awkward carriers of these ideas . . . the distinctions would not have made sense to the actors, and miss the coherence as well as the complexity of cultural practice at any given time' (p. 203).
2. On the Ulster Gaelic Society see Welch, 1988, pp. 90–1.
3. Hardiman, 1831, I, p. 218. The above follows Hardiman's text, rendered into roman script.
4. Burns, 1969, p. 141; Keats, 1970, p. 366. The Keats sonnet was not published until 1848. I am grateful to Hamish Mathison for pointing out Keats' allusion to Burns to me.

Bibliography

Brooke, Charlotte (1789) *Reliques of Irish Poetry* (Dublin: Bonham).
Burns, Robert (1969) *Poems and Songs*, ed. James Kinsley (Oxford: Oxford University Press).
Campbell, Matthew (2010) 'Davis, Mangan, Ferguson' in *The Blackwell Companion to Irish Literature*, ed. Julia M. Wright, 2 vols (Oxford: Blackwell).
Ferguson, Samuel (1833) 'A Dialogue Between the Head and Heart of an Irish Protestant', *Dublin University Magazine*, 2 (Nov.).
——. (1834) 'Hardiman's Irish Minstrelsy', I–IV, *Dublin University Magazine*, 3–4 (April to November).
——. (1845) 'Robert Burns', I–II, *Dublin University Magazine*, 25 (January and March).
——. (1847) 'Thomas Davis', *Dublin University Magazine*, 29 (February).
——. (1865) *Lays of the Western Gael* (London: Bell and Daldy).
Graham, Colin (2009) 'Hireling Strangers and the Wandering Throne: Ireland, Scotland and Samuel Ferguson', *Estudios Irlandeses*, 4 (2009), 23–31.
Hardiman, James, ed. (1831) *Irish Minstrelsy: Or Bardic Remains of Ireland, with English Poetical Translations*, 2 vols (London: Robins).
Hyde, Douglas (1893) *Abhráin grádh chúige Connacht: The Love Songs of Connacht* (Baile-Ath-Cliath: Gill).
Keats, John (1970) *The Complete Poems*, ed. Miriam Allott (London: Longman).
Leerssen, Joep (2002) *Hidden Ireland, Public Sphere* (Galway: Arlen House).

Lloyd, David (1987) *Nationalism and Minor Literature: James Clarence Mangan and the Emergence of Irish Cultural Nationalism* (Berkeley: University of California Press).

MacDonagh, Thomas (1996) *Literature in Ireland* (Nenagh: Relay Books).

Moore, Thomas (1824) *Memoirs of Captain Rock, the Celebrated Irish Chieftain, with some Account of his Ancestors, Written by Himself* (London: Longman).

Ó Buachalla, Brendan (1987) 'The Gaelic Background', in *Samuel Ferguson: A Centenary Tribute*, ed. Terence Brown and Barbara Hayley (Dublin: Royal Irish Academy), pp. 33–5.

Ó Ciosáin, Niall (1997) *Print and Popular Culture in Ireland, 1750–1850* (London: Macmillan).

Patten, Eve (2004) *Samuel Ferguson and the Culture of Nineteenth-Century Ireland* (Dublin: Four Courts Press).

Walsh, Edward (1847) *Irish Popular Songs* (Dublin: McGlashan).

Welch, Robert (1980) *Irish Poetry from Moore to Yeats* (Gerrard's Cross: Colin Smythe).

——. (1988) *A History of Verse Translation from the Irish, 1789–1897* (Gerrard's Cross: Colin Smythe).

Wordsworth, William (1969) *Poetical Works*, ed. Thomas Hutchinson and Ernest de Selincourt (Oxford: Oxford University Press).

Yeats, W. B. (1970) 'The Poetry of Sir Samuel Ferguson', from *The Irish Fireside*, 9 October 1886, in *Uncollected Prose*, 2 vols, ed. John P. Frayne (London: Macmillan), I.

——. (1952) *Collected Plays* (London: Macmillan).

——. (1957) *The Variorum Edition of the Poems of W. B. Yeats*, ed. Peter Allt and Russell K. Alspach (New York: Macmillan).

9
Courtly Lays or Democratic Songs? The Politics of Poetic Citation in Chartist Literary Criticism

Michael Sanders

> Poets and their poetry have, and will continue to exert an extensive influence on the destinies of mankind . . . [it is in order] to take an advantage of this great inherent power in our national poetry that we propose to bring before our readers the leading political principles developed in their writings.
> ('The Politics of Poets, I', 1840, *Chartist Circular*)

> What is Robert Browning doing . . . has he nothing to say for popular rights?
>
> Can Tennyson do no more than troll a courtly lay? His oak could tell other tales besides a love story.
> (*The Labourer* (Jones, 1847b, pp. 95–6))

Between them these two quotations, separated by a mere seven years, indicate Chartism's changing understanding of the political significance of poetry. As this chapter will show, Chartist literary theory conceived of poetry both as an agent of popular liberation and of popular oppression.[1] For the *Chartist Circular*, 'national poetry' represented a 'great inherent power' which only needed to be harnessed by Chartism. Conversely *The Labourer*, although sharing the *Circular*'s view of the power and significance of poetry, is more sceptical regarding its immediate usefulness to the movement. This chapter will trace the contours of this debate as manifested through the selection, citation and discussion of both historical and contemporaneous poetry in the pages of the Chartist press. In short, it will argue that there is a 'politics of citation' which reveals the close relationship between political and aesthetic theory in Chartist thinking.

In *Toward a Working-Class Canon*, Paul Murphy argues that the history of working-class literary criticism in the first half of the nineteenth century is one of a general broadening of attitudes from a sceptical, suspicious and, at times, openly hostile approach to literature (exemplified by Richard Carlile and William Cobbett) to a more generous recognition of the political importance of the 'aesthetic'. During the 1840s and 1850s, Murphy notes, many Chartist writers attested to their belief in 'the inseparable interconnection of the beautiful, the imaginative, and the truthful in literature and in the minds of readers' (Murphy, 1994, p. 58). Murphy also identifies a process of canon formation with 'working-class journalists disestablishing and recanonizing established writers, or sanctioning new, unestablished writers, to fit the values of their own class' (p. 3).

The pages of the *Chartist Circular* certainly provide evidence in support of Murphy's argument. Described by W. Hamish Fraser as 'an educational journal intended to bring a greater understanding of the aims of Chartism' (2005, p. 91), the *Chartist Circular* was a halfpenny, four-page weekly, printed in Glasgow and published under the superintendence of the Universal Suffrage Central Committee for Scotland (USCCS). Edited by William Thomson, who was the General Secretary to the USCCS,[2] the *Chartist Circular* ran for 146 issues from 28 September 1839 to 9 July 1842 (when debts forced its closure). It began publishing some five weeks before the Newport Uprising and ceased some two months after the presentation of the second Chartist petition and just over a month before the mass industrial unrest of August/September 1842. Thus, its existence coincided with the tumultuous early years of Chartism. At its peak it enjoyed a circulation in excess of 20,000 copies and played a key role in organizing Scottish Chartism at a national level.[3]

The front page of the *Chartist Circular* consisted of an original editorial while the rest of the journal offered a combination of longer articles on political, economic and social matters, shorter miscellaneous articles of an improving nature, brief extracts from a range of radical writers, humorous stories with a political/satirical edge, as well as original poetry and fiction.[4] A poetry column appeared on an almost weekly basis from the *Circular*'s third number onwards and during its lifetime it published around 150 poems by at least 67 poets. Over a similar period the *Northern Star* published around 350 poems by at least 120 poets. However, there appears to have been very little overlap between the two publications. Some fifteen identifiable poets contributed to both poetry columns and whilst these poets contributed around 130 poems in total across the two journals, a mere twelve appear in both.[5] Indeed, relative to their respective sizes, it can be argued that poetry played an even more significant role in the *Chartist Circular* than it did in the *Northern Star*.[6]

Where the *Chartist Circular* differs appreciably from the *Northern Star* is in the number of column-inches it devotes to constructing a 'Chartist canon' from the raw materials provided by the British poetic tradition. This process of canon formation occurred through two series, 'The Politics of Poets' and 'Literary Sketches', neither of which has an identified (or identifiable) author. 'The Politics of Poets' ran for ten numbers from 11 July 1840 to 13 March 1841, while 'Literary Sketches' ran for twenty-nine numbers from 13 February 1841 to 9 April 1842. 'The Politics of Poets' begins with Ebenezer Elliott's rejection of those critics who are already seeking to de-politicize the canon:

> The gentleman critics complain that the union of poetry with politics is always hurtful to the politics, and fatal to the poetry. But these great connoisseurs must be wrong, if Homer, Dante, Shakespeare, Milton, Cowper, and Burns were poets. ('The Politics of Poets, No. 1', 1840, p. 170)

Instead the *Chartist Circular* identifies poetry and politics, not only are all 'genuine poets . . . fervid politicians', but poetry itself is defined as 'impassioned truth' and the article emphatically declares 'All truth is radical'. The *Circular* strikes a recognizably Shelleyan note in its insistence that poets constitute the vanguard of humanity, proclaiming the truth of liberty in advance of its political realization. Noting that 'Poets and their poetry have, and will continue to exert an extensive influence on the destinies of mankind', the *Chartist Circular* declares that its intention in 'The Politics of Poets' series:

> is to take an advantage of this great inherent power in our national poetry . . . [by bringing] before our readers the leading political principles developed in their writings. ('The Politics of Poets, No. 1', 1840, p. 170)

The articles which follow focus initially on the Romantic poets who, in what will become a familiar gesture in Chartist literary criticism, are claimed as the poetic precursors of Chartism.[7] Shelley, Byron, Wordsworth, Coleridge and the young Southey are all discussed and praised for their republican and/or democratic tendencies.

The 'Literary Sketches' series which replaces 'The Politics of Poets' is far more ambitious in terms of its range and scope. It moves beyond the Romantics to discuss Milton, Henryson, Cowper and Goldsmith, it deals with a range of working-class poets, from the better-known such as Tannahill and Bloomfield, to more obscure Glasgow poets such as Walter Currie, Thomas Gillespie and Tom Atkenson. This series also examines some American poets and discusses a number of important historical figures such as John Knox and James I and James V of Scotland. James I, for example, is described as 'the literary royal radical of Scotland . . . assassinated by his rebellious nobles for being a political reformer' and the article concludes by calling on its readers to 'honour his virtues, venerate his politics, embalm and love his memory, read his poetry, [and] sing his music' ('Literary Sketches, James I', 1841, p. 394). Similarly, Robert Henryson (the fifteenth-century poet) is praised for having 'the bold sentiments of a Radical Reformer' although in an interesting recognition of historical difference the *Chartist Circular* notes that in the fifteenth century political notions were expressed by means of religious aspirations ('Literary Sketches, Robert Henryson', 1841, p. 378). John Knox is claimed as 'a zealous Radical Reformer – a Democrat – a Republican, and a physical-force Chartist' ('Literary Sketches, John Knox', 1841, p. 338).

What we are witnessing here is the construction of a 'national-popular' (or counter-hegemonic) poetic tradition, which functions as a reservoir of positive, democratic, values and aspirations that can be drawn on by the present movement. This view of the poetic tradition derives additional strength from its consonance with what we might call the 'Constitutionalist' metanarrative of Chartism's political discourse. Broadly speaking, Chartism often presented itself as a movement seeking the recovery of those ancient political rights 'lost' with the abrogation of the 'Anglo-Saxon Constitution'. It is hardly surprising, then, that it should represent the native poetic tradition as preserving those same liberties. Under this interpretation, the political and cultural exclusion of the working classes are structurally as well as historically related. It is possible to see how this logic might become reversible in the Chartist imagination. If the restoration of lost political rights necessarily includes access to the poetic tradition, might not access to the poetic tradition hasten the return of those same political rights? This view of the native poetic tradition as essentially democratic was widely held within Chartism, finding its most complete expression in the opening stanzas of the second book of Thomas Cooper's Chartist epic, *The Purgatory of Suicides* (1845), which identifies a tradition of patriot bards comprising Chaucer, Spenser, Shakespeare, Milton, Byron and Shelley.

However, 'Literary Sketches' also explicitly recognizes that poetry is a contested tradition and this is particularly evident in its treatment of Burns and Byron. The *Chartist Circular* finds it necessary to claim Burns as:

> a republican, a democrat; and in principle and practice, an honest Chartist. Ye who sneer at this assertion, read his 'Man was made to Mourn', 'A Man's a Man for a' that', 'The Twa Dogs', and 'A Winter Night', and your Whiggish doubts will vanish like the hoary mountain mist before the bright rays of the meridian summer sun. ('Literary Sketches, Robert Burns', 1841, pp. 309–10)

In the case of Byron the *Chartist Circular* makes it clear that it is necessary to retrieve his reputation from 'the malicious falsehoods with which ecclesiastical hypocrisy and political iniquity have dared to malign [his] honest intentions and noble character' ('Literary Sketches, Byron', 1841, pp. 473–4).

Given the importance accorded to poetry in such articles, the relative belatedness of both 'The Politics of Poets' and 'Literary Sketches' requires comment. As was noted earlier, the poetry column itself had appeared on an almost weekly basis from the third number, whereas 'The Politics of Poets' only begins with the forty-second number. Thus, whilst original Chartist poetry is published almost from the *Chartist Circular*'s inception, nearly ten months elapses before it begins to analyse and discuss poetry. Clearly priority is given to encouraging Chartist poetic production ahead of 'canonical engagement' and this follows the editorial policy pursued in the *Northern Star* at the same period.

Two articles published prior to 'The Politics of Poets' series provide a clue as to why the *Chartist Circular* made such an investment in poetry. The sixth number of the *Chartist Circular*, published 2 November 1839, contains an article entitled 'Morality of the Working Classes' written as a response to *Blackwood's Magazine*'s claim that the working classes are currently 'too ignorant, too drunk and improvident' to be trusted with the franchise. The *Chartist Circular* responds to this by citing the drive to self-education in working-class communities as evidence of intellectual and moral abilities, and by lambasting the government for failing to provide meaningful educational opportunities. In short, in the words of Fraser, '[t]he *Circular*'s argument was that the working class were *already* morally and intellectually worthy of the vote' (2005, p. 93).

Some months later, on 9 May 1840, in an article entitled 'The Genius of Working Men', the *Chartist Circular* claims that 'natural genius . . . is indigenous and belongs almost exclusively to working men. In every village we find an untaught poet, a painter, a musician.' Indeed, the writer claims that natural genius '*belong*[s] *almost exclusively to the working masses*' and cites, amongst others, Homer, Aesop, Socrates, Milton, Shakespeare, Burns, Tannahill and Bloomfield in support of this claim, before concluding, 'There is, therefore, no deficiency of *intellect* among the poor' ('Genius of Working Men', 1840, pp. 135–6). Taken together, these articles assert that the knowledge, intellect, literary judgement and creativity already displayed by the working classes demonstrate their inherent fitness to exercise the franchise.

Elsewhere, I have described this argument as the 'argument from culture' and have suggested that it performed a key role in Chartist strategic thinking in the interval between the rejection of the second petition and the emergence of the Chartist Land Plan (Sanders, 2009, pp. 76–7, 85). In this respect the dates of these articles are significant. 'The Morality of the Working Classes' appears just days before the 'Newport Uprising' exposed the limitations of an insurrectionary strategy, whilst the two series occupy the period before the second Chartist petition. The *Chartist Circular* is making the 'argument from culture' some three years ahead of the *Northern Star* (which starts to deploy this argument from 1844 onwards). The *Chartist Circular*'s precociousness in this regard opens the possibility that it may form a previously overlooked aspect of the 'New Move' of the early 1840s.[8] As Chartism recovered from the trauma of Newport and its aftermath, the movement engaged in a search for alternative strategies by means of which to secure its demands. 'Knowledge Chartism', 'Teetotal Chartism' and 'Christian Chartism' all had powerful advocates within the movement. Each of these strands envisaged the conquest of political power by broadly 'moral', even 'cultural', methods of suasion rather than through physical violence, and it is not difficult to see how 'Literary Chartism' might conceivably have belonged to the New Move in this respect.

An important strategic question facing the Chartist movement was how best to manage its relationship with the middle classes in general and middle-class radicalism in particular. Although some Chartists entertained fantasies of going it alone, many more recognized the necessity, perhaps the desirability, of securing middle-class support. The *Chartist Circular*'s investment in 'canonical' poetry might be seen as an attempt to lay the groundwork for negotiations with the middle classes by laying claim to forms of 'cultural capital' already acknowledged by the latter. Evidence of Chartism's ability to appreciate and create good poetry was intended to allay the kinds of anxieties expressed by *Blackwood's Magazine*. If this proposition sounds a little odd to twenty-first century ears, it is worth pointing out that just a few years later, middle-class radicals clearly regarded literature as an avenue for negotiation with working-class radicals.[9]

For the most part, the *Chartist Circular* prefers to theorize poetry as either 'prophetic' or 'bardic'. The 'canonical' Romantic poets, especially Byron and Shelley, exemplify the former, whilst most labouring-class poets are seen in bardic terms. In its sixth number, however, 'The Politics of Poets' turns its attention to what it describes as contemporary 'minor poets' (by which it appears to mean working-class poets). This article begins with the claim that 'Almost every town, village, and hamlet in Scotland has its poet, whose song in his own locality is listened to with feeling and respect' ('The Politics of Poets, No. VI', 1840, p. 231). Although obscure in their lifetimes and forgotten after death these local poets too are 'unacknowledged legislators' insofar as 'the influence of [their] talents can never be wholly lost to society'. The decision to look at contemporary working-class writers is justified on political rather than aesthetic grounds. The *Chartist Circular* makes it clear that its interest lies in the extent to which such poets represent 'the state of popular feeling' (p. 231). Furthermore, it argues, 'It matters, little, however rude the strain; like the feather it tells the way the wind blows.' The article claims that an ancient love of song and an independent spirit has generated an unquenchable desire for liberty amongst the Scottish people. The interchange between politics and poetry is understood as a two-way process. Poetry inspires and sustains political activity:

> Poetry is a lever of commanding influence when it grasps the subject that interests, or the elements that move the popular will. It penetrates to every nerve and fibre of society, stirring into irresistibility its undermost current. (p. 231)

As the invocation of 'nerve and fibre' suggests, poetry's political effect is continually theorized as affect. It is the multi-vocal yet essentially emotional nature of poetry which, for the *Chartist Circular*, plays a vital role in the struggle for democratic rights:

> The voices are many by which poetry speaks. At one time it appeals to all the soft and gentle feelings of our nature – at another it swells the heart with indignation against the ruthless oppressors of our species. At another time it speaks in the bold prophetic language of truth, singing of the increasing power and strength of the people . . . Again

it utters wrathful thundering against the proud and ambitious, who drench the earth in blood, and clothe the world with ruin, for the paltry purpose of winning a crown – anon it sings the jubilee hymn of freedom. ('Politics of Poets, No. VIII, 1840, p. 265)

However, political activity also exerts a pressure on poetic expression. The *Chartist Circular* argues that the ongoing struggle for popular rights has 'conveyed a corresponding spirit to our poetry, giving it a more intense and earnest feeling for the cause'. It then situates this change in a broader historical context, arguing that:

> Ever since the French Revolution mere sentiment in poetry has been giving way for that of principle – high, unbending principle . . . despotism deepens its gloom; the lights of fancy alone are inadequate to struggle with its darkness. Poetry needed, and received, a higher and a firmer tone; if it has lost in feeling, it has gained in power. ('Politics of Poets, No. VI', 1840, p. 231)

The slighting reference to 'mere sentiment' suggests a multi-layered and hierarchical model of affect. The *Chartist Circular* is suspicious of excessive emotional introspection, preferring Byron's interest in humankind to the inward focus of some of his contemporaries ('Politics of Poets, No. VIII', 1840, p. 265). It is 'fellow feeling' which the *Chartist Circular* prizes and it identifies a new social task for poetry which it describes as 'tracing through its ramified complications the development of the democratic principle which the minds of men, in the different nations of the world, had so largely imbibed, at and subsequent to the [French] Revolution' (p. 265).

However, this assertion of a seamless relationship between poetry and democracy is sometimes challenged within the pages of the *Chartist Circular* by a rather more problematic theorization of the political work performed by poetry. This dissident note first sounds in an article entitled 'Literary Reform' which begins, 'I do not know anything more essential for the improvement of mankind . . . than a Radical Literary Reform' ('Literary Reform', 1841, p. 299). This sounds a very different note from previous discussions, as it focuses on literature as an instrument of oppression rather than liberation. The central accusation is that literature has glorified and glamorized the actions of princes and heroes such that 'their selfishness, murders, battles, and massacres, have been falsely extolled for valour, magnanimity, and patriotism'. In a moment of Benjaminian insight, the article highlights a structural link between the actual violence perpetrated by class societies and the symbolic violence which underpins their modes of aesthetic representation:

> History does not condescend to extol the virtuous poor: it only venerates kings, priests, and generals . . . Poetry and romance delight to decorate the nobility . . . The poetry of humble life is not fashionable; a romance of cottagers would be a tale of nasty creatures which nobody would write, and few read. (p. 299)

It notes that lower-class characters only appear as either 'base and ignoble' or 'servile and sensual', and if a 'lower-class' hero ever demonstrates real virtue then you may be sure that their aristocratic origins will be quickly discovered. This analysis combines a rudimentary 'politics of narrative' with an understanding of the role of ideological misrecognition in securing the hegemonic effectiveness of literature. The result of this 'false philosophy' promulgated by 'literary authors' is that 'the masses, in ignorance, have worshipped their oppressors, as if they were incarnate divinities. So long as this literary vileness continues, so long will the people be led astray.' The remedy for this state of affairs is a 'Radical Literary Reform' which will extol the 'virtues of the masses' and expose and condemn 'the iniquities of the *titled*', and for the people to 'read only those good works which do them justice' (p. 299).

The alternative theorization of literature as an agent of political oppression and ideological mystification begun by 'Literary Reform' receives a fuller and more nuanced development in a number of articles devoted to Walter Scott, Allan Ramsay and John Home which appear as part of the 'Literary Sketches' series. Indeed, Walter Scott, the subject of the very first 'Literary Sketch', is criticized for the perceived political tendencies of his work:

> The subtle effect of his great historical panoramas is, to exalt the aristocracy, and debase the people; to excite veneration for Chiefs and Ladies, and contempt for the masses . . . He throws a false gloss over the political and social misery of . . . feudalism. ('Literary Sketches, Walter Scott', 1841, pp. 305–6)

It is the content and political implications of Scott's work that the *Chartist Circular* objects to, it does not dispute his skill as a writer:

> Sir Walter Scott is a popular author of great genius . . . But as he has written too much for the benefit of the oppressors, and the obloquy

of the oppressed, we gaze on his mighty enchantments with the painful emotions of pity and gloom. (pp. 305–6)

The *Circular*'s major anxiety is that Scott's success in aestheticizing feudalism will inculcate hostility to the 'democratic voice':

> The fascinating perusal of his popular works, in our early days, makes very false impressions on our youthful minds, and in manhood causes us to linger among the ruins of the past, and makes us shudder when we hear the democratic voice of the people rejoicing over feudal decay, and extolling, with laudable gladness, the march of equality among the human race. (pp. 305–6)

However, the article concludes by claiming that after 'Literary Reform' has occurred, the taste for Scott's works will decline:

> When the people shall have their own authors and press, to do them justice, they will sweep away the corruptions of literature from the haunts of social life, and the proud motto of Knowledge and Equality shall then wave triumphantly on the noble banner of Literary Reform. (pp. 305–6)

The *Chartist Circular*'s anxiety concerning Scott's influence might possibly be coloured (given Thomson's previous involvement in the Weavers' Union) by an awareness that such was the novelist's popularity that, according to Jonathan Rose, Dunfermline weavers 'were clubbing together to buy the Waverley novels' (2001, p. 116). Of particular concern to the *Chartist Circular* is the political effect of imaginative literature on young minds. Some of Scott's 'delusive romances' are, in the opinion of the *Chartist Circular*, 'unfit to be read by the junior masses, before their minds are matured with the knowledge of sound philosophy and political truth' ('Literary Sketches, Walter Scott', 1841, pp. 305–6). The subsequent discussion of Allan Ramsay's work identifies some of the *Chartist Circular*'s concerns. Ramsay's work, especially his *Gentle Shepherd*, is criticized not just for its 'unmanly adulation of the *titled* great' and its 'unmerited degradation of their vassals' or what it succinctly describes as its 'people-debasing politics'. The *Chartist Circular* also regrets the gaps in Ramsay's poem which, despite being set around the time of the English Revolution, 'contains no holy aspirations for civil and religious liberty, although the scene is laid at a time in Scottish history when the people were boldly struggling for their rights'. However, the principal objection to Ramsay's work lies in its capacity (particularly in the educational field) to inculcate 'Tory' values by stealth:

> When I was at school, the Gentle Shepherd, and the tragedy of Douglas, were read as schoolbooks, by the scholars. I did not then comprehend their political tendency, and the master never explained it. I admired Patie and Douglas, and thought them gallant and noble; the vassals I laughed at and despised.
> Thus was the intention of the teacher of Toryism fulfilled, – the minds of his pupils were poisoned with false political principles, and the seeds of Toryism were sown, which, like weeds in the garden, can never again be entirely eradicated from the soil. ('Literary Sketches, Allan Ramsay', 1841, p. 314)

The central political objection to Scott, Ramsay and Home is that through a process of emotional identification with a character, the values of Toryism are unknowingly internalized and possess greater political effect precisely because of this – as Althusser noted the successful ideology never proclaims 'I am ideological'.

In mounting such a critique, the *Chartist Circular* not only signals its opposition to the 'ideological work' performed by Scott's novels, but also betrays its anxiety that many Chartist readers may find it difficult to resist such sophisticated textual machinations. In his superb study *The Intellectual Life of the British Working Classes*, Rose demonstrates rather more confidence in the critical capacities of working-class readers by showing how they were able to produce politically radical interpretations of a range of 'conservative' writers including Scott. Indeed, there is a sense in which Rose deploys Scott as a test case, commenting that early nineteenth-century radical papers 'often assailed Walter Scott's conservatism, but their readers did not necessarily concur' (2001, p. 40). However, the overwhelming majority of Rose's examples of radical re-evaluation of Scott are drawn from readers born in the post-Chartist period, which suggests that this particular strategy was not readily available to Chartist readers. During this period it would seem that the 'intended' ideological pressures of the text were more difficult to resist and/or redirect than they were for subsequent generations of working-class readers.

The *Chartist Circular*, then, bequeaths a mixed legacy to subsequent Chartist critics. For the most part it represents the poetic tradition as existing in a largely unproblematic relationship to current Chartist values whilst sometimes theorizing literature as an agent of ruling-class hegemony. Generally speaking the *Northern Star* replicates this critical compound, identifying a poetic tradition (comprising Shakespeare, Milton, Cowper, Burns and Shelley) which is broadly consonant with Chartist values. At times though a very different version of literary history appears in its columns; witness the implicit criticisms which attend this celebration of a 'popular front of literature' in the *Northern Star* for 2 March 1844:

> Such a better state of things is in store for England when such bright stars of literature as Thomas Hood, Douglas Jerrold, &c., devote their heaven-gifted talents to the defence of the oppressed, and the advocacy of the wrong[ed]. Surely, the great wrongs of our social system are doomed, when men like these, instead of, as in past times, penning fulsome adulations to win the smiles and filthy lucre of the rich, dare to plead the cause of the helpless and the poor, heedless of aught save their *duty*. (p. 3)

It is the development of this critical inheritance in the pages of *The Labourer* that provides the focus for the final part of this chapter.

Edited by Feargus O'Connor and Ernest Jones and describing itself as a 'Monthly Magazine of Politics, Literature, Poetry, &c', *The Labourer* ran from January 1847 to December 1848. It reflected O'Connor's abiding interest in the 'land question' in general and the Chartist Land Plan in particular, whilst the literary and poetical sections of the paper, it is safe to assume, were conducted by Ernest Jones. In some respects *The Labourer* shares some common ground with the *Chartist Circular*; both journals champion Shelley and Byron, and both identify the aestheticization of feudalism with opposition to democracy. Similarly, both journals believe that poetry is (or ought to be) essentially democratic. However, where the *Circular* garners evidence for this proposition from the poetic archive, *The Labourer* examines the poetry of the present, and finds it sadly deficient. Indeed, in a review of T. Powell's *Poems*, *The Labourer* argues that many contemporary poets have abandoned poetry's traditional commitment to democracy in favour of 'writing for a class':

> They are class poets, the same as we have class-legislators. They seize some topic interesting only to the privileged few, or, more frequently, dwell on morbid, abstract theories, that never can claim, nor even deserve general attention. (Jones, 1847a, p. 284)

Two issues later, in an article entitled 'Literary Review', *The Labourer* boldly identifies and celebrates Chartist (or democratic) poetry as the most vital of the age: and, simultaneously, laments the tendency of non-Chartist poets to waste their poetic talents in pursuit of an exhausted aesthetic:

> [Chartist] poetry is, indeed the freshest and most stirring of the age; as in England, thus in France, America, Ireland, and Germany, the poetic spirit has struck the chords of liberty; and the fresh vigour of its productions contrasts proudly with the emasculated verses of a fashionable school. Yet, from many we have expected more. What is Robert Browning doing? He, who could fire the soul of a Luria, and develop the characters of a Victor and a Charles, – he, who could depict nature's nobility in a Colombe, – has he nothing to say for popular rights? Let him eschew his kings and queens, – let him quit the pageantry of courts – and *ascend* into the cottage of the poor.
>
> Can Tennyson do no more than troll a courtly lay? His oak could tell other tales besides a love story. (Jones, 1847b, pp. 95–6)

In addition to Browning and Tennyson, the review cites Knowles, Mackay, Gurney, Bailey, Horne and Powell as examples of wasted poetic talent. Drawing on established ideas of the poet as visionary, *The Labourer* comments 'Alas! it often happens that an author is before his age – these men are behind theirs' and continues by observing that historical oblivion is the usual fate of such writers. Throughout, the tone is one of sorrow rather than anger, and the article ends with an appeal to the aforementioned poets:

> We say to the great minds of the day, come among the people, write for the people, and your fame will live for ever. The people's instinct will give life to your philosophy, and the genius of the favoured few will hand down peace and plenty, knowledge and power, as an heirloom to posterity. (pp. 95–6)

The tensions which inform this analysis demand further comment. On the one hand Chartist poetry is proclaimed as 'the freshest and most stirring of the age', yet it appears as if 'the great minds of the day' are to be found beyond the Chartist ranks. *The Labourer* specifically appeals by name to the two of the most technically accomplished contemporary poets, Browning and Tennyson. This would seem to indicate a similar frustration at the discrepancy between political understanding and aesthetic achievement to that which is frequently voiced by the editor of the *Northern Star* at the poor quality of the verse he receives from aspiring Chartist poets. In addition, *The Labourer* (like the *Chartist Circular*) appears to endorse a surprisingly passive model of reading in which great truths realized by the poet are transferred to the reader's mind through the medium of poetry.

However, unlike the *Chartist Circular*, *The Labourer* does not insist on the existence of widespread 'natural genius' among the working classes. Neither does it devote its energies to excavating a politically supportive poetic tradition, nor pursue a study of contemporary working-class poets. Rather, it extends itself geographically by turning its attention to European literature. Over the course of its final thirteen numbers *The Labourer* publishes seven articles dealing with the literature of Poland, Russia and Germany, under the general title 'National Literature'. This series announces its intention of surveying the 'leading works' of a variety of national literatures because this will help *The Labourer*'s readers 'to judge of the characteristics of the people; since, as a general rule, those works only obtain a lasting popularity, which are a reflex of the popular mind and feeling' (Jones, 1847c, p. 279). Thus, in a significant modification of the thesis that all poetry is essentially democratic, *The Labourer* offers a more nuanced reading of the relationship between poetry and democracy in which the present condition of national literature provides a means of assessing a nation's desire and readiness for liberty.

The 'National Literature' series begins with two articles devoted to an extended analysis of Count Krasinski's *Infernal Comedy* which is described as a 'prophecy' set in the future (around AD 2000) and dealing with the last battle 'fought between democracy and chivalry'. *The Labourer* is especially interested in the scene in which Count Henry (the last defender of the feudal order) confronts the leader of the democrats, Pancrates. Jones notes the inherent difficulties of representing such a theme, especially with regard to political sympathies. Observing that a patriot might be too harsh on feudalism and an aristocrat too favourable to the aristocracy, Jones concludes that although Krasinski slightly favours the aristocracy, he nonetheless 'deals . . . fairly with the rival principles' (1847c, p. 281). This emphasis on even-handedness when representing competing political ideologies is not a precursor of Arnoldian disinterestedness. *The Labourer* does not believe that truth lies somewhere between or beyond the two represented positions. Rather, it is an assertion of the importance of truthful or objective representation, which in turn is understood as playing a vital role in promoting political understanding. Thus, *The Labourer* explains (possibly with an eye to the popularity of melodramatic tropes amongst radical writers), a portrayal of a vicious aristocrat does not constitute an argument against aristocracy as a form of government.

The Labourer then, like the *Chartist Circular*, understands poetry as a truth-telling activity. However, where the *Chartist Circular* subscribed to Ebenezer Elliott's definition of poetry as 'impassioned truth' and essentially regards poetry as a process whereby the understanding, knowledge and values belonging to the 'great mind' of the poet are transferred to the reader, a rather different theory of poetry begins to emerge in *The Labourer*. Towards the end of its analysis of the encounter between Count Henry and Pancrates *The Labourer* comments:

> This much for the social and political truth of this scene; in this point of view, it is a mistake; but unknown to himself, the author has read a lesson for the future, and pointed out the reason for the failure of past revolutions. (Jones, 1848, p. 40)

In particular, *The Labourer* argues, Krasinski has mistakenly universalized both the causes and the limitations of earlier revolutions. These misapprehensions are corrected by the critic:

> [Krasinski] has made the universal insurrection merely the ebullition of brute force, the cry of hunger for bread, of suffering for revenge. We confidently anticipate that mind will be the immediate agent of the future movement; that the desire after rights withheld will be greater than the mere physical craving; that the people's energies will take a nobler turn, and that, as they desire 'right to all', so they will inflict wrong on none. (Jones, 1847c, p. 283)

Here then, in a radical revision of the 'prophetic' (or 'great mind') theory of poetry, the truth of the text (implicitly understood as an essentially historical, rather than a transcendent, truth) is produced independently of authorial intention. Krasinski's errors are a function of his social and historical location rather than the result of his personal political affiliations. In effect, *The Labourer* is beginning to elaborate a theoretical position which anticipates Fredric Jameson's conception of the 'political unconscious'. Moreover, these truths can only be apprehended by an 'active' reader. In turn, this has possible implications for conceptions of the canon. If the political value of literature no longer resides in its ability to transmit great thoughts to its reader, but rather consists in its ability to provoke critical reflection on the part of the reader, then (unless aesthetic achievement is understood as a precondition for critical reflection) the canon becomes less important.

Furthermore, this reformulation of Chartist poetic theory points to emerging developments in the political metanarratives employed by Chartism. The critique of Krasinski rests on a conception of a (generally progressive) historical movement towards freedom, whose later phases are able to comprehend and thus correct the failings or limitations of earlier moments. This notion of progressive (or successive) struggles for freedom, whilst not absolutely incompatible with Chartism's original emphasis on the recovery of 'lost' political rights, does problematize the Constitutionalist metanarrative. In particular, it lends itself more to the discourse of 'natural rights' as discovered by human reason, which it then becomes the purpose of History to achieve.

The significance of the transition from 'lost' to 'natural' rights cannot be underestimated. In generic terms alone, it turns the struggle for political rights from a tragi-comedy (in which a primal unsullied constitution is first lost and then gradually recovered) into a comedy proper (a progressive movement towards political freedom). This generic disposition also alters the significance of the poetic tradition from a reservoir of relatively uncontaminated value to a record of historical error. In breaking with the *Chartist Circular*'s invocation of an essentially democratic British poetic tradition, *The Labourer* installs the unwritten poetry of the future rather than the poetry of the past as its implicit critical standard: 'democratic songs' not 'courtly lays' will become the focus for a new politics of poetic citation.

Notes

1. Some material used in this chapter has previously been published in '"Tracing the ramifications of the Democratic Principle": Literary Criticism and Theory in the *Chartist Circular*' in *Key Words*, 8 (2010). I am grateful to the editors of *Key Words* for permission to reprint this material.
2. For details of Thomson's career see Wilson, 1970, pp. 80–1, 131–5, 182–4, 195–6. For details of the relationship between Chartism and the Complete Suffrage Movement see Chase, 2007, pp. 198–238.
3. Like much of Scottish Chartism the *Chartist Circular* inclined to 'moral' rather than 'physical' force – a position influenced by the memory of the Scottish insurrection of 1820 (whose aftermath saw three hangings, sixteen transportations and numerous imprisonments). Fraser provides a helpful overview of the debate between 'moral' and 'physical' force Chartism in the Scottish Chartist press (2005, pp. 91–2).
4. A brief digest of no. 74 (20 Feb. 1841) offers a representative sample of the *Chartist Circular*'s contents: front page editorial, 'The Possession of Popular Rights the Elements of a Nation's Power', longer articles on 'Robert Burns',

'Casanova's Flight from the Lead-Chambers at Venice', 'Thoughts on the Dungeon, on the French Revolution', 'Political Catechism: On the Suffrage', 'Patriotism', the Poetry Column and a number of shorter miscellaneous articles on the Rev. Rowland Hill, the Bank of England, Catherine I of Russia, Second-hand Sermons and a brief extract from Wollstonecraft.
5. The twelve poems which appear in both journals are; Charles Davlin, 'Questions from the loom': James Syme, 'Labour Song': E. La Mont, 'The Land of the Brave and Free' & 'The Honest Working Man': Edward Polin, 'The Toilers' Homes of England' & 'Address to the Enslaved Millions': Argus, 'The Movement', 'Liberty – Universal Liberty', 'One Word for Louis-Phillipe', 'Whig Malignity – A Simile', 'Invocation to the Memory of Wallace', & 'The Past – The Present – The Future. A Prophecy'. Six of these poems appeared first in the *Northern Star* and six appeared first in the *Chartist Circular*.
6. The *Northern Star* was an eight-page broadsheet whilst the *Chartist Circular* appeared in a four-page 'Berliner' format. Thus, the former had at least twice as much space as the latter.
7. For a detailed discussion of the relationship between Romanticism and Chartist poetry see Janowitz, 1988.
8. For details of the 'New Move', see Chase, 2007, pp. 168–78.
9. For a discussion of the ways in which middle-class radicals saw poetry as a way of engaging with their working-class counterparts see Maidment, 1984, pp. 83–93.

Bibliography

Chase, Malcom (2007) *Chartism: A New History* (Manchester: Manchester University Press).
Fraser, W. Hamish (2005) 'The Chartist Press in Scotland', in *Papers for the People: A Study of the Chartist Press*, ed. Joan Allen and Owen R. Ashton (London: Merlin).
'The Genius of Working Men' (1840) *Chartist Circular*, 33 (May 9th), 135–6.
Jameson, Fredric (1991) *Postmodernism, or the Cultural Logic of Late Capitalism* (London: Verso).
Janowitz, Anne (1988) *Lyric and Labor in the Romantic Tradition* (Cambridge: Cambridge University Press).
Jones, Ernest (1847a) 'Review: T. Powell', *The Labourer*, 1:6, 284.
——. (1847b) 'Literary Review', *The Labourer*, 2:2, 95–6.
——. (1847c) 'National Literature', *The Labourer*, 2:6, 281.
——. (1848) 'National Literature', *The Labourer*, 3:1, 40.
'Literary Reform' (1841) *Chartist Circular*, 71 (Jan. 31st), 299.
'Literary Sketches, Allan Ramsay' (1841) *Chartist Circular*, 75 (Feb. 27th), 314.
'Literary Sketches, Byron' (1841) *Chartist Circular*, 114 (Nov. 27th), 473–4.
'Literary Sketches, James I of Scotland' (1841) *Chartist Circular*, 94 (July 10th), 394.
'Literary Sketches, John Knox' (1841) *Chartist Circular*, 80 (April 3rd), 338.
'Literary Sketches, Robert Burns' (1841) *Chartist Circular*, 74 (Feb. 20th), 309–10.
'Literary Sketches, Robert Henryson' (1841) *Chartist Circular*, 90 (June 12th), 378.

'Literary Sketches, Walter Scott' (1841) *Chartist Circular*, 73 (Feb. 13th), 305–6.

Maidment, Brian (1984) 'Magazines of Popular Progress and the Artisans', *Victorian Periodicals Review*, 17, 83–93.

'Morality of the Working Classes' (1839) *Chartist Circular*, 6 (Nov. 2nd), 22.

Murphy, Paul Thomas (1994) *Toward a Working-Class Canon: Literary Criticism in British Working-Class Periodicals, 1816–1858* (Athens: Ohio State University Press).

'The Politics of Poets. No. I' (1840) *Chartist Circular*, 42 (July 11th), 70.

'The Politics of Poets. No. VI' (1840) *Chartist Circular*, 57 (Oct. 24th), 231.

'The Politics of Poets. No. VIII' (1840) *Chartist Circular*, 65 (Dec. 19th), 265.

Rose, Jonathan (2001) *The Intellectual Life of the British Working Classes* (New Haven: Yale University Press).

Sanders, Mike (2009) *The Poetry of Chartism: Aesthetics, Politics, History* (Cambridge: Cambridge University Press).

Wilson, Alexander (1970) *The Chartist Movement in Scotland* (Manchester: Manchester University Press).

10
Edwin Waugh: The Social and Literary Standing of a Working-Class Icon

Brian Hollingworth

In the second half of the nineteenth century there was a great upsurge of dialect writing in Lancashire. Stimulated by a strengthening sense of regional identity, by the feelings for community consequent on the 'Cotton Famine' during the American Civil War, by increasing literacy among the working classes, and by growing national prosperity, publications of dialect writing in prose and verse multiplied remarkably. In particular three writers, Samuel Laycock, Ben Brierley and Edwin Waugh achieved considerable local fame. The latter two were even able to earn a precarious living as professional writers.

There can be no doubt that Edwin Waugh (1817–1890), often referred to as the Lancashire Burns, or the Poet Laureate of Lancashire, had a profound influence on the cultural life of a great number of ordinary working-class folk during his lifetime and well into more recent years. My own interest in his work comes from hearing frequent recitals of his poetry in the 1940s. He is well represented in the vigorous Northern folk music tradition of the later twentieth century, and to this day there is an Edwin Waugh Society holding regular meetings in his home town of Rochdale. Rochdale also boasts a Lancashire Dialect Writers Memorial, erected in 1900, featuring Waugh along with three other Rochdale writers, Margaret Rebecca Lahee, John Trafford Clegg and Oliver Ormerod.

His friend Francis Espinasse in *The Bookman* of July 1893 gave a description of Waugh's funeral which presents a remarkable account of his standing among the Lancashire populace at the time of his death:

> On the first Saturday of May 1890, a little more than three years ago, toiling and money-making Manchester presented an unusual spectacle. For two and a half miles from the railway station named after that busiest of human beehives, the Exchange of Manchester,

onwards and upwards towards Kersal Moor, from which there is a panoramic view of the great industrial city, with its church steeples and mill chimneys looming athwart a canopy of smoke, there stood on either side the roadway thousands of spectators reverently doffing their caps as a hearse with the coffined remains of one well known and endeared to them wended on its way towards Kersal Church and graveyard. As the hearse passed them the spectators fell in behind it to swell the funeral cortege, in which were the Mayors of Manchester and Salford in their carriages, with other representatives of local municipal officialism, and with deputations from most of the populous towns by which Manchester is belted. (Espinasse, 1893, p. 349)

Espinasse makes the claim here that this was the most striking funeral in Manchester since that of John Dalton forty-five years before, that Waugh's name was 'a household name throughout his native county', and that 'operatives and artizans' were 'conspicuous by their presence'. Yet this grand farewell was for a man who had entirely made his name by his writing in prose and verse largely in the medium of the Lancashire dialect, who had by repute little formal education, and had been completely unknown until he was almost forty.

The extent of his claim to being a significant regional writer in his later years can be judged by the success of the *Collected Edition* of his writings in prose and verse which Waugh himself published in ten volumes between 1881 and 1883, and to which he added another volume of *Poems and Songs* shortly before his death. Then, in 1893, under the editorship of his friend George Milner came a further *Collected Edition* in eight volumes which claimed a very large readership and is still widely available in second-hand bookshops. Concomitant with this project Milner gave a paper to the Manchester Literary Club of which he was President, an extension of his Introduction to the *Collected Edition*, which intelligently discussed the significance of provincial literature in general and of the work of Waugh in particular. In this lecture it is plain that Milner is attempting to legitimize the writings of Waugh as worthy of a place, if only a lowly place, in the established ranks of English literature.

Milner acknowledges Waugh's literary faults of padding and repetition in his prose writing, but nonetheless concludes that Waugh is an extremely good writer, especially when he moves into dialect: 'There he moves without restraint, and in an element which is entirely congenial to him' (Milner, 1893, p. 40). He also recognizes, rightly I believe, that, whatever the virtues of his prose writing, it is as a poet that 'his fame must rest'. This leads him to make the inevitable comparison, which was often made in Waugh's lifetime, with Robert Burns and discuss some of the issues of writing verse in the dialect. He finds that 'although the distance between them is confessedly great, our Lancashire moorland poet comes next in rank – not, of course, as poet pure and simple, but as a dialectal poet – to his great Scottish predecessor' (pp. 43-4). After a nod in the direction of Tennyson's Lincolnshire verse, he favourably compares Waugh with the other well-known dialect poet of the age, William Barnes. For Milner, Waugh is the superior. Barnes is 'more idyllic, but he has less humour, and the dramatic element in his poems is not sustained . . . While Barnes frequently gives you the impression of a poet expressing himself by intention, and with great skill, in a dialectal form, Waugh seems to be setting forth the ideas natural to his characters in the only language which either he or they had at command' (pp. 44-5).

Milner is worth quoting at some length because his account seems even today a just appraisal of the strengths of Waugh's dialect poetry. He is also to be applauded for recognizing that dialect writing has its own integrity and value:

> It is quite certain that sounder views have come into vogue, and one does not often meet now (at least among educated people) with the opinion, once so freely expressed, that all dialectal writing is necessarily synonymous with coarseness and vulgarity. (1893, p. 43)

Equally he fittingly asserts that the Lancashire dialect is 'capable of expressing poetic conceptions with delicacy and force' (p. 45). In effect Milner is happily, and successfully I believe, engaged in making Waugh into a writer worthy of respect, worthy of the attention of scholars and serious literary buffs. He is giving him a place within the canon: as indicated by the fact that the essay is surrounded in the proceedings of the Literary Club by presentations on Shelley and on Macbeth.

Milner had access to Waugh's unpublished 'An Old Man's Memories' and in his paper gives the most subtle and most complete contemporary account of Waugh's life, his triumphs and his failures during a career which saw him rise (if that is the correct word) from a cellar dwelling in Rochdale to a regional literary celebrity, the Grand Old Man of dialect literature. It is a very informative piece of writing, but it is through this biography that we can perhaps begin to see, by its emphases and also by its omissions, something of what Martha Vicinus in her seminal essay on Waugh has called the 'ambiguities' of his literary life.[1]

Powerful writing in the regional vernacular inevitably raises issues of placing within a canon which has been established in the standard language. Dialect codes have traditionally been seen as 'inferior' to standard forms, regarded, as Milner implies, as more limited in their means of expression, and covering a smaller range of emotions. Powerful writing in the vernacular also has implications beyond the boundaries of literature on issues of class and social acceptance. Dialect, when it appears on the page, is the speech of the ordinary man and woman written down: to many it lacks authentication and is a matter of embarrassment or incomprehensibility for the critical reader even before assessment of its quality begins. Alternatively, it is important for others to emphasize that the writer and the writing have not been uprooted from their working-class soil by their exposure within the written code to a more sophisticated environment. There is a perceived danger that they may become less 'authentic' by that very process.

Where Waugh is concerned certain features of his life, of his writing, and of his iconography, both during his life and afterwards, reflect the ambiguities of which Vicinus speaks. We can profitably consider accounts of his childhood and education, contemporary perceptions of his standing as a 'working-class' poet, and attitudes to sexual relationships in his poetry and in his iconography, as significations of the tensions which inevitably emerged and the responses which his contemporaries made to them. The comparisons with Burns are particularly cogent. Burns was perhaps the only labouring-class writer who had by general consent entered the canon, despite his lowly origins and his use of a regional language as his medium, and Waugh could aspire to take a place beside him there by hanging on to his plough handles assiduously. There is no doubt that Waugh himself was well aware of this, though one should not be too cynical about his motives. Between 1847 and 1851, well before he made any impression as a writer, he kept a diary from which it is plainly evident that Burns, of all the poets, was his favourite and his hero. Burns is frequently quoted verbatim, if not always accurately, and Waugh's aspirations as a writer are clearly sustained by the knowledge of the recognition which Burns had eventually received (see Waugh, 2008).

But it is in the later 1850s, after Waugh had begun to gain recognition as a writer, that one begins to see a development of Waugh's public persona which can only be interpreted as an attempt to mould himself on the template (suitably sanitized for a Victorian readership) of his Scottish hero. The first known photograph dates from 1861 and reveals a young-middle-aged, bow-tied and waistcoated man staring with some confidence at the camera. Yet the most significant item in the photograph lies in his left hand – he is holding a snuff box which he believed to have been owned by Robert Burns himself. This relic of the true cross is exhibited five years after the publication in the *Manchester Examiner* of the highly successful 'Come Whoam to thi Childer an' Me' and two years after his anthology *Poems and Songs* which had solidified his reputation as a dialect poet. To confirm the Burnsian connection over the years Waugh appears to have adopted a suitable uniform to match. In his prime Waugh must have been physically impressive. Milner reports:

> He walked with a slow firm step, and with his large hands spread out. He affected huge sticks, of which he had an immense collection, and he liked to throw a shepherd's plaid over his shoulder. His face, which was marked by quiet humour, was always ready to take a genial expression even when at its saddest; and, in a mirthful mood, it beamed all over with laughter. Like Bamford, he had the ease and natural manners of a born gentleman – a gentleman of the older sort, and his bearing showed no timidity or restraint in the presence of persons who were socially his superiors. No man had less of the morbid and puling poet about him. He was fond of clothing himself in honest homespun of the thickest texture, and of wearing huge broad-soled boots, guiltless of polish. It was not often that he attempted to get into evening dress, and when he did the attempt was only partially successful, and the result ludicrous. He was too large for such things, and always looked as if his next breath would burst his sable fetters. It used to be said that someone who went into his bedroom one morning found his tweed suit standing up on end in the middle of the floor without support; and I have heard him convulse a quiet household by giving, in a vein of richest humour, elaborate instructions overnight to the maid, about not having his boots spoiled with blacking. (Milner, 1893, pp. 62–3)

If manners makyth man, it is plain from this description that manners and clothes makyth the poet. Waugh seems to be clearly identifying himself by the plaid with Burns and by his honest homespun clothes and unpolished shoes with the kind of poetry – what many of his readers would have termed 'doric' – which he was writing. Few would be able to claim a homely suit as a carapace even as a tall story, but Waugh seems to have achieved the feat. A portrait of Waugh painted by William Percy in 1882 owned by the Manchester City Gallery (a copy of which accompanies his current O.D.N.B entry) reveals a patriarchal figure with a strong flowing beard, the plaid over his left shoulder and one of his sticks firmly grasped in his right hand – an impression quite in keeping with Milner's description. What makes this affectation (the word is almost used by Milner) more remarkable is that if we read the diary of his earlier years we find a very different potential poet. The real Waugh was wracked with self-doubt and melancholy, casting himself much more in the role of a Byronic fated hero than the hail-fellow-well-met of his later years.

It is noticeable that, at this stage in his account, Milner is also approving, in relation to his burial place at Kersal, another nomination frequently given to Waugh – 'the Moorland Poet':

> He lies on the edge of the moorland. The sun will shine freely over his grave and the moorland wind will blow over it; and that is well, for, as we have already said, no description fits him better than that of 'The Moorland Poet'. (Milner, 1893, p. 62)

Again there is an evident ambiguity behind Milner's sincere appellation. At one level this is a direct reference to Waugh's most famous poem in standard English, 'The Moorland Flower', which is the first poem in his *Poems and Lancashire Songs* of 1859, and it is true that much of Waugh's fictional prose writing reflects village life in the hills around Rochdale. Moreover, as Milner reminds us, Waugh was a keen rambler and spent many happy hours on the hills of Lancashire and the Lake District: to this day there is an annual pilgrimage by Waugh enthusiasts to Waugh's Well up on the moors near Edenfield. He was certainly a man of the moorlands. Yet Milner is not making his claim for Waugh as a significant poet because of the verse he wrote in standard English:

> With regard to his poems in ordinary English it may be admitted at once that they are sometimes common-place; and that, even when they rise to a higher level, all that we can venture to say of them is that they are graceful and pleasing. But in the dialect it is altogether different. (1893, p. 43)

And if we look at the dialect poems on which Waugh's reputation rests, though there are often idyllic hints of a pre-industrial past, the atmosphere is of the urban industrial present and their relevance is to the day to day life of people who are working in the mills. One might argue that Kersal churchyard was equally fitting for Waugh's burial because it was on the edge of the huge industrial conurbation in which he had spent most of his life. It is as though the poet and his readers or hearers are engaged in a conscious or unconscious scheme to present Waugh as a formidable figure within the pastoral tradition of a Bloomfield or a Burns, even when some of his most effective verse turns in another direction.

Similar ambiguities arise in at least two other areas of Waugh's life, where there is a recurring temptation for the Victorian admirer of Waugh's poetry, and for Waugh himself, to conceal or distort the factual details in order to idealize the man and his work. The first of these concerns his birth and upbringing and raises the issue of how far he fits into standard descriptions (then and now) of the 'labouring-class' or 'working-class' poet. With cotton providing the main source of employment for the Lancashire man and woman, the stereotypical poet can no longer compose at the plough tail, but rather must work to the clatter of the loom. Waugh's two major competitors, Laycock and Brierley, in this respect proved to have better credentials than Waugh. Laycock (1826–1893) came to the fore during the cotton panic of the early 1860s when he sold his poems to alleviate the sufferings of unemployment. He had been working in the mill since he was nine and claimed to have written the first of his twelve *Lyrics of the Cotton Famine* on the back of a cop ticket from a bale of cotton. Brierley (1825–96) had begun life as a handloom weaver – workers with considerable prestige during the mid years of the nineteenth century both because they were skilled craftsmen, and also because they had been driven from their cottages to the mills by the power loom.

Waugh, somewhat unfortunately for his poetic status, did not quite fit into this aristocracy. He had been poor enough but, as Milner makes clear, his background was decidedly bookish. Waugh's father died when he was nine and Milner tells us:

> Waugh had no schooling before he was seven years of age, but his mother taught him to read very early, and the books which his father had left were always handy on the window sill – the usual bookcase in a poor man's cottage. In 'An Old Man's Memories' – to which I am indebted for many of the facts included in this sketch – Waugh gives a list of these books – 'The Bible', 'The Book of Common Prayer', 'Wesley's Hymns', 'Baxter's Saint's Rest', 'Bunyan's Pilgrims Progress', 'Foxe's Book of Martyrs', a 'Compendium of the History of England', 'Culpepper's Herbal,' a large quarto copy of 'Barclay's Dictionary', and a few small elementary books.' (Milner, 1893, pp. 47–8)

This list no doubt reflects the interests of a mother who was intimately involved with the Methodist movement in its earlier years and a father who had received 'a good elementary education at Rochdale Grammar School' (p. 46). Milner gives a picture of a family which had originally come from Northumberland and had considerable standing in the local community before the problems of being, in Waugh's father's case, a seventh son, had reduced them to poverty. The death of his father increased the family's difficulties and consequently they were forced to live for several years in a cellar dwelling.

Nevertheless, Waugh's mother, who achieved saintly status in the eyes of her son, did her best to educate him:

> After he was seven years of age he seems to have received a little intermittent teaching at various schools – private, national, and commercial . . . As was almost invariably the case with boys of his class, at the time of which I am writing, the Sunday school and the night school were called in to make up for the deficiencies in day school training. (p. 50)

From other sources we learn further details of his formal education. When seven years old, Edwin was sent to the national Free School, and was afterwards transferred to Davenport's Commercial School, then considered one of the best in Rochdale. At this school, the boy (described by his master as 'rough and inattentive') received the ordinary middle-class education. He admits having been a failure in arithmetic, but he was a quick learner in other directions (*Great Thoughts*, 1891, p. 233). His circumstances were distressing enough, given the extreme poverty in which the family lived, but he certainly received some formal education and there is evidence that, given his background, Waugh himself never quite considered that he was 'working class'. Although some of his relations were employed in the mills and served King Cotton, all Waugh's career was concerned with print. At twelve he went to work for a printer, and a year later found employment with Thomas Holden, another Rochdale bookseller and printer. The opportunities which this gave him for reading inspired his lifelong interest in Lancashire folklore and history. He then became a journeyman printer, working in London, Durham and Wakefield before returning to Rochdale in the mid-1840s and briefly and acrimoniously working once more for Holden. In 1847 he gained a secretarial post with the Lancashire Public Schools Association and moved to Manchester from where, through contact with literary people of the provincial city, he began to build his literary career.

In Waugh's career, indeed, we see the slipperiness of the English class system when we try to define it. From Milner's point of view, though he himself might be described as 'only' a provincial intellectual, we have already seen evidence that he regarded Waugh as 'below' him. His notion, cited above, that Waugh 'showed no timidity or restraint in the presence of those who were socially his superiors' places his attitude quite clearly, as does his certainty about the education of 'boys of his class'. Yet Waugh from his earliest years writes down towards the working people from a superior height, even as he celebrates their activities and validates their turn of speech. There is a good example of this in his *Diary*, written well before he gained any literary success, when he describes meeting some drinkers in a public house near Littleborough. The Diary overall contains many examples of conversations with local people and is often a kind of testing ground of Waugh's ear for the dialect which is always entirely convincing. Here he clearly enjoys playing a class game with his interlocutors as they try to decide who he is:

> I had told the landlord to get me some eggs and ham cooked, for I was sincerely hungry. He popt his head out the parlor to say that all was ready in another room. I went mealwards and 'played a good stick'. – Returning to the parlor, old Race asked my leave to ask me a saucy sort of question. – He wished to know whether I was a native of Rochdale, or not. – I thought he remembered my face. – I told him I was at present a resident in Manchester, altho' a native of Rochdale. I saw in the faces about me a disposition to know more – my name and position, but partly for my own amusement, – partly because I wished to enjoy the deference which they paid to me unknown, which had they known my name and humble origin, they might have denied me – and then, I did not wish my errand into the neighbourhood to be known to everybody.[2] – Perceiving that I did not wish to be more communicative, – altho' with evidently unabated curiosity, they pushed it no further. Old Race and the doctor supt up, and departed, bidding me a respectful good night. (Waugh, 2008, p. 39)

This somewhat superior attitude to the local people he meets is replicated in his first major publication, *Sketches of Lancashire Life*, in 1855. As he travels to the cottage in Milnrow of the eighteenth-century Lancashire writer Tim Bobbin (real name John Collier), or visits one of his favourite moorland haunts, Blackstone Edge, the persona he adopts is distinctly superior to the country people he meets on the way. In turn, as he describes their reaction to his questioning, they are remarkably inclined to show him a suitable deference.

On the other side of the coin, we can see from the *Diary* that Waugh was not admitted beyond any class boundaries. When he gained his secretarial post with the Lancashire Public Schools Association his immediate boss was Francis Espinasse, a Scotsman who could claim connections with Carlyle. Apparently Espinasse, although considerably younger than Waugh, dubbed himself Don Quixote and Waugh Sancho Panza (Waugh, 2008, p. 113). In part, this was Espinasse's self-deprecating joke at the expense of his own gaunt appearance, but it certainly puts Waugh in his social place. That this epithet is largely a class distinction is supported by the fact that the *Diary* reveals a melancholy Waugh who in character terms is far from being the irrepressible servant of Cervantes' novel.[3]

Nevertheless many of his readers and hearers among the working classes of Lancashire were more than anxious to emphasize Waugh's position as a man of the people and a truly working class writer, a man who rose from the masses and triumphed over his lack of formal education. Consequently there is a continuing tendency to underplay the amount of education which Waugh actually received. For instance, an early biographer, otherwise informative about Waugh's career, emphasizes that 'whatever rudimentary education he received it was imparted to him by his mother and Sunday School teachers' (Robertson, 1881, p. 169). Espinasse, in his reminiscences, says no more than that he was 'of a humble birth and self educated', and other obituarists are equally reticent about his educational background. When Rochdale put on an exhibition in the Art Gallery to celebrate the centenary of his birth in 1917, his education is referred to as 'scant'.[4] Instead, to establish his working-class credentials they emphasize the extreme poverty in which the family lived after his father's death – that they lived in one of the notorious cellar dwellings of the time, that Waugh went selling shoes on Rochdale market. A picture is created, not untrue but possibly exaggerated, of a heroic childhood and a triumph over cultural adversity.

Most significantly, however, it is in the area of Victorian social conventionalities and personal sexual morality that the strains most markedly show in the distances between the public and private personas which were presented to the public by the poet and by his admirers. Waugh and his work were marketed to the reading and hearing public as a model of conventional domestic morality, whilst the misfortunes of his private life presented a very different picture. So that this discrepancy should not affect Waugh as an iconic figure in the local canon, details of his private life, both during his lifetime and after his death, were deftly removed from the record.

Waugh gained dramatic local fame when his poem 'Come Whoam to thi childer an' Me' was published in the *Manchester Examiner* in 1856. It proved an immediate hit with the readers and since then has become well nigh synonymous with his name in local folklore. The poem is so typical of both Waugh's strengths and of his weaknesses as a dialect poet that it should be quoted in full.

> Aw've just mended th' fire wi' a cob;
> Owd Swaddle has brought thi new shoon;   *shoes*
> There's some nice bacon-collops o'th'hob,
> An' a quart o'ale-posset i'th'oon;   *oven*
> Aw've brought thi top-cwot, doesta know,
> For th'rains comin' deawn very dree   *drearily*
> An' har-stone's as white as new snow; –
> Come whoam to thi childer an'me.
>
> When aw put little Sally to bed,
> Hoo cried' cose her feyther weren't theer,
> So aw kiss'd little thing, an' aw said
> Thae'd bring her a ribbin fro'th'fair;
> An aw gav' her her doll, an' some rags,
> An' a nice little white cotton-bo';
> An' aw kiss'd her again; but hoo said
> 'At hoo wanted to kiss *thee* an'o.
>
> An' Dick, too, aw'd sich wark wi' him,
> Afore aw could get him upstairs;
> Thae towd him thae'd bring him a drum,
> He said, when he're sayin' his prayers;
> Then he looked i'my face, an' he said,
> 'Has th'boggarts taen houd o'my dad?'   *devils*
> An' he cried whol his e'en were quite red; –
> He likes thee some weel, does yon lad!
>
> At th'lung-length, aw geet 'em laid still;
> An' aw hearken't folks' feet that went by;

So aw iron't o'my cloas reet weel,
An' aw hang'd' em o'th'maiden to dry;   *clothes rack*
When aw'd mended thi stockin's an' shirts,
Aw sit deawn to knit i'my cheer,
An'aw rayley did feel rather hurt, –
Mon, aw'm *one*-ly when theaw artn't theer.

'Aw've a drum an' a trumpet for Dick;
Aw've a yard o'blue ribbin for Sal;
Aw've a book full o'babs; an' a stick,   *pictures*
An'some' bacco an'pipes for myself;
Aw've brought thee some coffee an'tay, –
Iv thae'll *feel* i'my pocket thae'll *see*;
An'aw've bought tho a new cap today, –
For aw al'ays bring summat for *thee*!

'God bless tho'my lass; aw'll go whoam
An'aw'll kiss thee an'th'childer o'round;
Thae knows that wherever aw roam,
Aw'm fain to get back to th'owd ground;
Aw can do wi' a crack o'er a glass;
Aw can do wi' a bit of a spree;
But aw've no gradely comfort, my lass,
Except wi' yon childer an' thee.'

In a poem such as this his appeal to the local audience is very evident. He manages to capture, within the cadences of the verse, not just the vocabulary of dialect but also its idiom. These are idioms which, if translated into the standard language, lose much of their 'homely' force. 'Mended th'fire wi' a cob' – improved the fire with a piece of coal: 'aw'd sich wark wi'him' – I'd so much trouble with him: 'aw'm *one*-ly' – I'm lonely: 'aw've no gradely comfort' – I've no proper enjoyment. Dialect gains linguistic distinctiveness in the poetry of Waugh. It is easy to see how the readers (and perhaps more commonly the hearers) would closely identify with the situations described and the feelings expressed. In addition, Waugh characteristically catches the 'Dutch interior' of a Lancashire working-class home with its fireside oven and hearthstone, and the little, cheap, 'cotto-bo' toys that the children might play with. Waugh's poetry appeals because of the way his close observation of working-class lives is seamlessly integrated into his use of dialectal idiom and verse.

Moreover, the poem is a dialogue, with the first four verses given to the woman, and the last two to the man. This dialogue form is very common in Waugh's poetry and gives it a dramatic edge that is often lacking in other writers. It is to this quality that Milner is referring when he ranks Waugh above Barnes as a vernacular poet. On the other hand, to modern eyes the poem has a typically Victorian idealized sentimentality, which even Waugh's friends and contemporaries recognized. Ben Brierley soon wrote a parody entitled 'Go Tak' thi' Ragged Childer an' Flit' (i.e. move house). Several others followed. Moreover, written only six years after the Chartist gathering at Kennington, this poem must surely stand as an ur-text in the controversial issue of the apparent domestication in the social values of the radical working classes in the second half of the nineteenth century – the apparent subjection of the working classes to middle class values. In the *Dictionary of National Biography* (1899 edn) Espinasse informs us that, recognizing the poem's local popularity, Lady Burdett Coutts, the social reformer and friend of Dickens, actively promoted sales of the poem not only in England but abroad as well. It is safe to assume that her enthusiasm for the poem was connected to its exemplary moral teaching rather than its qualities as a fine piece of dialect writing. Similarly *The Saturday Review* in a laudatory acknowledgement of the poem when John Harland published his *Ballads and Songs of Lancashire* in 1865 remarks: 'We wonder how many of the four million sermons preached annually in our happy country have as wholesome effect as this simple piece has had, and continues to have.'[5]

Indeed, the popularity of the poem as a moral exemplum may well lead us to look sceptically at Milner's claim, earlier quoted more positively, that in 1903 educated people no longer felt that dialect writing was synonymous with coarseness and vulgarity. One reason for this surely is that Laycock, Brierley and Waugh cleaned the dialect up. Dialect poems of the earlier nineteenth century, such as the well-known traditional poem 'Jone o'Grinfilt' and its many successors, or the *Songs* of the Wilson family in Manchester, might not only be accused of a roughness which emanated from their oral origin, but also of a subversive morality which threatened the establishment, sometimes in no uncertain terms. Yet, although the three outstanding dialect writers of the second half of the century came to the fore at a time of considerable social suffering with the Cotton Famine caused by the American Civil War, and radical tendencies might have been expected, their sentiments are uniformly exemplary and unthreatening.

However, whatever opinion one forms of the significance of its moral stance, it cannot be denied that 'Come Whoam' was tremendously popular with the ordinary working people of Lancashire and the surrounding counties. After it appeared in the newspaper a Manchester publisher, Kelly and Slater, persuaded Waugh, rather reluctantly apparently, to issue it on fly sheets. They sold 20,000 copies directly 'out of their own shop' and others were printed by 'several private persons' and 'sold on tobacco papers'.[6] Espinasse, in his description of Waugh's funeral, claims that the poem sold 'literally by the million not only in Lancashire but throughout England and the colonies' (1893, p. 361). Surely an exaggeration, but there can be no doubt that the poem had a tremendous impact, established Waugh as a writer and a working-class hero, and gave an impetus to Lancashire writing which extended for well over fifty years. Waugh became the poet of the hearth and home, and the iconic image which he attained among Lancashire working folk was largely painted upon this emblematic poem. Unfortunately, through no particular hypocrisy on his part, Waugh's own private life seriously failed to match up to the idyllic pictures set forth in this and much of his dialect poetry. And the thoroughness with which this failure was concealed from his reading and hearing public tells us a great deal about the conventions of respectable Victorian morality and the means by which public knowledge could be manipulated to hide uncomfortable facts. In this area of the presentation of Waugh's public persona, the means adopted were not those of exaggeration, selection or emphasis but rather absence and averted vision.

Waugh married Mary Ann Hill in May 1847 at Rochdale Parish Church. Within a very short time their relationship deteriorated and his diary records in vivid detail the dramatic consequences. In September 1847, after a brief period of unemployment, he gained his job with the Lancashire Public Schools Association and moved with Mary Ann to Manchester. As we have seen, the post brought him in contact with Espinasse, and a number of other literary men such as Alexander Ireland, the editor of the *Manchester Examiner*. It proved the foundation for his literary career. But Waugh found Mary Ann feckless and sluttish. In all probability she found him workshy and certainly in serious and continuing debt. A pattern emerged of Mary Ann returning to her mother, who lived beyond Rochdale near Littleborough, and Edwin going there to persuade her to return. At one point in the diary Waugh gives a dramatic description of what in effect is a midnight brawl in the street between himself and some of Mary Ann's relatives (Waugh, 2008, pp. 65–7). There is considerable evidence in the number of times that she did go back to Manchester of a strong affection between them. On at least one occasion she walked all the way from Rochdale to Manchester to do so. But, in the longer run, although they had three children, the marriage collapsed (Vicinus, 1983, pp. 12–14).

When 'Come Whoam' was published, therefore, Waugh's personal circumstances regarding marriage and home could hardly have been more different from those depicted in the poem. Samuel Bamford, the old radical of Peterloo, who had an antipathy to Waugh which Waugh fully reciprocated, confided to a friend that the poem was written 'whilst his wife and children were at the very time in the Marland Workhouse and he living with another woman in Strangeways' (qtd Vicinus, 1983, p. 14). Bamford cannot be taken as a reliable witness but Mary Ann had already spent time in the Marland Workhouse during the time Waugh was writing his diary, so this may well be true in greater or lesser part. Certainly Waugh never experienced a conventional married life again. His personal life becomes shrouded in reticence and ambiguity. In some ways he becomes an itinerant single man, partly because of his writing, which is often based on extended visits to local places such as Preston during the Cotton Famine or the Lake District for his various 'rambles' there, and partly because of his ambiguous marital status. It is indicative that on the day of the 1881 census, Mary Ann Waugh, Head of Household, is still living in her native village of Shore near Littleborough while Waugh himself, though still styling himself a married man, is staying in a hotel in Grange-over-Sands in the Lake District. Indeed, as Milner tells us, for several years he lived in a hotel in the Manchester suburb of Kersal where he was eventually buried (1893, p. 59). In his later years he seems to have established a permanent relationship with another woman, Rosanna, who took his surname and is buried near him, not with him, in Kersal Churchyard.[7] The records are, one might say, deliberately scanty in regard to this part of his life and contemporary accounts of his doings after 1856 are always concerning homosocial activities – rambles on the moors with his male friends, the meetings of the Manchester Literary Club, and other club activities, his readings with Ben Brierley or by himself around Lancashire and further afield. Women disappear from the record and Waugh is presented as a cheerful and entertaining bachelor, a much less threatening public image for the writer of 'Come Whoam' than a man who had deserted his wife and children.

Such absences are particularly conspicuous in accounts of his final years when he was suffering from cancer of the tongue and had moved from Manchester to New Brighton on the Mersey estuary for his health.

Milner, typically, records the support given to him by his doctor and male friends but there is no mention of Rosanna's role or whether she went from Manchester to New Brighton with him or attended his funeral. Espinasse's account of Waugh's life and death has the same glaring absences. An immediate memoir in the *Manchester City News* (3 May 1890) which had wide circulation is equally reticent. Waugh's death provoked obituaries in almost all the town newspapers in Lancashire, but all seem to have been silent on this significant feature of Waugh's life. The nearest acknowledgement of Mary Ann's existence is a coy sentence in the *Rochdale Times*, also on 3 May 1890, admitting that 'in his early days Waugh married a Rochdale lady'.

Given the gritty circumstances of Waugh's life, Milner's summing up of his character and work in his otherwise excellent paper to the Manchester Literary Club is cloying and typical of the fashion in which Waugh was projected to his admirers and friends during his years of literary success and also after his death. Post-Victorian sanctimoniousness is used to avoid awkward truths and confirm Waugh's claim to iconic status. Typically, however, as so often in such eulogies, there is a hint of secrets suppressed, in that almost revealing phrase 'his better self':

> The child was father of the man, and the influence of his mother's simple piety is unmistakable in his work. Through all his passages of boisterous humour there is never found either immoral taint or sinister suggestion. His books, like his bodily presence and his better self, are conspicuously clean and healthy. His real worth may be estimated by the number of those who loved him when living, and who honour him now he is gone. Few men possessed in a higher degree the faculty of gaining friends; but he had also that much rarer gift which enables a man to keep them when they have been gained. (Milner, 1893, p. 66)

By such means was Waugh's status as a Lancashire poet and writer established, and by such means was it maintained in later years. In the twentieth century one might discern almost active resistance among his devotees to any information which questioned Waugh's personal behaviour and moral status. His manifest strengths as a poet were inextricably linked with the perceived wholesomeness of his message, and closely related to the perceived gallantry of his character in his working-class struggle from obscurity to local celebration. However, although entirely understandable, indeed inevitable, given the moral climate and the mores of disclosure and retention which surrounded

Victorian social and literary culture, these ambiguities, it seems to me, may now prevent a true assessment of Waugh's claims to that place within the canon of literature which Milner was seeking. It is sufficient to say that Waugh is a very good poet in the Lancashire dialect – to read 'Tum Rindle' or 'Down Again' or 'The Dules i'this Bonnet o'Mine' or many others is to prove the point. Those interested in vernacular literature should read the poems. There is no need today to stand in reverence before his doubtful image, nor, on the other hand, to scorn the poet because of the idealistic misrepresentations imposed upon him by his virtuous contemporaries.

Notes

1. Vicinus, 1984. See also Vicinus 1974 for further discussion of Waugh.
2. He was trying to persuade his estranged wife to come back to him.
3. Espinasse refers to this again in his memoir (1893, pp. 349–65).
4. See Folder 5 of the Edwin Waugh Papers in the Selborne Collection, Birmingham University Library.
5. Quoted in the memoir on Waugh's death in *Manchester City News*, May 3rd 1890.
6. Note from publishers Kelly and Slater in Waugh documents, Manchester Central Library.
7. See Folder 7 of the Edwin Waugh papers in the Selborne collection, Birmingham University Library.

Bibliography

Espinasse, Francis (1893) *Literary Recollections and Sketches* (London: Hodder & Stoughton).
Great Thoughts (1891) VI: 145 (11 April), 233.
Milner, George (1893) 'Edwin Waugh', in *Manchester Literary Club Papers*, XII.
Robertson, W. (1881) *Old and New Rochdale and its People* (Rochdale: n.pub)
Vicinus, Martha (1984) *The Lancashire Dialect Writer Edwin Waugh; The Ambiguities of Self-Help* (Rochdale: George Kelsall).
——. (1974) *The Industrial Muse* (London: Croom Helm).
Waugh, Edwin (1893) *Collected Edition of the Works of Edwin Waugh*, ed. George Milner (Manchester: J. Heywood).
——. (2008) *The Diary of Edwin Waugh: Life in Victorian Manchester and Rochdale, 1847–51*, ed. Brian Hollingworth (Lancaster: Scotforth Books).

11
William Barnes's Place and Dialects of Connection

Sue Edney

In their paper on the use of dialect and the literary canon, Tom Burton and Ken Ruthven consider the 'markedness' of Victorian dialect use – it is working class.

> In canonical Victorian literature, regional speech is acceptable only when restricted to working-class characters and embedded in a standard English narrative, as the Yorkshire dialect is in Emily Brontë's *Wuthering Heights* (1847) or the North Staffordshire and Derbyshire dialects are in George Eliot's *Adam Bede* (1859). (Burton and Ruthven, 2009, pp. 313, 311)

Throughout the nineteenth century attitudes to language formation varied, but there was a common assumption that labourers spoke 'badly'.[1] Dialect use, in poetry, can be potentially awkward for both dialect and non-dialect audiences alike: it draws an audience into a place which is not necessarily 'their' place but contributes to a sometimes problematic notion of belonging to a community that is 'placed'. On one hand, reading and writing in dialect provides a linguistic interaction that might bolster the cultural and social construction of a local community. Yet, on the other, the use of local language can push wider audiences away. Under these combined circumstances, the use of dialect, however skilful and imaginative, limits a poem's reception. More importantly in terms of minority status, it can limit the dialect writer's circulation within the poetic marketplace, including his or her potential influence on other poets.

William Barnes is important in the study of Victorian dialect writing not simply because his poetry, never out of print since its first publication, provides some of the finest examples of dialect poetry in the period, but also because his class position complicates this standard view of dialect as 'working-class'. Barnes was a self-educated Victorian rural schoolmaster, part of whose role was to train students for the Indian Civil Service. His semi-literate parents were fractionally above agricultural labourers, renting a holding so small that Barnes called it a 'farmling', just outside Sturminster Newton in Dorset.[2] A mixture of fortune, physical frailty and early success in copperplate meant that Barnes was taken on as a solicitor's clerk at around fourteen years old, instead of joining his brothers in a search for diminishing work in the fields. He *became* middle class through sheer determination, the first one of his family, forcing himself through Oxford University in middle age as a 'ten years man' in order to gain a degree in Divinity. He was not like his middle-class contemporaries, therefore, such as Alfred Tennyson, or even the much younger Dorset man, Thomas Hardy, who was from a fully literate family, and whose father ran an established building trade. Both Tennyson and Hardy strongly admired Barnes's poetry, and both were also notable users of dialect. Yet Tennyson's dialect poems were a small part of his large and varied body of work, through which he could address his childhood's difficulties as well as his Lincolnshire roots. They were not undertaken until he had a solid presence within the literary establishment, from 1860 onwards. Those readers who found dialect difficult could pass over these works, and many remain unaware of them. Barnes's use of dialect is, in contrast, uncompromising. Although he was urged to produce 'translations' and in 1868 published one volume of poetry in 'common' English, they were unsuccessful and the volume was never reprinted in England. There were, however, three volumes of dialect poetry, the 1879 collection running into seven editions by 1905 (Chedzoy, 2010, p. 169).

The vast majority of Barnes's poems deal with the specificities of rural labouring-class life in a particular part of England, using a language also specific to that place. It is not possible to engage with his poetry without engaging with the complexities of Dorset dialect. Through hard work, helped by a loving and beneficial marriage to Julia Miles, who was the daughter of an excise officer, Barnes successfully created a middle-class position for himself and his family, but in doing so he effectively excluded his poetic works from the 'canon' of labouring or working-class poetics, then and now. As Coventry Patmore observed, he did not even have 'the advantage of being able to demand the admiration of the sympathizing public on the score that he is a chimney-sweep, or a rat-catcher, and has never learned to read' (Patmore, 1862, p. 155). Yet in his choice of language and material, he consciously wrote within a tradition primarily associated, for Victorian readers and for recent literary critics, with working-class poetics. Barnes shows how problematic these distinctions are, and how our attempts to categorize particular forms of language as indicative of class status are inevitably limiting. This essay considers how Barnes negotiated these contradictions in his 'affective' lyrics, casting an establishment form in unorthodox language. Geoffrey Grigson described Barnes's insistent use of dialect as a 'learned perversity' (see Barnes, 1950, p. 11). And yet for Barnes, writing lyrical poems in local language gave new life to an existing form while preserving the language and culture of a local community, one that he was concerned might be disintegrating and fragmenting. At the same time, the 'learned' part of his perversity – Barnes's considerable and eclectic self-instruction in all branches of academic and practical interest – keeps him at the forefront of nineteenth-century intellectual engagement, alongside his admirers. This alone ought to ensure his place in the canon of nineteenth-century poetry; so much of his poetry speaks directly to contemporary anxieties and enthusiasms. His poetic skill, furthermore, pre-figured the 'modern' poetry of the early twentieth century, using 'highly artificial verse-forms and metrical devices to meet the rhythm of ordinary spoken English', something Robert Frost and Edward Thomas were trying to achieve seventy years after Barnes's first collection in 1844, as David Wright has shown (1969, p. 147). Interestingly, Wright includes Barnes in his selection of 'seven Victorian poets' alongside Matthew Arnold, arguably the one Victorian figure responsible for instituting the notion of 'canonical' English writers. Barnes, he argues, evaded canonization partly because he avoided 'the artificial "poetical"' (p. 8)

The Victorian lyric held an important cultural position as an expression of *connected* individual and societal pressures and pleasures. Barnes emphasized a classless lyrical basis for his own writing as a way of elevating the local labouring culture that formed his subject-matter, as well as educating his middle class audience into a better understanding of what was lost in the general drive towards industrial efficiency at the expense of family farming practices, local customs, childhood freedoms and a life perspective viewed from a specific locality. However, the importance of this message was not always understood by his contemporaries who wanted pleasant nostalgic pastoral, and is only now beginning to be realized against a background of increased concern surrounding cultural and environmental diversity. Barnes's use of dialect obscures as well as develops the message, and in much of the nineteenth century its reception as an authentic *aesthetic* medium was often confused in trying to pin down its philological accuracy. Attempts to separate the poetry from its orthography, or to use dialect poetry as a linguistic exercise alone are becoming less frequent in twenty-first century academic research, although there is still some way to go in re-uniting linguistic and literary studies.[3]

Although he was highly learned, Barnes's poetry has much in common with nineteenth-century labouring-class and self-taught dialect poetry, sharing a commitment to the home, family and community. Such poetry seemed (and arguably often was) uncontroversial, yet simultaneously carried political force in its attacks on perceived injustices and its strong support for social cohesion. In as much as nineteenth-century labouring-class dialect verse is still read, within and outwith the academy, linguistic and biographical concerns have tended to dominate discussion. In literary criticism, Florence Boos has commented on the difficulty of situating self-taught and working-class poetry within theoretical frameworks such as 'structuralism, deconstruction, "postmodernism" and the like': the fact that such poetry might respond best to a historicist approach, she argues, potentially limited its use by twentieth-century critics and relegated it to 'minor' literature (2007, p. 224). There is no objection to minority status in itself, as Guillory, Deleuze and Guattari have extensively argued, nor does minor inevitably mean 'second-rate', as James Najarian discusses (Najarian, 2003, p. 571). On the other hand, problems arise when it appears that minority status relates solely to a linguistic appraisal.

In the 'Dissertation' prefacing his first volume of poetry, Barnes declared his intentions for the poems with care: they were not written 'to show up the simplicity of rural life as an object of sport'. Barnes made use of what he knew to be available to his community when considering their needs, poems with 'the associations of an early youth that was passed among rural families in a secluded part of the county':

> As he has not written for readers who have had their lots cast in town-occupations of a highly civilized community, and cannot sympathize with the rustic mind, he can hardly hope that they will understand either his poems or his intention; since, with the not uncommon notion that every change from the plough towards the desk . . . is an onward step toward happiness . . . they will most likely find it very hard to conceive that wisdom and goodness would be found speaking in a dialect which may seem to them a fit vehicle only for the animal wants and passions of a boor. (Barnes, 'Dissertation', 1844, pp. 36–7)

Much of the available anthologized eighteenth-century and ballad poetry was sometimes coupled to the generally benign impression of a 'golden age' when England was a better 'place' altogether, a cultural false memory famously described by Raymond Williams as the 'escalator' effect.[4] There was also, as a result, a pervasive georgic impulse throughout self-taught poetry in the early nineteenth-century, even in small lyrics and songs, in which stewardship and the didactic value of labour and self-education could be promoted.

Anne Janowitz points to the 'dialectic' in which 'categories of self and community differentiate and depend upon each other' during the early nineteenth century, producing the 'communitarian lyric' (1998, p. 12). In all his writing, Barnes focuses on the working community; he identified himself as a 'working man' in his everyday life, and celebrated the potential of virtuous labour depicted in earlier georgic writing (Chedzoy, 1985, pp. 138–9). People in the landscape create the georgic connection of place and environment to humanity. There is no easy way to express this persistent connection in poetic terms except to use the term 'georgic' as shorthand, meaning an aesthetic, but also an ethical, enclosure of 'people-in-landscape'. Barnes believed his poems 'had a didactic purpose', as Valerie Shepherd points out, in similar georgic fashion, and using dialect provided a pragmatic setting for what he considered a realistic portrayal of rural working life. Shepherd quotes the phrase Barnes used himself about teaching poetry, 'setting forth the good and loveworthy that men's minds would more readily take and hold it'.[5]

Barnes's use of an apparently outdated language to write about the minutia of a valley in Dorset indicates another feature of Victorian culture: a passion for antiquarianism and historicism. Hilary Fraser points to both sides of this 'historicist turn' in the nineteenth century: history could serve 'as a means of legitimacy' for self-conscious Victorian modernity, yet historical knowledge also contributed to a gradual realization of the lack of stability in 'pastness' (2000, pp. 116–17). One of Barnes's affinities with another Dorset poet, Thomas Hardy, was in their mutual 'sense of the irretrievable pastness of the past', apparently expressed by Barnes in his poetic language (Zietlow, 1969, p. 298). Yet Barnes recognized that local language could explore Victorian modernity as well as it could evoke the past. Barnes's use of dialect was one route into a 'pragmatic poetry', as John Parham terms Gerard Manley Hopkins' writing, one in which it might become possible to translate 'romantic sensibility into pragmatic critique' of the Victorian condition while 'retaining an ecocentric or romantic sentiment' (2010, pp. 75–6). The construction of place in this project was linked to cultural interpretations of faith, nation and society. In all this Barnes, in common with other analysts of Victorian modernity, recognized 'that the physical environment is connected to other – cultural economic, social, and moral – components of society and, ultimately, to political organisation', as Parham argues in his recent study of 'Victorian ecology' (p. 70). Using dialect enabled Barnes to make what he believed were concrete connections between situations and the communities involved in them: between words and things. For many readers and writers from whatever background in the early nineteenth century, stability of language was as important as security of place. Patrick Joyce summarizes the common position for labouring-class and self-taught writers:

> Language was the bearer of values and ideas, in stories and proverbs, for example. But it was more than merely bearer or vehicle: it was in fact the embodiment or substance of value, itself a form of symbolic meaning standing for all manner of desires, associations, beliefs, conscious and unconscious. (Joyce, 1991, p. 279)

The influence of present-day linguistic theories makes us wary of such concrete embeddedness of language; we tend to see a more slippery relationship between signifier and signified. And there were plenty of Victorian philological scholars and poets who recognized the ambiguities of words and things; it was something Tennyson, for example, exploited in his poetry. However, for the self-taught poet, a secure relationship between local language and place was important, as a constituent part of an identity bound to place and circumstance.

Barnes believed that if a lyric could re-create a place imaginatively it could help to stabilize communal and individual memories, as well as contributing to its continuity. It was not just the place, but 'the pliace a tiale's a-tuold o'', as he wrote in 1844, that mattered:

> Why tidden vields an runnen brooks,
>   Nar trees in spring ar fall;
> An' tidden woody slopes an' nooks'
>   Da touch us muost ov all;
> An' tidden ivy that da cling
>   By housen big an' wold, O,
> But this is, a'ter all, the thing, –
>   The pliace a tiale's a tuold o'.
>
> (Barnes, 1844, pp. 249–50)

Telling the tales of places in local language helped to crystallize the relationship between people and their environments. In this poem, the experience of sympathetic re-connection is strong enough to constitute a physical response: in the 'squier's house, an evr'y groun' / That now his son ha' zuold, O'.

> The mâid a-lov'd to our heart's core,
> The dearest of our kin,
> Da miake us like the very door
> Wher thā went out an' in.
> 'Tis zummat touchèn that bevel
> Poor flesh an' blood o' wold, O
> Da miake us like to zee so well
> The pliace a tiale's a-tuold o'.

The memory of love and its link to physical loss magnifies even the *idea* of a door into a beloved object, and the movement 'out an' in' implies the emotional swing of pleasure and pain invoked by telling the tale. The absence of 'flesh and blood' is pointed up by the use of a common word like 'touchèn', rather than 'poignant', or 'affecting' – there is no more touching to be done.[6]

Encouraging sympathy in an audience was a central concern of the Victorian writer.[7] In Barnes's concrete language 'heart's core' is more fundamental than sentimental; blood – both actual and as a figure for the related community – moves 'out an' in' through the heart's door.[8] Barnes's poetry was written in 'good heart', from a position of exhortation in favour of community stewardship and personal effort. In later writers, such as Matthew Arnold, anxiety overtakes 'the curative properties of affective literature', as Kirstie Blair notes (2006, pp. 8–9). Barnes, instinctively in touch with his community, makes maximum use of affective suggestion to provoke a moral sympathy.

One of the reasons change and decay has overtaken places like the Blackmore Vale is that new blood has sold out the old. During the 1840s, when Barnes wrote this poem, and throughout the economically depressed period between the end of the Napoleonic Wars and the mid-nineteenth century, houses and lands were often sold to pay family debts and to turn small farms into larger ones for greater profit. Barnes wrote about both, and witnessed the effects of both in his locality and among members of his own family. Homes 'vell into han'', and the people scattered:

> An' zome ō'm be a wantèn bread,
> Zome, better off, ha' died
>
> (Barnes, 1844, pp. 258–60)

In 'The Huomestead A-Vell into Han", Barnes employs a dramatic device that runs through much of his poetry, that of engaging us in conversation. We are addressed, along with a companion, 'John', and conducted around the ghosts of home where the speaker is all that is left of the family: 'Var we can't get a life put in / Var mine, when I be gone'. The 'archet' and 'groun' var carn' become shades made of words. They represent ghosts of former productivity, alongside the work enjoyed to 'better ouer lan's, John'.

> An' in the archet out behine
>   The apple-trees in row, John,
> Did swây wi' upright stems, ar leine
>   Wi' heads a-noddèn low, John.
> An' there, bezide some groun' var carn,
>   Two strips did skirt the road;
> In oone the cow did toss her harn,
>   While t'other wer a-mow'd
>   In June, below
>   The lofty row
> Ov trees that in the hedge did grow.

Elegy is here matched with the topicality of land loss to create a poetic memorial; thus, the place can never be forgotten because the memories are re-created in what Barnes considered to be 'living' language; language that revives the specific constituents of place and community. In the last verse, elegy unites past and present, and triumphs over the bitterness of scattering, poverty and death. Barnes was not given to resentment and anger; even when writing of his own misfortune sorrow tends to be the dominant note. In this case, the sorrow is stirred by our sympathetic relationship to it. Barnes uses his metrically arranged, yet naturalistic speech cadences to grab our attention, the 'sound of sense' that would later become the strength of Robert Frost's poetry. Matthew Hollis summarizes part of Frost's idea as follows: 'We use cadence to indicate and understand meaning in a way that goes deeper than the content of individual words into the arena of moods and atmospheres' (2011, pp. 72–3). Although largely unacknowledged by later poets and critics, Barnes was an early exponent of the 'sound of sense', as well as the sense of sound as an affective force.

> An' I coo'd lead ye now all roun'
>   The parish, if I woo'd, John,

> An' show ye still the very groun'
> Where vive good housen stood, John.
> In broken archets near the spot,
> A vew wold trees da stan';
> But dew da val wher vo'ke oonce zot
> About the burnen bran'
> In housen warm,
> A-kep vrom harm
> By elems that did break the starm.

Like John Clare, Barnes links trees to continuity and the protection bestowed by belonging to a place. 'To a Fallen Elm' was written on the occasion of a proposal to cut down two elms at the side of Clare's cottage in Helpston (in fact, they were spared because the owner changed his mind). The horror of their potential loss drives Clare to a poetic rage in which all his hated symbols of oppression are condemned:

> The common heath became the spoilers prey
> The rabbit had not where to make his den
> And labours only cow was drove away
> No matter – wrong was right and right was wrong
> And freedoms brawl was sanction to the song.
>
> ('To a Fallen Elm, 1831, ll.60–4,
> in Clare, 2004, pp. 96–8)

There is no possibility of Barnes writing or, probably, thinking in these terms. Barnes attempts to see both sides of the landed/landless debate, and celebrates the hierarchy of rural life although condemning some of its effects. For Barnes, eliciting sympathy requires an appeal to the greatest number. Clare, in this poem at least, appealed to the disaffected. His elm is both a real tree and a symbol of 'freedom': the freedom of customary rights afforded to those living on the margins of convention; gipsies, travellers, animals and all the poor cowherds and horse-boys that Clare saw everyday on their solitary rounds.

The elm in Barnes's poem also symbolizes the care and security afforded *by* the community to those who dwell in it, 'warm', 'harm' and 'starm', linked in euphony. Now, the elm is broken, and the storm is free to rage; 'harm' has overtaken the 'housen warm', yet because Barnes ends his poem with an image of stability and strength, he illuminates the foregoing verses with the *potential* offered by supportive communities – we have been invited in as a *part* of it, if only as witnesses – even while he laments their actual destruction. There is also the advantage of Dorset grammar in lyrics that extol the virtue of continuity in the use of the auxiliary verb 'do': trees 'da stan", dew 'da vall'. The sense of time continuing in this use implies something more than the present tense, or present historic, can convey. 'Trees stand' or 'dew falls' have a completeness about them that the imperfect auxiliary avoids; 'do' extends the movement of the verse into a timeless moment – trees regularly stand, and dew regularly falls. In his quiet way, Barnes reaches deeply into communal memory in order to re-create a sense of permanence destroyed through economic and social flux. The use of dialect fostered a sense of collective identity that could be used politically, but was more often used to reinforce social solidarity, in favour of community rather than against authority.[9]

In his study of Victorian pastoral, Owen Schur points to Hardy's celebration of Barnes as 'a part of the great British tradition' of pastoral, not simply 'a minor dialectal poet', but a poet who 'resituates himself in pastoral through the use of dialect' (1989, p. 168). Possibly, Schur is not coupling 'minor' to 'dialectal', only stating that Barnes was always considered 'minor' and he also wrote in dialect. He seems to imply that Barnes's pastoral as celebrated by Hardy was indeed 'great', part of the perceived cultural need that classical pastoral demonstrated: 'a product of the changing relationship between . . . the ideal and the real' as John Barrell and John Bull note in their introduction to *English Pastoral Verse* (1982, p. 8). These same authors, however, apparently despairing at the pointlessness of pastoral in industrial and post-industrial societies, also accuse Barnes (and Tennyson, in his dialect poems) 'of disguising, while compounding, their artificiality' in a pastoral 'too hopelessly nostalgic' to be of any use (p. 431). But by using dialect to 'resituate' himself within pastoral, as Schur suggests, we might argue that Barnes also gave the pastoral genre greater situated and communal significance.

Restoring local language in poems of place can have a totemic effect, re-making the place in our imaginations; this was certainly an attribute that appealed to Barnes's contemporary readers, especially working people. Alan Chedzoy quotes from a typical letter to Barnes, written in 1869: 'The old Home of my Youth and all my dear ones now mouldering in the earth came back to mind.' This comes from a Dorset-born servant, 'in the gloom of an underground London Kitchen' (2010, p. 9). His middle-class readers came to respect his scholarship, and many poets admired his literary skill, from William Allingham and Tennyson to Coventry Patmore and Hardy. But he was also regularly encouraged to 'translate' his writing into standard English to make the sentiments more accessible 'for the sake of the more unfortunate', as Alexander MacMillan delicately requested, who couldn't understand them – or perhaps did not feel it was appropriate to try.[10]

Even while Barnes's pastoral poetry sounds a familiar lament for the past, he is tracking change in language and landscapes. As Chedzoy points out, even by the time Barnes's first volume of poetry was published in 1844, Dorset speech was 'no more than an embarrassing relic' for many of its aspirational workers. Chedzoy relates Hardy's personal experience of childhood living in Higher Bockhampton near Dorchester: 'though both Jemima [Hardy] and her husband spoke with broad accents, her son Thomas later remembered that the dialect "was not spoken in his mother's house, but only when necessary to the cottagers, and by his father to the workmen"', adding that the perception was that '[p]eople going up in the world wanted nothing to do with Barnes's old homely talk' (2010, p. 102). It is important, though, to recognize Barnes's own ambivalence about the positive values of local language set against the inevitability of loss or 'corruption' of 'pure' forms. These are the two fronts on which Barnes was operating: he wanted to promote dialect use in order to give Dorset people (and by implication Dorset the place) a literature they could call their own. In doing this he had to allow for linguistic instability in order to keep hold of his audience. He needed to modify and adapt as the years went on.

At the same time, much of his prose concerned the origins of English in Wessex, and his belief that West Country speech exhibited a 'purity' that other regional and, of course, urban dialects lacked. Just as historical and scientific investigation could confer legitimacy on Victorian modernity even while it exposed Victorian instability and self-doubt, the many linguistic projects of the period, including early forms of what we might now term 'dialectology', enabled our present understanding of language evolution alongside species evolution. Legitimacy could be conferred by elevating the status of English itself, which could then achieve the same status for academic study as Latin and Greek, partly because of its ancient origins. As Patrick Joyce states:

> It is easy now to lose sight of just how significant for contemporaries was the model of culture and history to be found in language. Notions of language shaped the whole mental framework of nineteenth-century intellectual life. (1991, p. 206)

Barnes's dialect poetry can be viewed as part of a historicist project to educate the English in their own *linguistic* history, thereby encouraging a deeper appreciation of national and local identities. For Barnes at least, this had little to do with class, but everything to do with community. The relationship between words and things, so regularly under academic and popular scrutiny in the early nineteenth century, provided him with an analogy connected to the intricate shifts in fortune and status in rural communities. He attempted to recover a relationship between local words and local things that emphasized stability even through adversity, and then to write a literature for that relationship – a literature for a people who could otherwise only read poetry in what Barnes called 'National English'. A 'national' poetry could apply equally to Sturminster Newton or Cambridge but could not imaginatively re-create a specific place belonging to 'real' people. As Elizabeth Helsinger writes: 'The nation as home or nation as community commits itself to excluding what it cannot assimilate' (1997, pp. 16–17). Although the majority of these excluded people were inevitably 'workers' and many were among the landless poor in Barnes's parish, the language remained a custom in common. For Barnes, dialect was not one of 'the marks of the beast' that Hardy's Elizabeth Henchard was forced to eliminate from her everyday conversation (Hardy, 1912, p. 148). And yet his desire to straddle the orthodox and the uneducated in order to create a vision of a place and people for themselves as well as the establishment meant he had no real fit in either category.

For most poets who admired Barnes, it was the 'naturalness' of his language that attracted them, as Philip Larkin describes it; 'the natural words in their natural order' (1983, p. 149). There is, however, a difference between his early dialect poems, begun in the 1830s, and his later versions of the same poems. While this does not materially affect his best poems from the later volumes of 1859 and 1862, readers are given 'watered down' versions of his first collection (1844), as Tom Burton calls them, reproduced in the final collection of 1879, although this remained the most popular edition (2007, p. 348). Literary dialect use is inevitably different, especially in poetry, from colloquial dialects: the self-conscious process of writing for an unknown audience takes account of what is acceptable and intelligible. Although Barnes himself, while not 'class-blind', took no personal measure of someone's social position, his audience wanted something more genteel. They had gone up in the world since 1844 and they did not want to be laughed at. The linguistic position was complicated, as is usual, by sociological formations of language and community. Through 'code switching', communities might speak in ways that differed from an individual's speech.[11] Burton and Ruthven point to aspirational aspects that affect any assessment of local usage, including the isolation that stems from increased mobility – our village may use those words, but I do not wish to (2009, p. 318, pp. 336–7).

This presented Barnes with a dilemma. Dialect *literature* could be directed at more than one audience, yet could also include expressions and constructions that were only fully appreciated by certain sections, whereas standard English potentially diluted the effect of using different sociolinguistic codes. Barnes's poems should be read aloud; they are intended to be and were, in Barnes's middle years, *performed*. 'If the 1844 spellings are like those in a pronouncing dictionary, it is precisely because Barnes wanted readers to know what the poems should sound like', writes Burton (2007, p. 351). Barnes's confidence in his own voice meant he could use the lyrical ballad in dialect as a commentary on the use of language itself, as well as on the potential fragmentation of the language community, as expressed in 'Jenny out Vrom Hwome'. Barnes wrote many 'dramatic monologues', miniatures of rural activity, including hay-making and Christmas festivities, for example. This poem is among a different group of lyrics in that Barnes dramatizes a mood or condition rather than a personal character. Although 'Jenny' is the portrayal of an unhappy young girl 'placed' in service, the poem is also a subtle exploration of the performance of language as part of the construction of place. His poetic dialect enables him to combine social critique with lyric depth:

> O wild-riavèn west winds! as you da roar on,
>   The elems da rock an' the poplars da ply,
> An' wiave da drēve wiave in the dark-water'd pon', –
>   Oh! wher do ye rise vrom, an wher do ye die?
>
> O wild-riavèn winds! I da wish I cood vlee
>   Wi' you, lik' a bird o' the clouds, up above
> The rudge o' the hill an' the top o' the tree,
>   To wher I da long var an' vo'kes I da love.
>
> Ar else that in under *th*eos rock I cood hear,
>   In the soft-zwellèn sounds ya da leäve in your road,
> Zome words ya mid bring me, vrom tongues that be dear,
>   Vrom friends that da love me, all scatter'd abrode.
>
> O wild-riavèn winds! if ya ever da roar
>   By the house an' the elems vrom wher I'm a-come,
> Breathe up at the winder ar call at the door,
>   An' tell ya've a-voun' me a-*th*inkèn o' huome.[12]

In this poem the loss of language *connected* to place is something to be feared. The speaking winds are asked to remind Jenny's community that she still speaks the familiar 'tongues that be dear'; whether her friends 'scatter'd abrode' do or not is something she wonders. Dislocation, arising from the poverty of rural life and the subsequent dilution of speech and customs, informs the poem's troubled tone: 'wiave da drēve wiave' relentlessly, highlighting the impotence felt by the girl and rural communities. Although the metre implies stresses on 'wiave' here, Dorset pronunciation requires a length in 'drēve' that renders the whole phrase stressed in every sense.[13] The raving wind plays an ambiguous role – it is unknown, and impersonal: 'wher do ye rise vrom, an' wher do ye die?' is a question that underlies the poet's whole examination of how communities fragment, blown apart by strange winds (cultural, economic, political) that roar in alien (standard English) tongues and scatter the familiar.

But it also gathers together, with 'soft-zwellèn sounds', characteristic of Dorset's landscape and accent, bringing poignant hope, 'zome words ya mid bring me'. A notion of concrete transmission (by the wind) is underscored by the physicality of the printed voice; the poem on the page. Printing enables poems to be spoken internally, with or without an accent.[14] This is difficult to do with a non-standard poem as it invites reading in a particular way, in Barnes's case to the benefit of the poet's insider knowledge of place, educating us into a better understanding of the vitality of connection. Yet the spoken voice is scattered to the winds. Printing the voice offers a permanent record and acts as a testament to those who need proof – children, grandchildren – that any of these events, people or places are 'true'.

Although Clare was supremely literate he understood the *sound* of his locality as experienced by the community of place and people who had little or no literacy. Barnes had to re-establish his oral links with place and community, and then to interpret the community for an audience whose first reference point was more likely than not to be textual. His conflation of oral and written forms inevitably had to evolve with changing receptions of his work. If he wanted this local voice to be heard he had no choice but to refine in order to conserve – a pragmatic approach. Barnes spoke through working-class characters without being one of them. His personal lyrics are often more poetically powerful than his social commentary; both are committed to expressing the connection between land and people, language and community, concentrated in Dorset dialect.

One of Barnes's best lyrics emphasizing the value of home and the specificity of place is also a deeply personal evocation of loss, 'The Wife

A-Lost', written after the death of his wife, Julia, in 1852. It is still anthologized as a poem of universal and powerful appeal, full of 'sensibility' without sentimentality. Bernard Richards points out how the dialect 'distances' while it also 'expresses a depth of feeling' (1980, p. 34):

> Since I noo mwore do zee your feäce,
>   Up steärs or down below,
> I'll zit me in the lwonesome pleäce,
>   Where flat-bough'd beech do grow :
> Below the beeches' bough, my love,
>   Where you did never come,
> An' I don't look to meet ye now,
>   As I do look at hwome.
>
> Since you noo mwore be at my zide,
>   In walks in zummer het,
> I'll goo alwone where mist do ride,
>   Droo trees a-drippèn wet:
> Below the raïn-wet bough, my love,
>   Where you did never come,
> An' I don't grieve to miss ye now,
>   As I do grieve at hwome.
>
> Since now bezide my dinner-bwoard
>   Your vaïce do never sound,
> I'll eat the bit I can avword,
>   A-vield upon the ground;
> Below the darksome bough, my love,
>   Where you did never dine,
> An' I don't grieve to miss ye now,
>   As I at hwome do pine.
>
> (Barnes, 1859, pp. 154–5)

There is very little non-standard English in this poem that cannot be understood. It possesses an accent rather than exhibits a dialect, yet in that accent Barnes sets a twofold elegy; for Julia and for the place that constitutes 'home'. Seamus Perry sums up the 'quiet brilliance' of this poem 'in the way it brings things home' (2007, p. 128). This is exactly right: home, for Barnes, is made of connections between things, people and the environment in which they belong and thrive. As Alan Hertz comments: 'In a sense, his characters are not individuals; certainly, they often see themselves as cells in a social organism composed of things as well as people' (1985, p. 122).

In 'The Wife A-Lost' Barnes is, in fact, unable to bring things home, because home is no longer the place he wants to be. All the 'homely' details point to the intricate interdependence of rural labourer and local environment; outside in all weathers, food that he 'can avword' eaten in the fields, the sheltering tree, so often a symbol of loving care. In this instance he has nowhere else to call home; all the symbols of home remind him of what he has lost, and he seeks out the least comforting features of rural subsistence to bring him some sense of 'day-to-day coping': rain, mist and dark. 'The final stage in any adequate response to loss' writes Perry, 'is persuading yourself, and perhaps others too, that the attenuated world is still worth persisting with' (2007, pp. 129, 116). There is almost, in this poem, a sense that Barnes is unsure that his 'pleäce' can still support him, because his 'place' has altered so radically. Barnes's poetry is not complacent. As Hertz notes, the Blackmore Vale 'is not the unchanging, untroubled backwater that some critics have described: people are evicted from their homes; they grow up and marry; they grow old and die':

> These changes can be catastrophic, for to lose a home is to wreck the family, and to lose a wife or child is to make home uninhabitable. (1985, p. 122)

As an elegy for a place that no longer brings solace or support, it has become an ecosystem of 'darksome', 'lwonesome' connections, an unusually 'solipsistic' landscape, comments Hertz (p. 121). And yet, Barnes did recover some sense of equilibrium, even in his grief, and this poem also hints at the power of what Seamus Heaney has termed 'the awful necessity of the gift for keeping going' that he recognized in John Clare's sonnets (1996, p. 78). The regular iambic rhythm is the heart beat of the poem, in keeping with 'the insistent return to a few unshiftable points of reference – "hwome", "love", "now"' (Perry, 2007, p. 129).

'Home' is always the edge against which to test 'away', and vice versa. Very often, the experience of dislocation is the trigger for exploration of past and place, as it was for Clare – even the dislocation arising from writing down his place added to his sense of loss. In making the vernacular choice, there is an implication that dialect is 'at home' already. Local words can develop a metonymic relationship with fragile communities, helping to reinforce their significance. Regional 'listing', the repetition of local details in dialect poetry, acts as a signal of 'authentic local identity' that has a link to a named place.[15] Joan Beal comments on how the 'linguistic repertoire' of dialect 'provides models for the *performance of local identity*' [my emphasis]. In some measure, this includes the performance of *place* by using language closely connected to it (2009, p. 140). For Barnes the literature was as important as the language; the imaginative coupling united the people with their place. Parham writes that Hopkins was impressed by Barnes's poetry because it was 'a more general "embodiment" of a regional inscape whereby a clear link is forged between writer and environment' (2010, p. 151). Hopkins saw in Barnes's work 'the possibility for a more concrete language grounded in our affinity with the rest of nature' (although Barnes was too much a poet of one kind of place for Hopkins' poetic project). In his 1980 anthology of Victorian poetry, Richards suggests that the best of Barnes's poetry is 'fresh and distinct, relying on direct experience':

> Twentieth-century taste, re-aligned by the focus on Hopkins, is now more attuned to some of the principles that Barnes stood for . . . both were interested in forging a new poetic idiom that would be clearly based on folk origins, but would also be in a long and eclectic tradition of poetic artifice. (p. 28)

Romantic standards still have much to answer for in a variety of critical assumptions about the judgement of poetry's value. Margaret Russett distinguishes the minor from the 'marginal', using John Clare as an example of a poet who, once 'rescued' from the margins (although he is paradoxically celebrated as a poet of the marginal) 'their canonization will nonetheless take the majority form of an ascription to textual difficulty, the institutional trace of the Romantic reading standard' (1997, p. 5). Much of Barnes's poetry was celebrated in its own time as 'major' in quality, while remaining handicapped by its linguistic idiosyncrasy. Barnes's apparently simple lyrics are, as Hardy noted, as serious a form of poetry as Tennyson's: he 'belonged to the literary school of such poets as Tennyson, Gray, and Collins' (Hardy, 1993, p. 196). Indeed, the only poetic influences we are aware of were those of his teenage years, read in the collection of Dorchester rector, Henry John Richman; Pope, Collins and Gray among them. These canonical poets formed the background to his early attempts at standard English verse, used as a 'passport' to his future position. 'He could turn a rhyme, shape a stanza, quote Pope and assume the pastoral style', comments Chedzoy (2010, pp. 27, 30). And yet Barnes understood that his true voice was that which connected him to his place and his community, interpreting the people and the landscape through the everyday poetry of local speech.

Notes

1. See Smith, 1984, p. 12, and pp. 75–6 on establishment 'fear' surrounding labourers' increasing ability to read and write.
2. Chedzoy, 2010, p. 16. Biographical references are to this text unless otherwise stated.
3. See Burton and Ruthven, 2009, p. 309: 'the academic study of English dialect poetry' has fallen through 'the gap created by the historic compartmentalization of university English into "literature" and "language" components'.
4. Williams is careful to point out the awkward relationship between 'real history' and the 'escalator' of community and personal memories, while he also states that the 'apparent resting places' of better days and ways 'have some actual significance'; 1985, pp. 1, 12.
5. See Shepherd in Barnes, 1998, p. 23, quoting Barnes: 'a note defining the purpose of "Poetry" and sub-titled "Teaching",' also in Levy, 1960, p. 17.
6. Austin and Jones, 2002, point out that the '"grave" accent in *-èn* endings indicates the "ing" /iŋ/ of standard pronunciation' distinguishing, for example 'falling' from 'fallen' (p. 58).
7. See, for example, Jaffe, 2000 and Ratcliffe, 2008.
8. See Blair, 2006, especially pp. 188–89 on the heart's 'core' in Tennyson's *In Memoriam*.
9. For a discussion of Barnes's political position in relation to his poems of more obvious social commentary, see Edney, 2009, p. 216.
10. Chedzoy, 2010, p. 166; Chedzoy is quoting a letter from MacMillan to Barnes in 1864, who had already contributed a few standard English poems to *MacMillan's Magazine*, urging him to 'abandon the dialect'.
11. See Trudgill, 2000, pp. 81–104 on 'Language and Context'.
12. Barnes, 1844, pp. 154–5; *th* was a later substitute for /ð/ throughout.
13. In fact, 'wiave' is certainly pronounced as two syllables, 'wee' and '[w]ave', but also with an emphasis on the 've' ending.
14. See Griffiths, 1989, p. 95: 'a reader must be influenced by what was of moment to the writer of that work. Accent is the sound of what was of moment in writing'.
15. Beal, 2009, p. 141. Beal discusses research that examines how the use of local terms, even in non-dialect speakers, 'can be used to project localness', including Agha's influential 2003 study.

Bibliography

Agha, Asif (2003) 'The Social Life of Cultural Value, *Language and Communication*, 23, 231–73.
Austin, F. and B. Jones (2002) *The Language and Craft of William Barnes, English Poet and Philologist (1801–1886)* (Lampeter: Edwin Mellen Press).
Barnes, William (1844) *Poems of Rural Life in the Dorset Dialect* (London: John Russell Smith).
——. (1859) *Homely Rhymes: A Second Collection of Poems in the Dorset Dialect* (London: John Russell Smith).

——. (1950) *Selected Poems of William Barnes 1800–1886*, ed. Geoffrey Grigson (London: Routledge and Kegan Paul).
——. (1998) *The Poems of William Barnes*, ed. Valerie Shepherd (Nottingham: Trent Editions).
Barrell, J. and J. Bull, eds. (1982) *The Penguin Book of English Pastoral Verse* (Harmondsworth: Penguin).
Beal, J. C. (2009) 'Enregisterment, Commodification, and Historical Context: "Geordie" versus "Sheffieldish"', *American Speech*, 84, 138–56.
Blair, Kirstie (2006) *Victorian Poetry and the Culture of the Heart* (Oxford: Oxford University Press).
Boos, Florence (2007) 'Working-Class Poetry' in *A Companion to Victorian Poetry*, ed. Richard Cronin, Alison Chapman and Antony H. Harrison (Oxford: Blackwell), pp. 204–29.
Burton, T. L. (2007) 'What William Barnes Done: Dilution of the Dialect in Later Versions of the Poems of Rural Life', *Review of English Studies*, 58, 338–63.
——. and K. K. Ruthven (2009) 'Dialect Poetry, William Barnes and the Literary Canon', *ELH*, 76, 309–34.
Chedzoy, Alan (1985) *William Barnes: A Life of the Dorset Poet* (Wimborne: Dovecote Press).
——. (2010) *The People's Poet: William Barnes of Dorset* (Stroud: The History Press).
Clare, John (2004) *John Clare: Major Works*, ed. E. Robinson and D. Powell (Oxford: Oxford University Press).
Deleuze, G. and F. Guattari (1986) *Kafka: Toward a Minor Literature*, trans. D. Polan (Minneapolis, MN: University of Minnesota Press).
Edney, Sue (2009) '"Times be Badish vor the Poor": William Barnes and his Dialect of Disturbance in the Dorset "Eclogues"', *English*, 58, 206–29.
Fraser, Hilary (2000) 'Victorian Poetry and Historicism', in *The Cambridge Companion to Victorian Poetry*, ed. Joseph Bristow (Cambridge: Cambridge University Press), pp. 114–36.
Griffiths, Eric (1989) *The Printed Voice of Victorian Poetry* (Oxford: Clarendon Press).
Guillory, John (1993) *Cultural Capital: The Problem of Literary Canon Formation* (Chicago: University of Chicago Press).
Hardy, Thomas (1912) *The Life and Death of the Mayor of Casterbridge* (London: Macmillan).
——. (1993) *Thomas Hardy: Selected Poems*, ed. H. Thomas (London: Penguin).
Heaney, Seamus (1996) *The Redress of Poetry* (New York: Noonday Press).
Helsinger, Elizabeth K. (1997) *Rural Scenes and National Representation: Britain, 1815–1850* (Princeton: Princeton University Press).
Hertz, Alan (1985) 'The Hallowed Pleäces of William Barnes', *Victorian Poetry*, 23, 109–24.
Hollis, Matthew (2011) *Now All Roads Lead to France: The Last Years of Edward Thomas* (London: Faber and Faber).
Jaffe, Audrey (2000) *Scenes of Sympathy: Identity and Representation in Victorian Fiction* (New York: Cornell University Press).
Janowitz, Anne (1998) *Lyric and Labour in the Romantic Tradition* (Cambridge: Cambridge University Press).
Joyce, Patrick (1991) *Visions of the People: Industrial England and the Question of Class 1848–1914* (Cambridge: Cambridge University Press).

Larkin, Philip (1983) 'The Poetry of William Barnes' in *Required Writing: Miscellaneous Pieces, 1955–1982* (New York: Farrar, Straus, Giroux), pp. 149–52.

Lucas, John (1994) 'Clare's Politics', in *John Clare in Context*, ed. H. Haughton, A. Phillips and G. Summerfield (Cambridge: Cambridge University Press), pp. 148–77.

Najarian, James (2003) 'Canonicity, Marginality, and the Celebration of the Minor', *Victorian Poetry*, 41, 570–4.

Parham, John (2010) *Green Man Hopkins: Poetry and the Victorian Ecological Imagination* (Amsterdam/New York: Rodopi).

Patmore, Coventry (1862) 'William Barnes, the Dorsetshire Poet', *Macmillan's Magazine*, 6, 154–63.

Perry, Seamus (2007) 'Elegy' in *A Companion to Victorian Poetry*, ed. Richard Cronin, Alison Chapman and Antony H. Harrison (Oxford: Blackwell), pp. 115–34.

Ratcliffe, Sophie (2008) *On Sympathy* (Oxford: Oxford University Press).

Richards, Bernard, ed. (1980) *English Verse, 1830–1890* (Harlow: Longman).

Russett, Margaret (1997) *De Quincey's Romanticism: Canonical Minority and the Forms of Transmission* (Cambridge: Cambridge University Press).

Schur, Owen (1989) *Victorian Pastoral: Tennyson, Hardy, and the Subversion of Forms* (Columbus: Ohio State University Press).

Smith, Olivia (1984) *The Politics of Language, 1791–1819* (Oxford: Clarendon Press).

Trudgill, Peter (2000) *Sociolinguistics: An Introduction to Language and Society*, 4th edn (London: Penguin).

Williams, Raymond (1985) *The Country and the City* (London: Hogarth).

Wright, David, ed. (1969) *Seven Victorian Poets* (London: Heinemann).

Zietlow, Paul (1969) 'Thomas Hardy and William Barnes: Two Dorset Poets', *PMLA*, 84, 291–303.

Index

Aesop 161
Agha, Asif 208n
Aitken, Jean Carlyle 131n
Allingham, William 200
Anderson, Alexander 1
Anderson, Robert 20
Andrews, Kerri 4, 11
'Argus' 172n
Arnold, Matthew 139, 151, 169, 193, 197
Ashby, M. K. 66
Athenaeum 125
Atkenson, Tom 159
Austin, F. 208n
Austin, Sarah 131n

Bailey, Philip James 168
Bamford, Samuel 188
Barbauld, Anna 20
Barnes, William 4, 10, 12, 131n, 132n, 176, 186, 191–208; 'The Pliace a Tiale's A-Tuold O' 196–7, 'The Huomestead A-Vell into Han" 198–200, 'Jenny out Vrom Hwome' 203–4, 'The Wife A-Lost' 204–6
Barrell, John 86, 200
Bate, Jonathan 74n, 75n
Beal, Joan 206–7, 208n
Beattie, James 17, 20, 39, 49
Beddoes, Thomas 96, 107
Benjamin, Walter 163
Bennion, Thomas 61
Bentham, Jeremy 133n
Berkeley, George 98
Binfield, Kevin 3
Bird, James 1–2
Bishop, Elizabeth 92
Blackwood's Edinburgh Magazine 6, 140, 160, 162
Blair, Hugh 17, 20, 23, 82
Blair, Kirstie 197, 208n
Blake, William 20

Blane, John 28
Bloomfield, Hannah 69, 71, 74n
Bloomfield, Nathaniel 55, 69
Bloomfield, Robert 3, 11, 18, 24, 27, 32n, 55–74, 159, 161, 180; *May Day with the Muses* 63–5, *The Farmer's Boy* 65–6, 80–1, 'Rosy Hannah' 72–3
Blunden, Edmund 92
Bonnell, Thomas F. 5
Bookman, The 174–5
Boos, Florence S. 3, 194
Bowles, W. L. 55
Boyle, Robert 99
Brierley, Ben 174, 180, 186, 188
Briggs, Asa 131n
Brontë, Emily 191
Brooke, Charlotte 149, 151, 152
Brown, Agnes 22
Brown, Simon 127
Browning, Robert 156, 168
Buchan, Earl of 18
Bull, John 200
Bulwer, Edward 125, 132n
Burdett-Coutts, Angela 186
Burke, Edmund 23, 91
Burke, Tim 13n, 17, 32n, 37, 43
Burns, Gilbert 25, 30
Burns, Robert 4, 5, 10, 11, 16–32, 34, 38–9, 44, 47, 48–53, 79–81, 82, 84, 116, 119, 139, 140, 141, 146, 154n, 158, 160, 161, 167, 171n, 174, 176, 177–8, 180; 'To James Tennant of Glenconner' 19, 'Second Epistle to Lapraik' 22, 'The Inventory' 25, 'The Vision' 26–30, 'The Twa Dogs' 48–53
Burns, William 25, 28, 30
Burton, Tom 191, 202–3, 208n
Byron, George Gordon 1, 57, 69, 127, 132n, 136, 158, 159, 160, 162, 163, 167, 179

212 Index

Caine, Hall 93n
Calder, Grace J. 131n
Campbell, Ian 116
Campbell, James 40
Campbell, John 84
Campbell, Matthew 6, 12
Capern, Edward 5
Carlile, Richard 157
Carlyle, Alexander 131n
Carlyle, James 116–20
Carlyle, Jane 121
Carlyle, John A. 131n
Carlyle, Thomas 5, 6, 11–12, 24–5, 116–33, 183
Cary, Henry 69
Cervantes, Miguel de 183
Chartism 5, 6, 8, 12, 13n, 117–18, 129, 156–72, 186
Chartist Circular 12, 156–72
Chase, Malcolm 131n, 171n, 172n
Chatterton, Thomas 73
Chaucer, Geoffrey 64, 159
Chedzoy, Alan 192, 195, 200, 201, 207, 208n
Chirico, Paul 74n
Christmas, William J. 3, 5, 6–7, 13n, 32n
Clare, John 3, 7, 10–11, 18, 24, 27, 32n, 55–74, 77–93, 199, 204, 206, 207; *The Shepherd's Calendar* 66–7, 'Song' ['The rushbeds touched the boiling spring'] 70–3, 'Bumbarrel's Nest' 77–8, 'A Sudden Shower' 83–5, 'Sedge Birds Nest' 85–6, 'The Flitting' 89–91
Clegg, John Trafford 174
Cobbett, William 51, 157
Coleridge, S. T. 55, 96, 107, 112–13, 114n, 152, 158
Collier, John ('Tim Bobbin') 182
Collier, Mary 7
Collins, William 207
Cooper, Thomas 159
Corkery, Daniel 36
Cottle, Joseph 96, 114n
Cowper, William 95–114, 158, 159, 167; *The Task* 95, 97, 101–2, 104–5, 111, 113–14
Crabbe, George 39, 69

Creech, William 19, 30
Cunningham, Allan 55, 69, 74n, 121
Cunningham, Valentine 87, 91–2
Currie, James 18, 24
Currie, Walter 159

Dahlmann, F. C. 131n
Dalrymple, James 44
Dalton, John 175
D'Alton, John 147–8
Dante 158
Darling, George 67
Davis, Thomas 150
Davlin, Charles 172n
Day, A. 37
DeLaura, David 113
Deleuze, Gilles 194
Demers, Patricia 114
Dennis, John 93n
Dermody, Thomas 16, 55
Devine, Tom (T. M.) 22, 134n
Dickens, Charles 125, 126, 186
Dickinson, Emily 90
Dobson, N. 37
Dowling, William 34
Drury, Edward 59–60
Dryden, John 20
Dublin University Magazine 6, 137–9, 141, 149–50
Duck, Stephen 6–7, 16, 27–8, 32n, 132n
Duff, William 17
Dunlop, Frances 18, 23

Edinburgh Review 16
Edney, Sue 12
Eliot, George 191
Elliott, Ebenezer 1, 5, 11–12, 116–33, 158, 170
Emmerson, Eliza 56
Espinasse, Francis 174–5, 183, 186, 187, 189, 190n
European Magazine, The 92
Evans, John 55

Ferguson, Samuel 6, 10, 12, 136–54; 'Pastheen Finn' ('Páistín Fionn'), 142–8
Fergusson, Robert 17, 20, 47, 48

Fitzwilliam, Earl 132n
Franklin, Benjamin 41
Fraser, Hilary 195
Fraser, W. Hamish 157, 160, 171n
Fraser's Magazine 121
Friendship's Offering 91
Frost, Robert 193, 198
Fulford, Tim 32n
Furniss, Tom 107

Gaskell, Elizabeth 122, 125
Gilchrist, Octavius 59, 67, 81–2
Gill, Stephen 86
Gillespie, Thomas 159
Gladstone, William 117, 137
Glass, James 45, 46–7
Godwin, William 96, 112
Goethe, Johann Wolfgang von 116, 124
Goldsmith, Oliver 20, 39, 64, 159
Goodridge, John 2, 3, 7, 10–11, 13n, 131n
Gorji, Mina 7, 11
Graham, Colin 140
Gray, Thomas 56, 207
Griffin, Dustin 32n
Griffiths, Eric 208n
Grigson, Geoffrey 193
Guattari, Felix 194
Guest, Kristen 123
Guillory, John 9, 79, 194
Gurney, Archer 168

Hall, Marie Boas 99
Hamilton, Gavin 25, 29, 30
Hardiman, James 143–9, 152, 154n
Hardy, Jemima 201
Hardy, Thomas 92, 192, 195, 200, 201, 202, 207
Harland, John 186
Hartman, Geoffrey 105, 114n
Haywood, Ian 65
Hazlitt, William 80, 83
Heaney, Seamus 35, 83, 206
Hearne, Ray 126, 130, 132n
Helsinger, Elizabeth 202
Henderson, Joseph 64
Henryson, Robert 159

Heringman, Noah 114n
Hertz, Alan 205, 206
Hessey, James 62, 64
Hewitt, John 35, 36–7, 38
Hill, Mary Ann 187–9
Hill, Rowland 172n
Hogg, James 18
Hoggart, Richard 131n
Holden, Thomas 181
Holden's Dollar Magazine 132n
Holland, Isaiah Knowles 59
Hollingworth, Brian 12
Hollis, Matthew 198
Home, John 164, 166
Homer 158, 161
Hood, Thomas 167
Hopkins, Gerard Manley 92, 195, 207
Horne, R. H. 168
Hoskins, Philip 74n
Houghton, Walter 131n
Household Words 125
Houston, Natalie 86
Howard, John 66
Hume, David 23
Hutton, James 107–8
Hyde, Douglas 142

Ikeler, A. Abbott 121–2
Inskip, Thomas 58, 61–2, 67–8, 69, 71, 74n
Ireland, Alexander 187

Jaffe, Audrey 208n
James I 159
James V 159
Jameson, Fredric 170
Jamie, Kathleen 77
Janowitz, Anne 8, 13n, 172n, 195
Jay, Mike 108
Jeffrey, Francis 16, 20, 24, 27
Jerrold, Douglas 167
Johnson, Samuel 78
Johnston, Ellen 1
Johnston, Freya 81
Jones, B. 208n
Jones, Ernest 156, 167–71
Jones, Gareth Stedman 4–5, 13n
Joyce, Patrick 196, 201

Index

Keats, John 7–9, 61, 74n, 146, 154n
Keegan, Bridget 3, 5, 37, 75n
Kemp, Alexander 40–1, 48, 51
King, J. W. 125, 132n
Knowles, Sheridan 168
Knox, John 159
Kramnick, Jonathan Brody 5
Krasinski, Count Zygmunt 169–71
Krishnamurthy, Aruna 6

Labbe, Jacqueline 114
Labourer, The 156, 167–71
Lahee, Margaret Rebecca 174
Lamont, Aeneas 41
La Mont, E. 172n
Landon, Letitia Elizabeth (L.E.L.) 55
Landry, Donna 3–4, 7, 114n
Lapraik, John 21, 22, 29
Larkin, Philip 202
Laycock, Samuel 174, 180, 186
Leapor, Mary 7
Leask, Nigel 4, 10, 11
Lee, Hermione 74n
Leerson, Joep 137
Levy, W. T. 208n
Lithgow, R. A. Douglas 13n
Little, Janet 18
Lloyd, David 151
Lodge, Sara 85
London Magazine 59, 61, 73, 81, 83, 93
Lounger, The 16
Low, Donald 16, 20, 25, 82
Lowell, Robert 92
Lucas, John 64–5

MacDonagh, Thomas 142, 153
Mackay, Charles 168
Mackay, James 28
Mackenzie, Henry 16–17, 24, 84
Macmillan, Alexander 201, 208n
Maidment, Brian 13n, 172n
Main, David M. 93n
Manchester City News 189, 190n
Manchester Examiner 178, 184, 187
Martin, Frederick 58
Massey, Gerald 3
Mathison, Hamish 154n
McBride, Ian 40

McClure, David 30
McEathron, Scott 1, 2
McGuirk, Carol 17–18, 32n
McHugh, Heather 98
McIlvanney, Liam 20, 22, 31
McWilliams, P. 37
Miles, Julia 192
Mill, John Stuart 117, 121, 132n
Miller, Patrick 25
Milner, George 175–82, 186, 188–90
Milton, John 5, 20, 28, 158, 159, 161, 167
Montagu, Elizabeth 96, 114n
Montgomery, James 55–6, 92
Moore, John 18
Moore, Thomas 136, 138
More, Hannah 96, 97, 114n
Morris, Keith 126, 130, 132n
Morris, William 117
Mullan, Luke 40, 41, 44
Murphy, Andrew 13n
Murphy, Paul Thomas 5–6, 157

Najarian, James 194
Napier, Macvey 126–7, 132n
Nation, The 141
New Monthly Magazine 125
Norbrook, David 79
Northern Star (Belfast) 41, 42, 43, 45
Northern Star (Chartist periodical) 157–8, 160, 161, 167, 169, 172n

Ó Buachalla, Brendan 146
Ó Ciosáin, Niall 154
O'Connell, Daniel 137
O'Connor, Feargus 167
O'Hagan, Thomas 137
Ormerod, Oliver 174
Orr, James 40, 41
Orr, Jennifer 10, 11

Paine, Thomas (Tom) 23, 43
Parham, John 195–6, 207
Patmore, Coventry 192, 200
Paton, Elizabeth 22
Patten, Eve 139, 140
Percy, William 178
Perry, Seamus 205, 206

Index

Pitt, William   23, 25
Pittock, Murray   20–1
Polin, Edward   172n
Pope, Alexander   7, 20, 39, 45, 52, 59, 152, 207
Powell, T.   167, 168
Pratt, Lynda   32n
Preston, Edward Baily   74n
Prince, John Critchley   7–10, 13n
Prince, Kathryn   13n
Prynne, Jeremy   132n

Ramsay, Allan   17, 20, 22, 38, 48, 164–6
Ranken, James   21
Ratcliffe, Sophie   208n
Reid, Thomas   189
Richards, Bernard   205, 207
Richman, Henry John   207
Riddell, Robert   23
Rippingille, Edward   61
Robertson, William (Enlightenment churchman)   23
Robertson, William (Rochdale historian)   183
Robinson, Jeffrey C.   114n
Robinson, Philip   37, 40
Rochdale Times   189
Roe, Nicholas   114
Rose, Jonathan   7, 13n, 131n, 165, 166
Rousseau, Jean-Jacques   50
Ruskin, John   130, 131n
Russett, Margaret   207
Ruthven, Ken   191, 202–3, 208n

Sales, Roger   58
Salmon, Richard   131n
Sanders, Michael (Mike)   6, 12, 13n, 131n
Saturday Review, The   186
Schiller, Friedrich   116
Schorr, Naomi   82
Schur, Owen   200
Scott, Ernest   37
Scott, Walter   20, 150, 164–6
Scrivener, Michael   7, 13
Searle, January   125, 128, 133n
Seary, E. R.   127

Shakespeare, William   5, 13n, 20, 57, 61, 125, 158, 159, 161, 167, 176
Sharp, William   87, 88, 93n
Sheffield Independent   132n, 133n
Shelley, Percy Bysshe   129, 158, 159, 162, 167, 176
Shenstone, William   20, 39
Shepherd, Valerie   195, 208n
Shiells, James   100, 102, 104–9, 112, 114n
Sillar, Davie   21
Sinclair, Sir John   23
Smith, Adam   19, 29, 30
Smith, Charlotte   55, 114
Smith, Jeremy   20
Smith, Olivia   208n
Socrates   161
Southey, Robert   3, 6, 55, 96, 112, 125, 127, 132n, 158
Sowerby, James   127
Spenser, Edmund   5, 7, 39, 84, 159
Sprott, Gavin   29
Stamford Champion, The   85
St Clair, William   7, 13n
Stewart, Dugald   24
Storey, Mark   64, 81, 82, 92, 132n
Stott, Anne   114n
Strachey, Edward   122
Strang, Barbara M. H.   93n
Syme, James   172n

Tannahill, Robert   159, 161
Taylor, John   61, 62, 82, 83
Templeton, Viscount of Upton   43–4, 45, 46
Tennant, David   19
Tennant, James   19
Tennyson, Alfred   64, 91, 156, 168, 176, 192, 196, 200, 207
Theocritus   39, 69
Thomas, Edward   193
Thompson, E. P.   4, 18–19, 21
Thomson, James   66, 74n, 127
Thomson, Samuel   4, 10, 18, 35–53; 'Lyle's Hill'   39–40, 'Allan, Damon, Sylvander and Edwin: a Pastoral'   48–53
Thomson, William   157, 165, 171n
Thoreau, Henry   131n

Thornton, Kelsey 57
Tibble, J. W. 57
Tibble, Anne 57
Tompkins, J. M. S. 97, 108
Treadwell, James 131n
Trudgill, Peter 208n

United Irishmen 42–3, 46, 137

Vicinus, Martha 3, 176, 177, 188, 190n

Waddington, Samuel 93n
Waithe, Marcus 5, 6, 11–12
Waldron, Mary 97, 100, 108, 114n
Walsh, Edward 153
Walton, Isaac 73
Ward, C. A. 119
Ward, Sam 74n, 75n
Ward, Thomas Aline 132n
Watkins, John 125, 126, 128, 129, 132n, 133n
Watts, Alaric 55
Waugh, Edwin 10, 12, 174–90; 'Come Whoam to thi childer an' Me' 184–7
Waugh, Mary Ann (*see* Hill, Mary Ann)
Welch, Robert 151–2, 154n

Westminster Review 124
Weston, Joseph 69
White, Simon J. 11, 65
Williams, Edward ('Iolo Morgangw') 18
Williams, John 74n
Williams, Raymond 129, 195, 208n
Wilson, Alexander 171n
Wilson, Michael, Alexander and Thomas ('Wilson Family') 186
Wollstonecraft, Mary 172n
Wolven, Karen 124, 128
Woolf, Virginia 56
Wordsworth, William 11, 16–17, 20, 24, 39, 86, 92, 95–114, 139, 140, 152–3, 158; *The Prelude* 95–6, 102–4, 105, 110–11, 113–14
Wright, David 193

Yearsley, Ann 1, 4, 11, 55, 95–114; 'Soliloquy' 95–114, 'To the Memory of James Shiells, Esq.' 106–9, 112
Yeats, W. B. 136, 142–3, 145
Young, Edward 112
Young Irelanders 137

Zietlow, Paul 195